Presidents
of the
United States
America's Heritage

By
Willis J. Ehlert

Presidents of the United States: America's Heritage
By Willis J. Ehlert

State House Publishing
4022 Paunack Avenue
Madison, WI 53711-1625

First Edition
2001

Printed in the United States by United Graphics

Library of Congress Control Number 00-092

ISBN 0-9634908-5-0

Cover Design by Boelter & Lincoln

For my wife and family
and
to everyone who enjoys American history.

It all began as an exercise for the mind five years ago and eventually evolved into this book. My thanks go out to all who have helped me to run sources down and have found answers for questions asked. Our librarians are a treasure. A special thanks goes to Norma Wehlitz for her early suggestions and initial reading of the text. It started me on the right track of what I hoped to do. A heart-felt thank you goes to my wife, Reva, for her many hours of reading and suggestions. If there are still errors, the fault is mine alone.

It would be amiss on my part not to acknowledge all the historians who have compiled and written the many source books that I used in gathering the information for this book. I want to especially acknowledge William A. Degregorio whose book <u>The Complete Book of U. S. Presidents</u> was the inspiration and general source book for me. His book had all the answers.

Finally, effort has been made to provide accurate and concise information on the presidents. Often sources did not agree, so the consensus was used. Hopefully all is accurate after six proof-readings and data checking. Neither the author or publisher shall have liability or responsibility to anyone or any entity for liability or loss because of information contained in this book. The bibliography and presidential libraries and historical sites information was current at publication time. Changes will occur so neither the author or publisher can accept liability or responsibility for those changes.

Table of Contents

George Washington's Mount Vernon

Preface

Throughout my life I have had an abiding interest in the presidency. As a youth I remember my mother turning on the radio and listening to Franklin Roosevelt's fireside chats. I vividly recall sitting in our high school assembly the day after the bombing of Pearl Harbor, and hearing President Roosevelt declare war in his "Day of Infamy" speech to Congress.

While serving in the Army Air Corps overseas during World War II, I remember the moment when word came that President Roosevelt had died and the shock of losing a leader who had led the nation throughout the war. Then came the speculation about President Truman and how he would finish the job of victory.

I was on a ship returning to the United States when we received word that Truman had ordered the atomic bombing of Japan. It was a shock to suddenly realize that my army service might be ending.

Later at college, I vividly recall the political campaign of President Truman and the "Give 'em hell, Harry" cries as I watched him drive by in a campaign motorcade .

Remembering seeing and hearing Richard Nixon campaigning from the back of his campaign train as it stopped in an East side Madison railroad yard is another vivid memory.

Several years later when I met and shook his hand at a campaign visit, I was startled by firm handshake and the facial makeup

he wore for the bright television lights.

These memories of presidents and now the total immersion into the campaigns conducted on television today, have resulted in a lifelong interest in the presidency of the United States.

A few years ago while visiting an antique shop, I found a set of books, The Messages and Papers of the Presidents published by James D. Richardson in 1897. They have made fascinating reading as well as excellent primary sources for American historical events. Reading the proclamations, letters, and addresses that presidents have made, added a dimension to American history from a different point of view.

Through the years I have collected many drawings and books about the presidents. The finest group of drawings was found in Messages and Papers of the Presidents, an eleven volume set containing excellent engravings of the presidents Washington through William Howard Taft. I wanted to introduce them once again.

The presidency and its presence and importance in American life is an accepted fact. Books have constantly been written about the office and the individuals who have served as the chief executive of the most powerful nation in history.

I found that most books about the presidency were either too lengthy and or too costly for general use in libraries and schools. There is a need for an intermediate, comprehensive reference book that would provide general information for those who want to check a fact or begin a study of a particular president before going into more lengthly detail about that president.

I have attempted in my book to delineate in a definitive manner what the Presidency is about, but I have made no attempt to render a judgment on the merits or failure of how a particular president carried out the duties of the office.

My primary goal is to present a readable, inexpensive book to be used as a basic reference in schools and libraries, and to creating an interest in the presidency for readers of all ages

I wanted to provide a capsule picture of each president's life, how he served and used the office, and how he led the country during his presidency.

The totality of how the presidency evolved should become apparent. I made no attempt at trying to directly answer the question of what the presidency is about. My hope is that the arrangement of the book will encourage the reader to do further reading and come to his or her own conclusions about the presidency.

In considering the men who held the office of president, we can only marvel that anyone would aspire to becoming president. I intended that the reader might come to some understanding of the complexity of the presidency and how fulfilling and certainly, how frustrating it can be.

At the same time by my listing and describing some of the major historical events that occurred during a president's term, I hoped to give the reader more insight into how a president fits into the fabric

of a period in the nation's history.

Previous books on the presidents have approached the presidency with other aims. Some have presented capsule renditions of the lives of the presidents while others have carefully chronicled in minute detail every nuance of a president's life and service. These large, expensive books have been helpful and were used as references.

Occasionally it was found that they disagreed on a date or event. When this occurred, the consensus has been the reference for my book.

It is important for all citizens to renew their interest in the political process of nominating and electing a president. After the events of the November 2000 presidential election, it is vital that citizens become once more cognizant of how important one vote can be.

This book is an attempt to present the information and events to illustrate how our American heritage is based upon one of the more important factors that make up the historical fabric of the United States, the American presidency.

Willis J. Ehlert
April 2001

Presidents of the United States: America's Heritage
By
Willis J. Ehlert

Introduction

"I do solemnly swear (or affirm) that I will faithfully execute the Office of President of the United States, and will to the best of my Ability, preserve, protect and defend the Constitution of the United States."

For more than two hundred years, elected presidents of the United States have repeated these solemn words at their inauguration.

Since the founders created the office, the presidency has grown more complex. From a small group of men who dreamed of establishing a new country with an entirely new concept of a people governing themselves to the twenty-first century when a president must deal with a shrinking world, each president has had to develop a new strategy for dealing with current challenges during their terms.

Some presidents have clearly seen the needs and problems and acted decisively, while others have at times struggled and often failed. In varying degrees all have been conscious of the power of the presidency and the responsibility they had to the office.

Much of what we know about the success or failure of a president depends upon historians' views as they present a president's life and accomplishments. Many presidents are conscious of this. A prime example is President Clinton in the final year of his presidency. His was a conscious need to leave office on a positive note so that history will remember him for the excellent economy with budget surpluses and his attempts to bring peace to the Middle East and Ireland, and not the scandals and aborted national health plan of the first term or the events leading to the impeachment attempt of the second term.

Because of this executive change every four or eight years, we as a nation are living the adventure of democracy in the United States. It is the first and only true experiment in the history of the world where a diverse people have banded together to create a new way of voluntarily governing themselves.

The United States is still an experiment in the dynamic social enterprise called a democracy which in every year, every month, and every day, finds the nation changing in some way. Sometimes these changes are sudden and disruptive, such as when a president has been assassinated or died while in office. Mostly the changes are subtle with citizens noting little day to day differences.

Central to this change is the ritual of electing a new leader who will be the political and social leader for four years. How we choose and whom we choose is ours to determine. We have to live with our decision.

Even though the United States is one of the most admired democracies in the world, the turnout for national elections rank as one of the lowest in world. In prosperous times the percentage of voters falls below fifty percent. It is certain that if restrictions were put on who could and who could not vote, there would be not only an incredible outcry by citizens, but marches, talk show discussions, newspaper and magazine editorials and even strikes protesting the ruling.

The truth is that many citizens ignore the political races and blithely go about their daily living. This lack of participation in the election process by voting age citizens is a danger to our free democracy. History is filled with examples of citizens allowing others to conduct the affairs of government while they ignore the one true privilege that is the salient feature of our representative democracy, the privilege to vote for candidates they wish to lead them. By not voting, they run the danger of the rise of a demagogue who in time could lead the nation down the path to dictatorship.

It is a frightening prospect but all citizens must be vigilant and participate in the election process by voting. In recent years, the eligible voter participation has remained near the fifty percent mark. The percentage rises slightly if there is a specific concern such as war, inflation, or recession. Since 1932, we have had 60% of the eligible voters cast ballots in only four presidential elections. The lowest percentage of 49% was cast in 1996. In 2000, it was 51%.

The presidency over the span of years from Colonial times to the present has become more complicated and more demanding. The president at all times represents to the world as well as to the citizens of the United States, the power, the stature, and the influence of the United States.

Most presidents have been torn between dealing with events in the United States and dealing with foreign affairs. A number have succeeded in both areas. Ronald Reagan and Theodore Roosevelt are examples. Therefore, no president can be considered without noting the major events that occurred during his presidency both in the United States and the world. A listing or description of some of the major historical events that occurred during each president's term, should give the reader better insight into how a president fits into the fabric of his presidency and in the nation's history.

The totality of how the presidency evolved should become apparent and that should help the reader arrive at some conclusions about what the office of the president is or should be.

We really do not hold to a particular mold when we choose our president. Our presidents have come from all levels of society, from all areas of our nation. They have brought to the office a variety of viewpoints and purposes. So to attempt to specify a particular model of what we as a nation might choose as our leader is impossible. Rather we should view the presidency as a dynamic office in which we as a nation focus our dreams and hopes on the direction that our nation will take based upon our past and our vision of the future.

Each president approaches the office differently. Some have entered the office of the presidency with reluctance, while others with enthusiasm. Each president has to literally "invent" the office for himself. Some presidents have contributed much, while others have offered less. Some presidents accomplished a great deal while in office, while others accomplished little. A number of presidents have had some control over events and reacted to them positively; while other presidents have had little control over events and reacted to a situation often to their regret.

Presidents develop an internal vision of their role that is influenced by their family backgrounds and the moral and social values that were instilled as they grew to adulthood. Their vision of the presidency is always their individual interpretation based upon the values and moral standards they bring to the office. Some held to uplifting standards, but many were less flattering and almost self depreciating.

Each president comes to the office with standards of judgment which he brings to bear on national and international events that he must and does deal with. He is a human being like the rest of us, but circumstances have placed him in the center of events that can have far reaching effects upon the citizens of the United States and the world.

In 1981, Ronald Reagan said of the presidency that he saw the office as a place where the president could make "Americans believe in themselves again."

Woodrow Wilson said that "the President is a kind of slave.." Another viewpoint of how a president views himself was expressed by Andrew Jackson when he stated, "I know what I am fit for. I can command a body of men in a rough way; but I am not fit to be President."

A rather cynical view of the role was given by William Howard Taft when he stated the "major part of the President is to increase gate receipts of expositions and fairs..." Lyndon Johnson stated that election to the presidency gives the president the responsibility to govern, but he must earn the right to govern.

The most important criteria for a president is that he or she must have a sincere desire to serve, to guide the nation, and present a moral role model of integrity, honesty, and forthrightness as the nation's leader. Near the end of his first term, William McKinley declared that he had had enough of the fame and the struggles of the office, still because of his dedication to serve the country, he decided to seek a second term.

In the final analysis, each president contributes some aspect of the vision he has for the United States. In doing so, each becomes an important part of the fabric of our country's history

So the final conclusion about the presidency is that the responsibility lies with the nation's citizens, to choose responsibly the person they want to lead the country and to represent the nation in world events. If we fail to take our responsibility to vote as we at times do, the blame must be ours as a people. If we accept the responsibility and vote, if we seriously consider the accomplishments and character of the individual who aspires to the presidency, and if we choose well, we will be rewarded by a period of time that is peaceful and fulfilling to all.

This book is about the choices American citizens have made for this high office. Read the accounts carefully and you may see a pattern for our country as it moves toward the Nirvana of a perfect government led by a person of noble ideas and compassionate nature.

Whether we achieve such a success always remains in the future because the president is merely a mirror of society and his individual interpretation of the values of that society at a particular time in our country's history.

Therefore, a better understanding of the office of the presidency and the men who have occupied the office will help us come to an understanding of a current president as he or she struggles today in total public view to carry out the duties of the office.

As we move into the 21st century, the president who is chosen to lead our country will be totally different in nature and vision from a Washington or a Roosevelt, from a Hayes or a Reagan. What they all share in common will be the aim to lead our complex society in a positive, prosperous, and peaceful way.

It is important that we study the presidents and their times with the goal of learning what drives an individual to vie for this most prestigious and humbling office. It is each citizen's responsibility to become more informed about the history of the United States, but most of all, deciding what attributes and goals an elected president must possess. As each presidential term ends and an election is held, we witness the strength of our democracy when we perform the ritual of electing a leader for four years without ranker and bloodshed. Regardless of how angry and divisive a presidential campaign becomes, when the moment arrives for the new president to take the oath of office, the power is passed peacefully from one individual to another without recriminations and revolution

The 2000 presidential election and the ballot chaos that occurred in Florida can be a civics lesson for all Americans and for the Congress. A uniform national ballot and an informed citizenry is needed. Every vote is important and every citizen should look upon his or her vote as a sacred duty to perform when given the opportunity.

An orderly and uniform national balloting process would assure us that we will continue to have a smooth transition from one administration to another.

This peaceful passage of power of the most powerful office in the world must be preserved, for it is the salient feature of democracy, American style.

The White House

Since 1791 when Washington and L'Enfant decided on the location of the President's House, the Executive Mansion, the White House has become a symbol of a man's and a nation's power in the world. The official president's residence became known as the White House during Theodore Roosevelt's term. Until then it was unofficially called the White House because it was constructed of light colored painted sandstone.

Since the early 1800's when President John Adams moved into this austere building, the building has become the center of the world where its occupant's every expression and utterance often affects events world wide. His actions and decisions become history. "The White House" is then often synonymous with "the President."

What exactly is the White House besides the residence of the leader of the United States? While most of the White House is closed to the public, visitors to the first floor view an art gallery of historical portraits and objects that are a part of American history. The building and its contents belong to the American people, but for a span of one or two terms, the White House becomes "home" to a president. In the upper floors, the president, takes up residence and lives his private life in the midst of history. The White House, a place of temporary residence, is the focal point as each president serves his term of office. Each leaves a legacy that adds to the building's image. In times of peace and in times of crisis, the world focuses on this most unique yet architecturally simple mansion, the White House.

History of the White House

It was George Washington and Pierre Charles L'Enfant, the French designer of what was to become Washington, D. C., who in 1791, selected the site of the future residence of the President of the United States. They selected the high ground above Goose Creek to build the Executive home that became known as the White House. However, years would pass before the Federal District was approved and constructed. In the meantime, the government was moved from New York city, where Washington had taken the oath of office for his first term, to Philadelphia where he took the oath for his second term. There the government remained until John Adams and his wife, Abigail, moved into the partially completed president's house in 1800. Here Adams finished out the last months of his Presidency.

Washington dismissed Major L'Enfant over disagreements and his obstinate nature that was slowing the construction of the capital district. Thomas Jefferson convinced Washington to hold a competition for the design of the Executive Mansion. Five hundred dollars or a gold medal would go to the winner of the design competition. Jefferson entered a design signing it "A. L." Washington favored and modified a design by a young architect, James Hoban, whom he had encouraged to enter. The three judges agreed with Washington and awarded the prize to Hoban. His design was simple but elegant. The building would become the most luxurious building in the young nation.

The Design

James Hoban's design for the President's House was a simple box-like three story Georgian structure that would be erected on the eighty acre site that Washington and L'Enfant had chosen. The structure would be 170 feet long and 85 feet wide. The front entrance would face the north. It was European in design and had a simple dignity befitting a head of state. The most interesting feature of the building was the design of an egg-shaped oval drawing room in the center of the rear of the building. Today it is the Blue Room. The original structure contained thirty-six rooms. Seven rooms were on the first floor along with the entrance hall. This was to be at ground level and face what was to become Pennsylvania Avenue. Today the first floor is where the president on occasions meets the public. The family quarters and offices are on the second floor. The ground floor is where the servants' quarters and the kitchens are located.

The President's House or White House is a rectangular box-like structure. It is fronted by a two story portico with plain Ionic columns that hold up a plain pediment with simple dentils outlining its form. This portico is over the entrance that has a bas relief carved stone garland above the curved fan-shaped ornate glass over the doorway. Three windows are under the portico on the second floor. On each side of the portico are four windows with twelve panes. These windows are matched on the first floor by windows with fifteen panes. The decorative lintels above each window on the second story are simple. Under each window are small paired corbels acting as supports. The larger first floor windows are more ornate. Curved and triangular lintels crown each window casement supported by longer corbels on each side at the window bottom. A simple balustrade runs around the entire roof. The simple edging below the balustrade is broken up by plain dentil ornamentation.

This simple exterior has not appreciably changed since it was completed. Matthew Brady's first photograph of the president's home serves as a good reference for its early appearance.

It is the interior that has changed most. Several major changes, modifications and improvements have been made. Originally there were no bathrooms because outhouses were used. There was no inside water system. Baths had to taken in tubs with heated water brought in by servants. The East Room was not completed until about 1827. This elegant and decorated room has been used for state funerals when presidents have died while in office.

Building the White House

Ground breaking for the 170 by 85 foot mansion took place in 1792.

Foundation stone was brought in from Aquia Creek near the site.

By fall of 1792, the walls were beginning to rise and the building began to take on its future shape. On October 13, 1792, officials and residents put an engraved brass plate set in mortar on the foundation which read: "This first stone of the President's House was laid the 13th day of October 1792, and in the seventeenth year of the independence of the United States of America." This was followed by the names George Washington, President; Thomas Jefferson, and Doctor Stewart and Daniel Carroll, Commissioners; James Hoban, Architect and Collen Williamson, Master Mason. The inscription "Vivat Republica" meaning "Long Live the Republic" followed.

Construction went slowly. The exterior was finished in tan Virginia sandstone. By 1800, the interior was still not completed when John and Abigail Adams moved in. It was drafty, had no interior conveniences such as bathrooms, and the roof leaked from the heavy slate that bore down on the stone walls, cracking them. President Jefferson hired the Capitol architect, Benjamin Henry Latrobe who designed a sheet-iron roof to replace the slate.

It was Jefferson who had the building white-washed hence the name, White House, although this name would not become official until 1902, during Theodore Roosevelt's presidency.

During the War of 1812, in retaliation for the United States' burning government buildings in what is now Toronto, Canada, British troops in Washington burned the President's House and the partially completed Capitol building. After the war, architect James Hoban began the rebuilding of the President's House.

The presidents who moved in after Adams had no better accommodations than he had had. Slowly changes and improvements were made and by 1824, Monroe, after consulting with architect Charles Bulfinch, completed the South Portico. It was a circular extension with Ionic columns patterned after the portico of Chateau de Rastignac in France. The North Portico was built five years later and finished in 1830. With the completion of the North Portico, the building took on the appearance as we know it today.

The White House Through the Years

The White House could be described as a work in progress. While the exterior was basically completed in the early 1800's, over the years many changes were made to the interior.

Fire was the one disaster that destroyed much of the initial interior. Less than thirty years after the Revolutionary War victory, the War of 1812 occurred and on August, 24, 1814, the British entered Washington and set fire to the White House after Dolley Madison had fled to safety. The entire interior of the building was destroyed and the only thing that saved the outer stone walls from total destruction was a great rain storm that put out the fire and drove the British troops to their ships.

In 1815, Congress voted to have the White House rebuilt and Hoban was again hired to complete the structure. He discovered that the rains and the two years since the fire, had weakened most of the shell and all except a portion of the east wall had to be replaced. However, a section of the north front including the front door and four columns were saved and on the south most of the wall was used. The entire west wall and much of the east wall had to be replaced.

By March, 1817, the walls were up and a temporary roof was in place and during the summer of that year, Hoban had the windows installed, put in the staircases, and generally tried to make the building livable for James Monroe to move into in October of 1817. Monroe moved in but for almost two years he put up with work on the building's interior while he lived and conducted the affairs of the presidency.

On New Years Day, 1818, citizens of Washington turned out to meet President Monroe and his wife, Elizabeth, as they opened the almost completed President's House for public viewing. During his term, Monroe furnished the White House with French furnishings including the Monroes' furniture acquired while he was Ambassador to France.

Building was begun on the two porticoes that had been in the original plans but were never built. By 1820, the White House except for the two porticoes was completed. It remained for Andrew Jackson to hire Hoban again to finish the rectangular North Portico that measured 40 by 59 feet. The portico with its 50 foot columns was the last exterior change to the White House for years to come.

Renovation

As the years passed, there was only nominal upkeep and few additions or changes the building. No one gave a thought to the overall condition of the building until President Harry Truman. He had observed that when he walked in his office, the floor not only creaked, by swayed. Finally when his daughter's piano leg went through the floor and appeared in the ceiling of the dining room, he decided that something had to be done. After his reelection, Truman formed a committee of prominent architects along with the official architect to survey the White House's condition. What they found was appalling. The foundation of the building sat on eight feet of soft clay that caused the interior walls to settle and crack. Beams were giving way. The grand staircase was near collapse, the roof and third floor that was added in 1927, were supported only by crumbling walls. They found that only the outer walls could be saved.

The result of this analysis was that the Trumans spent the second term living in nearby Blair House. The entire interior of the White House was taken out. A steel framework was built inside against the exterior walls, and the interior of the White House was completed and supported on this framework. The interior decorations were taken down and crated and later put back when the work was completed.

Four years later on March 27, 1952, the Truman's moved in. They found a sparkling, structurally sound building.

Each President and First Lady who come to live in the White House during the president's term of office, uses the living quarters for their interests and as a place to relax.

In recent years each presidential couple has added their own touch to the White House.

Dwight Eisenhower had one room turned into an artist's studio where he could paint at his leisure.

Each president redoes the Oval Office to his own tastes. Usually with new carpeting, new colors, and furniture. President Reagan had it done in Southwest colors and Western art. John Kennedy had a favorite rocking chair and the "Resolute " desk given to President Hayes by the British in 1880, put in the oval office. The desk was a gift from Queen Victoria for the rescue of the abandoned ice-bound British ship by American whalers. The desk was made from oak timbers from the ship.

In 2001, one of George W. Bush's first priorities was to decide how he wanted the Oval Office decorated. He would keep using the *Resolute* desk. Presidents Reagan, Carter, and Clinton used the desk. The oval rug will be Southwestern colors of sage and melon.

In recent years many of the rooms have been returned to their original state by First Ladies re-decorating and adding antiques and adding to the extensive art collection throughout the White House. Truly, the White House has become America's National treasure house.

The Presidency

The Concept and Creation of the Presidency

Background

The Articles of Confederation document was the beginning point on the road to establishing the presidency. Ratified in 1781, it gave one vote to each member state that joined the "firm league of friendship," with all member states retaining most of their individual sovereignty. The Confederation was a loose fabric of agreement that had all the power lodged with the Continental Congress. This led to constant quarrels between the states. The Revolutionary War was fought under it so it is understandable why it was so difficult to carry on a war.

Following the Revolution and still under the Confederation, the country suffered a severe depression. There was a debt of forty million dollars, the markets for farm products was almost gone, and trade with England was minimal. Hard money was scarce so states began issuing paper money thus inflating the common currency. Property owners saw their investments decline in value. Farmers protested when two thousand farmers participated in Shay's Rebellion that had to be put down by armed militia.

Consequently, the time was ripe for anarchy to reign. Fearing the fulfillment of the old adage, "Win the war, but lose the peace," men of property like George Washington called for a stronger central government, a new government. For this purpose a group of property owners from several colonies met to consider ways to proceed to correct the shortcomings of the Confederation.

First Constitutional Convention

On February 21, 1787, representatives in the Congress under the Articles of Confederation called for a convention to revise the Articles. Thus the first Constitutional Convention was convened on May 14, 1787, eleven years after the end of the Revolutionary War, but it was postponed for lack of a quorum. A week later it did convene with the necessary quorum.

The greatest problem in the beginning of the deliberations was the balance of power. It lay with the eight larger states representing 3,800,000 people. These states were Virginia, Massachusetts, Pennsylvania, North Carolina, New York, Maryland, South Carolina, and Connecticut. The five smaller states included Rhode Island which sent no representatives, New Jersey, New Hampshire, Georgia, and Delaware. Their total population was 534, 000.

Highly respected George Washington was elected president of the Convention. The governor of Virginia, Edmund Randolph, presented a group of fifteen resolutions known as the Virginia Plan. It contained the basis for our present government which is a balance of power between the executive, the judiciary and the legislative. The seventh resolution called for an elected national executive elected by the legislature. It is the first reference at the Convention to the office of the presidency. Charles Pinckney of South Carolina called for this executive to be called the President of the United States.

All deliberations were done in secrecy. James Madison, who had earlier argued for a new constitution, made extensive notes of the discussions, noting that little could be accomplished if the debates were made public.

The main debate about the presidency concerned the perimeters of the office. At the start many felt that several persons should hold the office so they discussed how many; next, how should they be chosen; then how long a term should last; and finally, what would be the duties?

On June 1, 1787, James Wilson of Pennsylvania proposed that the executive should be a single person. Pinckney seconded the proposal. The debate that followed showed the delegates' fears. A single executive reminded them of George III from whom they had won freedom. Some wanted a triumvirate while others argued that such an arrangement would bring about disagreements. The question of a single executive was put off while they discussed the powers of the office.

How the executive was to be elected and for how long was another major point of debate. Few of the delegates trusted the people and a popular vote. The smaller states feared that the larger states would dominate the office.

The term of office discussed was between three years and seven years and whether a reelection should be allowed, or a nine year term with no reelection. James Wilson then proposed the electoral system we have today. Simply, it avoided a partisan legislative election as well as a direct popular vote that the smaller states feared.

A decision on the office of president was set aside until the problem of the representation between larger and smaller states was resolved.

On July 16, 1787, the states reached a compromise of equal representation in an upper house and representation by population in a lower house. Thus the greatest obstacle to moving toward a constitution was resolved by establishing the bicameral system.

Discussions and debate continued during the summer of 1787. Resolutions were proposed, debated, and defeated. The electoral system was agreed to on July 19, 1787. A Committee of Five was formed to review all proposals for term length.

On August 6, they proposed seven years with no reelection. Then on September 4, a larger committee proposed a four year term with no mention of reelection. This was agreed to along with the election by electors from each state. Electors would be the total number of senators and representatives. In these two committee reports reference was made to a single executive and so by tacit agreement the resolutions that followed referred only to one person. The larger committee also proposed the Electoral College system. With these resolutions agreed to, movement for a Constitution that all could sign occurred.

The Constitution was signed on September 17, 1787, by thirty-nine delegates with only George Mason of Virginia abstaining. The signing established the office of president.

Choosing the President

Electing the president was not always the highly organized, media driven event it is today.

At the Constitutional Convention that convened in 1787, the debates centered on electing a single executive or multiple leaders. A single executive, the president, was eventually agreed upon. Then the method of election had to be considered. What came out of the deliberations was the electoral college that would elect the president thus reserving power to the states where state legislatures would select the electors. These early state legislative elections were by landed gentry and men with high economic status who paid taxes and thus were on the public record and could vote. In this way the American democracy became an indirect democracy with the people electing state legislatures.

The creators of the Constitution envisioned the election of the president and vice-president, the only federal offices not directly elected, to be non-partisan.

However, in spite of George Washington's warning against political factions in his Farewell Address, it soon became evident that a political party system would evolve. During the debate over the adoption of the proposed Constitution, proponents of the Constitution stood for a strong central government which gave some powers to the states. Opponents of adoption were against a strong Federal government that assumed power over the states.

Constitutional electors were appointed or elected primarily by state legislatures and not by a direct vote of the people. Soon after the adoption of the Constitution, the Federalist party of Alexander Hamilton and the Democratic-Republican party of Thomas Jefferson and James Madison developed. These political parties were supported by the newspaper media with the *Gazette*, a Federalist newspaper on one side and the *Aurora*, a Democratic-Republican paper that attacked George Washington and the Federalists on the other.

Popular vote by land-owning and tax paying men became the norm in all states except South Carolina while Massachusetts added a religious requirement. The adopted Constitution left it up to the states to determine who might vote.

By 1824, this had begun to change and electors in most states were elected by popular vote from nominations made by political parties or legislatures. All states except South Carolina used the popular vote to determine the electors. The electors are not proportioned following the popular vote, but they are awarded to the winning party with winner gaining all the electoral votes. Today two states, Maine and Nebraska proportion electoral votes. There is one vote for each congressional district and two votes for whomever wins the state popular vote. However, there has never been a divided vote in these two states.

In essence when a voter casts a ballot for president and vice-president, he is voting for electors.

The winners meet at the state capitols on the first Monday after the second Wednesday in December and cast their ballots for president and vice-president. The sealed results are sent to Washington, the ballots are opened by the president of the Senate and tabulated at a joint session of Congress on the following January 6. There are a total of 538 electoral votes with 270 needed to become the president.

The early elections did not have well defined results. As early as 1796, ticket balancing occurred. The Democratic-Republicans chose Thomas Jefferson. The Federalists chose John Adams, but in order to take Southern votes away from Jefferson, they chose Thomas Pinckney of South Carolina to run for vice-president. The result was less than satisfactory. Because the two candidates with the most votes gained the offices, John Adams, Federalist, became president and Thomas Jefferson, a Democratic-Republican, became vice-president

The 1800 election again showed the need to revise the system when Jefferson and Aaron Burr tied. The ensuing political maneuvering caused future political recriminations by Burr. The vote was made in the House of Representatives, and with political maneuvering, Jefferson was elected.

By 1828, the two party system was fully entrenched with Andrew Jackson's popular election. The two party system resulted primarily because of two specific issues that would be a part of the political scene in years to come, import tariffs and slavery. Federalists were for higher tariffs to protect Northern industries; Democratic-Republicans wanted lower tariffs to aid the exporting of Southern raw materials.

The second issue was slavery. In 1856, the Republican party, founded in February, 1854, opposed the Kansas-Nebraska Act of 1854, which repealed the Compromise of 1820, thus allowing settlers in a territory decide whether to permit slavery.

Until the advent of the national convention, nominees for president and vice-president were selected either by an informal meeting of party leaders, or a caucus was held by party members of Congress.

Andrew Jackson was nominated by his state legislature. Later, state conventions or caucuses seconded his running mate, Martin Van Buren, for vice-president.

In 1832, both Republicans and Democrats met in Baltimore for a national nominating convention.

The Democrats added another segment to the national convention in 1840 by creating a national Democratic platform for the candidates.

The year 1856, marks the start of the more formal national political conventions. The Republican party's first national convention met on June 17, 1856, in Philadelphia. The purpose was to give direction to the party as well as to nominate John Fremont for president.

The Democrats met in a formal party convention in Baltimore and nominated James Buchanan.

Over the years both parties held conventions that were often free-for-all affairs with many candidates available. Many ballots were taken at these conventions until a winner was declared. Walkouts by dissident groups within a party occurred.

These groups often held their own nominating conventions. The result was that a national party might end up with an unknown and unelectable ticket. An example is the 1868 Democratic convention in New York. Over forty-five possible candidates were available. From these, came a compromise candidate Horatio Seymour for president against Republican U. S. Grant.

Throughout the 1880's and into the 1890's, conventions continued to be brokered to fit the best possible candidates in both parties. In 1880 it took the Republicans thirty-six ballots to nominate James Garfield. Again in 1924, the Democrats held a marathon convention and after ninety-nine ballots, John W. Davis was nominated.

The nomination process became much easier in 1936 for the Democrats when they did away with the two-thirds majority vote for nomination, in favor of the more easily attainable majority. The Republicans had had this rule for decades.

With the coming of television the entire convention format changed. There is little internal bargaining for the nominations. Most states have primary elections for president. Delegates to the national nominating convention are chosen by popular vote. Maine and Iowa still hold a type of local caucus to select delegates. Some states hold state conventions and endorse candidates.

Overall , primaries are the major road for a candidate to line up pledged delegates to call on at the convention for nomination. The result is that no longer are conventions held to broker various possible candidates, but rather the national nominating conventions have become media events where the leaders as well as ordinary party citizens are showcased. Speeches, films, and party personalities are paraded before the cameras during prime time. There might be some drama at occasional conventions such as Dwight Eisenhower's duel with Robert Taft at the 1952 Republican convention. However, in recent years, the party nominees are known well before the convention convenes. All that needs to be done is to adopt platforms, hear keynote and nominating speeches, ballot for the nominees, and listen to acceptance speeches.

The clearest example of this is the precise and forgone conclusion of the 2000 presidential campaign. It began more than a year before the nominating conventions. Both Vice-President Al Gore and Texas Governor George W. Bush went through the primaries with few problems, emerging with full blown campaigns months before the July and August conventions.

So the national nominating conventions evolved and replaced the unworkable non-partisan system of choosing the president.

Today there is speculation about the usefulness and the need for national nominating conventions in today's media saturated world. After the 2000 national conventions, many media sources indicated that this may be the last conventions they will cover.

The Presidents of the United States

George Washington
1st President (1789-1797)

No president has been more revered or trusted than George Washington. The 6 feet, 2 inch tall, Washington quietly led our country in peace and war. He was the guiding leader who helped bring about the establishment of the United Sates of America. Washington served as the commander of the Continental Army during the Revolutionary War, President of the Constitutional Convention, and later was a unanimous choice for two terms as president. His most important trait was his ability to mold divisive factions into a consensus and bring about stability to a new nation.

Upon learning of his election to the presidency, the retired Washington, left his home at Mount Vernon to serve his country again. Under his guidance and leadership, he helped the new nation adopt a constitution and then with Congress, he helped create a functioning government. Together they set about establishing the legitimacy of the United States of America in the world. Washington's strong moral nature demanded that he be conscious of the precedents he was setting for presidents who would follow him. He was truly the "Father of our country."

Biography

George Washington was born on February 22, 1732, on a family estate near the Potomac River in Virginia. His childhood was centered upon his older brother, Lawrence, who helped raise him after his father died. At sixteen, Washington went to live with Lawrence at Mount Vernon where Lawrence trained him to be a surveyor.

Washington grew to be a tall, imposing man with a quiet, dignified personality that through the years impressed all who met him. He attended Colonial schools and had no formal university training.

George Washington's military career began with his duties in the Virginia militia where he was appointed a major and rose to the rank of colonel. During the French and Indian War (1754-1763), Washington oversaw the building of Fort Necessity in Pennsylvania. He later surrendered the Fort to the French forces in June, 1754.

He served with General Braddock and led his forces in retreat after the death of Braddock at the Battle of the Wilderness on July 9, 1754.

In December, 1758, Colonel Washington resigned from the militia after he was elected to the Virginia House of Burgesses in July of that year.

At age 26, Washington married the widow, Martha Dandridge Custis, a prominent, wealthy lady who lived near Williamsburg, Virginia. While they had no children of their own, Washington treated his wife's son and daughter as his own. With his election, Washington's life of public service began.

For the next thirty-three years he would serve in various capacities in public life. He was in the House of Burgesses from 1759 to 1774. Here he joined in the protests to England's colonial policies. He was a member of Virginia's delegation to the First and Second Continental Congresses where he became military advisor and chairman of the committee to raise arms and ammunition for the Continental Army. In 1775, Washington was named Commander-in-Chief of the Continental Army.

During the Revolution, Washington led an untrained military force of militia against a highly trained British army. Major battles were Trenton (December, 1776), Princeton (January, 1777), Brandywine (September 1777), and Georgetown (October 1777). His greatest accomplishment was marshaling his forces after the cold, desperate winter at Valley Forge in December, 1777.

After Valley Forge, Washington with the aid of Frenchman, Baron Friedrich Von Steuben, revitalized the army by drilling the militia into a disciplined fighting force. This new army challenged the British forces and eventually surrounded the British at Yorktown in 1781, bringing the American Revolution to a close.

After the war, Washington went back to Mount Vernon to retire but was asked to come to serve his country one more time as a delegate to the Constitutional Convention.

Here he served as president of the Convention of 1787, leading the delegates who wanted a strong central government. With the establishment of the United States and the adoption of a constitution, the only real choice the nation's delegates had was to elect Washington president. He served two terms as president.

At age 65, Washington again retired to Mount Vernon, to run his estate.

In early December, 1799, Washington rode on horseback around his plantation in a cold, sleet rain. He returned in wet clothes and caught a severe cold. His health declined and he died on December 14, 1799.

Presidential Election-1789

A proven, trusted leader, Washington, a Federalist, was selected by all sixty-nine electors from the ten states that had ratified the Constitution. During his first term (1789-1793) he supported Alexander Hamilton in his efforts to set the young nation on solid fiscal base by raising taxes and paying off the debt of more than seventy-five million dollars. At this time the country's population was about four million. Washington surprised everyone by nominating Thomas Jefferson, a diplomat serving in France, as his Secretary of State. During his first term President Washington began meeting with his department heads, establishing the cabinet system that remains part of today's Executive branch.

Presidential Election-1792

Washington's first term as president was so successful that he was again elected to serve as the president from 1793-1797.

It is notable that both the Federalists and the Democratic-Republicans urged his unanimous reelection. All 132 elector representatives from fifteen states voted for him. John Adams again became the vice-president with 77 votes.

Major Legislation During Presidency

On July 4, 1789, the United States passed the first tariff laws on imported goods. The tariff law gave U. S. ships carrying imported goods a break, while equally taxing, English and French ships carrying foreign goods.

In September, 1789, Congress passed the Federal Judiciary Act, creating the Supreme Court and the lower federal courts.

On November 21, 1789, North Carolina became the twelfth state to ratify the Constitution.

On May 29, 1790, Rhode Island became the thirteenth state to ratify the Constitution

Philadelphia was made the temporary capital of the United States on December 6, 1790.

On September 15, 1791, Congress submitted the Bill of Rights to the states for ratification. By December 15, 1791, the Bill of Rights was ratified as the first ten amendments to the Constitution.

On June 1, 1792, Kentucky became the fifteenth state to join the United States.

George Washington's Proclamation of Neutrality, 1793, kept the young American nation out of the war between the French and the British.

Washington's administration established the Departments of State, War, and Treasury, and set up the early post office system. The first judges and attorney-general of the United States were appointed.

On June 1, 1796, Tennessee joined the Union as the sixteenth state.

In 1797, the Bank of the United States was established.

Major Events During Presidency

In 1790, the first official complete census of the population of the U.S. was taken. The total population was 3,929,625 including a half million slaves and 60,000 free blacks.

To help pay the national debt, Congress approved an excise tax on liquor. Western Pennsylvania farmers whose corn crops were used for liquor refused to pay. They armed themselves and in 1794 created the Whiskey Rebellion, the the first challenge to Federal authority. Washington sent 15,000 Federal troops. This show of force quelled the uprising. Two leaders were tried, convicted and later pardoned by President Washington.

The 1795, the controversial Jay's Treaty laid the foundation that led to the War of 1812. Under the Treaty, Britain withdrew its forces in the Northwest Territory as promised in the Treaty of Paris of 1783, which had ended the Revolutionary War.

France looked on Jay's Treaty as an affront and they too began harassing American ships.

In turn, in order to avoid an open conflict with England so soon after the recovery from the Revolution, George Washington agreed to give up the neutrality of the seas, thus allowing Britain to board and search U. S. ships on the high seas and impress U. S. sailors into their navy. This action would become the basis for the War of 1812 with England. It also allowed the United States to use the Mississippi River and New Orleans for commerce.

Pinckney's Treaty of 1795, created normal relations with Spain by establishing the boundary between the U. S. and Spanish Florida.

Throughout his presidency, Washington understood that he and the Congress were setting precedents by many of their acts or actions. Executive privilege was one presidential precedent that Washington set.

In 1796, the House of Representatives questioned the wisdom of Jay's Treaty. They passed a resolution in March, 1796, asking Washington for the papers dealing with the treaty. In his reply on March 30, 1796, Washington stated that the Senate had seen the papers before ratifying the treaty. He indicated that to turn the papers over to the House would not be in the best interests of the country. Therefore he had to turn down their request. He did so in a special message to the House. He understood that the consent to a treaty was not necessary by the House and therefore "under all circumstances of this case forbids a compliance with your request."[1]

_____

[1] *Messages and Papers of the Presidents* Vol. 1 pp. 186-188

John Adams
2nd President (1797-1801)

The shy, quick-tempered and tenacious 5 feet, 6 inches tall John Adams was a tireless patriot who spent his life helping to establish the United States of America. Called the Atlas of Independence, Adams became a voluntary caretaker of the process of independence from England before and during the Revolutionary War. He had a high sense of justice and used his innate sense of independence to lead the new country through difficult times. Adams was often called autocratic because of his mistrust of the common people and what he felt was their lack of ability to rule themselves.

Biography

John Adams was born on October 30, 1735, to a Massachusetts farm family in Braintree (now Quincy). His father, John Adams, was a farmer and leather craftsman. His mother was Susanne Boylston Adams. He was the great, great grandson of the Pilgrims, John and Priscilla Alden. His ancestors came to the early colonies in 1640. John

Adams grew up on the farm, attended Harvard, and graduated in 1755. He studied law and became the lawyer who chose to defend British Captain Prescott and the soldiers who perpetrated the Boston Massacre on March 5, 1770. All were acquitted except two who were branded for manslaughter.

On October 25, 1764, Adams married Abigail Smith. They had five children during the marriage. One son, John Quincy Adams, became the sixth president of the United States.

Early on in his public life, Adams was a spokesman against the actions of the British crown. He spoke out against the Stamp Act and established himself as a spokesman against English rule. As a representative at the two Continental Congresses, Adams spoke out for independence. He served on the committee to draft the Declaration of Independence and urged Thomas Jefferson to write the document.

After it was adopted, Adams was one of the fifty-six delegates who signed it. He and Thomas Jefferson were the only future presidents to sign it.

It was Adams who nominated and urged the Continental Congress to appoint George Washington commander in chief of the army. Later in 1798, after Adams became president and Washington had retired to Mount Vernon at the height of the disagreement with France, he sent to the Senate the nomination of Washington "to be Lieutenant-General and Commander-in-Chief of all armies raised or to be raised in the United States."[1]

Adams later served on several diplomatic missions for the United States which included Dutch recognition of the new nation. He also drafted the Massachusetts constitution during the 1780's. However, his greatest triumph was on the diplomatic mission to Paris to conclude the Revolution and obtain a peace treaty with Britain. Adams, Benjamin Franklin, and John Jay concluded the Treaty of Paris which was signed on September 3, 1783. It established the Mississippi River as the nation's western boundary.

After a three year term as the first minister to Britain, Adams returned home in 1788, and the following year was elected vice-president during Washington's two terms as president.

In 1796, he was elected president for one term and served until March 4, 1801. Adams and his wife, Abigail, were the first to live in the White House where Abigail tried to establish something of a home. No single room was totally finished nor were there adequate lamps for light. She could not hang her wash outside because of a lack of a yard so she used the East Room to do so.[2]

In retirement, Adams spent much time in reading and corresponding with Dr. Benjamin Rush of Philadelphia and renewing his friendship with Thomas Jefferson. In 1820, he served as a Massachusetts selector and voted for James Monroe. At age 89, he saw his son, John Quincy elected president.

John Adams died on July 4, 1826, the fiftieth anniversary of the founding of the United States. His last words were, "Jefferson still..."

---

[1] Op. Cit. *Messages Vol. 1* p. 257

[2] Kenneth W.. Leish, *The White House*, p. 20

The last indistinct word was perhaps " lives." The irony is that Jefferson preceded Adams in death by only a few hours.

John Adams' character and values can be summed up in a letter he sent his wife, Abigail, while serving in the Continental Congress. In it he stated that he wished her to instill in their sons the absolute need to "revere nothing but religion, morality, and liberty."

Presidential Campaign-1796

John Adams was never formally nominated, but had the tacit endorsement of Washington as the candidate for the Federalists. His opponent was Thomas Jefferson for the Democratic-Republicans. Aaron Burr was the vice-president candidate.

The campaign of 1796 perhaps set the tone of many campaigns to come. It was a vicious series of character attacks by both Jeffersonians and supporters of Adams. The attacks were in letters and pamphlets distributed by both Adams and Jefferson supporters.

Adams was portrayed as a despot who distrusted the people. He was portrayed as wanting to retain central power in Washington with a Senate elected for life in order to thwart the common masses who elected the House members every two years.

Jefferson was portrayed by the Federalists as a demagogue who deceived the people by appealing to their fears.

The ballots in 1796 did not distinguish between president and vice-president. The candidate with the highest number of votes became president; the next highest, the vice-president regardless of differing political beliefs. Even the Federalist Hamilton plotted against Adams by encouraging the Southern electors to vote for Adams as a vice-presidential candidate

Presidential Election-1796

John Adams won the majority of electors in 9 states, for a total of 71 votes. Jefferson won 68 votes with a majority in 7 states. The Federalist Thomas Pinckney received 59 and Aaron Burr, 30 votes. Many others received votes including Samuel Adams with 15. Consequently Thomas Jefferson, Democratic-Republican, became the vice-president under the Federalist President John Adams.

Major Legislation During Presidency

In 1793, during Washington's first term, Congress passed an act to recognize the use of foreign coins for a period of three years until such time as the government could begin minting its own coins. On July 22, 1797, one of the first proclamations that John Adams made was to declare the end of the use of foreign gold and silver coins. At that time the U. S. began minting coins for legal tender.[3]

Adams was vehement in his efforts to keep the United States out of a war with France over the stopping and search of our ships in France's war with Britain. The undeclared Quasi-War with France reached crisis status with many in the United States wanting to go to

---

3 Op cit. *Messages.* p. 239

war. Adams remained firm and urged a more tempered solution.

In 1799, his peace mission to France, headed by Patrick Henry, succeeded with the Convention of 1800 that established neutrality on the seas and gave France most favored nation trading rights.

The Logan Act of 1799 remains in effect today. It prevents citizens from privately negotiating with foreign powers.

To encourage the settlement of Western lands, the Congress enacted the Land Act of 1800. It allowed individual settlers to purchase up to 320 acres at local land offices. This act eliminated the land speculator.

Major Events During Presidency

In October, 1797, American commissioners went to Paris. The XYZ Affair was the name given to the report that Adams sent to Congress telling of the attempt by the French to bribe the American peace delegation with $240,000 if they would agree to France's terms of declaring war on England. The French indicated that they would show respect for the American flag. The U. S. could not accept any of this because of the Jay Treaty with England.

Consequently, the Treaty of 1778 with France was suspended and an undeclared naval war carried on with both sides seizing ships. Adams' report[4] created in the United States a hatred for the French and many urged war against France.

Adams continued to negotiate while putting the U. S. on a war preparation status by creating the Un-

ited States Navy Department to carry on the naval war that might occur. The affair caused Congress to pass the Alien and Sedition Acts of 1798 that were directed primarily at the French.

The four acts were the Naturalization Act that made it more difficult for immigrants to become citizens.

The Alien Act allowed the president to deport any alien who was deemed dangerous.

The Alien Enemies Act authorized the president to round up and imprison enemies during war time.

The Sedition Act made it a Federal offense to write and criticize the government.

The penalties were fines and imprisonment. These acts had a two year expiration date and expired in 1800. The Naturalization Act was repealed in 1802.

The public reaction to these Acts was so negative that it was one of the reasons for the rise of the Jeffersonians or Democrat-Republicans. Their rise brought about the demise of the Federalists.

In September, 1800, Emperor Napoleon and the U. S. signed a peace treaty, but the final settlement in the damages to American ships was not completed until Andrew Jackson's presidency.

The Fries Rebellion of 1799 was an uprising by Pennsylvanians against the levying of federal taxes on property. John Fries was arrested and convicted of treason and was to be hanged, but Adams in 1800, pardoned him and others who had taken a part in the rebellion.

---

4 Ibid. pp.254-255

Thomas Jefferson
3rd President (1801-1809)

Thomas Jefferson was a thin, 6 feet, 2 inches tall, somewhat awkward man with reddish hair and an angular face. His life was one of continuous study and learning as shown in his myriad interests in philosophy, language, architecture, science, and politics. His mind remained active his entire 83 years of life. The legacy he left is one that is the essence of our democratic America. He believed strongly in man's ability to govern himself and wholeheartedly in the personal liberty of all individuals.

Biography

Thomas Jefferson was born on April 13, 1743, at Shadwell plantation in Virginia to Colonel Peter Jefferson and Jane Randolph Jefferson. He grew up in the rural setting of his father's 5,000 acre plantation which he inherited at age 14 upon his 49 year old father's death. After several years of private tutoring, the 17 year old Jefferson went to college at William and Mary in Williamsburg and graduated at age 19 in 1762. He was learned in Latin, Greek, French, Italian, and Spanish.

While attending college in Williamsburg, he saw government in action. Later he studied law under George Wythe and was admitted to the bar in 1767 at age 24.

At 25, Jefferson was elected to the Virginia House of Burgesses and remained a member until the Revolution. There he supported the move to break free of British rule.

On January 1, 1772, he married Martha Wayles Skelton, a wealthy widow who doubled Jefferson's wealth with her inheritance, but she also brought indebtedness. Only two daughters of six children lived to adulthood. His home at Monticello on top of a mountain near Charlottesville was designed, built, and remodeled by him. Eventually, Jefferson owned nearly 10,000 acres and 200 slaves in spite of his stand against slavery.

In 1775, at age 33, Jefferson was chosen to be a delegate to the Continental Congress. There he had his greatest achievement. He wrote the Declaration of Independence in 1776. In it he put all his passion for protecting and gaining liberty for the colonists. His immortal words have become a litany of liberty for the human spirit. It was adopted on July 4, 1776, by the thirteen colonies with fifty-six delegates signing the document.

During the Revolution, Jefferson was elected governor of Virginia in 1779. Jefferson proposed the separation of church and state in an Ordinance of Religious Freedom. It was not passed, but in 1785, Virginia did pass the same type of measure. His term was uneventful except for the British invasion of the state in 1781. Jefferson was blamed for failing to adequately defend Virginia and resigned.

In 1783, after the death of his wife, he served as Virginia's representative to Congress. There he proposed the decimal monetary system. His report on the western part of the country anticipated the Northwest Ordinance of 1787 and the Louisiana Purchase in 1803 during his presidency.

Following service in the Continental Congress, Jefferson accepted the ministership to France in 1785 and spent five years living in Paris. During those years, Jefferson absorbed the culture and learning of Europe, visiting famous scientists, learning more about agriculture, enjoying the French cuisine, and reading the literature. He came into contact with the revival of Greek architecture and later introduced it into the United States, beginning the Greek revival movement that continued into the nineteenth century. His design of the state capitol at Richmond is based upon a temple in Nimes, France. It was the first public building in the U. S. built in the classical revival style.

In 1790, Jefferson was called home by Washington to become his Secretary of State. He served as Secretary until 1793. Alexander Hamilton was in the same cabinet. He and Jefferson often clashed on the Federal role of a centralized government. Jefferson agreed with Washington's isolationist policy.

In 1796, Jefferson, a Democrat-Republican, was elected vice-president under John Adams, a Federalist. The irony was that he and

Adams disagreed about the role of government. Federalist Adams followed Washington's strong central government and Jefferson espoused a more laissez faire approach, giving more power to the states. The Federalists were declining in power and in the 1800 election, Jefferson became president ending the Federalists as a political power.

After serving two terms as president from 1801 to 1809, Jefferson retired to his Monticello home. His final public service was designing and building the University of Virginia at Charlottesville in 1819.

Jefferson's wife's debts plagued him his entire life so that he died almost penniless, owning only his home and lands.

Jefferson died on July 4, 1826, preceding John Adams in death by a few hours. The date marked the fiftieth anniversary of the signing of the Declaration of Independence, Thomas Jefferson's greatest legacy.

Jefferson wrote his own epitaph: "Here was buried Thomas Jefferson, author of the Declaration of Independence, of the statute of Virginia for Religious Freedom, and father of the University of Virginia."

Presidential Campaign-1800

The presidential campaign of 1800 between Democrat-Republican Jefferson and Federalist John Adams was a divisive and nastily fought war of words carried out in the press. Neither candidate made public speeches, but their views were well known. The Sedition Act of 1798 passed by a Federalist Congress was invoked many times against editors and writers who spoke out against Federalist policies. The Federalists portrayed Jefferson as a hedonistic man who if elected would allow pillage and rape to run rampant in the land. They painted him as a man with no religious beliefs.

Virginia and Kentucky had written resolutions condemning the Alien and Sedition Acts so the campaign was a debate over whether the states had the right to nullify Federal laws. When the Republicans defeated the New York legislature Federalists, it assured Jefferson the twelve New York electoral votes.

Election-1800

Both Jefferson and Aaron Burr, his vice-president running mate on the Democrat-Republican ticket, received 73 electoral votes. John Adams received 65 votes. Even though Jefferson was the agreed upon presidential candidate, the tie with Burr, who refused to give in to Jefferson, threw the election into the Federalist dominated House of Representatives. Jefferson and Burr had won 8 states.

During the week of February 11-17, 1801, the House of Representatives with each state casting one vote based upon the state delegate majority, voted 36 times before finally electing Jefferson to the presidency. The Federalists decided to back Burr, but Hamilton lobbied for Jefferson and won ten states over to Jefferson. Burr won four states. Delaware and South Carolina did not vote.

Because of this deadlock, the Twelfth Amendment to the Constitution was passed in 1804. It provided separate balloting for the president and vice-president.

Presidential Campaign-1804

The Republicans in Congress nominated Jefferson for president and George Clinton of New York for vice-president. Their opponents were Federalist Charles Pinckney of South Carolina for president and Rufus King of New York for vice-president.

The campaign was nothing like the previous one. The Federalists had lost favor with the people and Jefferson had made inroads into the Northern Federalist states, so he faced little challenge.

Presidential Election-1804

In 1804 the 12th Amendment established a separate ballot for president and vice-president.

In the first election held under the 12th Amendment, Jefferson received 162 electoral votes to Pinckney's 14. Jefferson carried 15 states. The Federalist Pinckney carried two states indicating the total decline of the Federalists as a political party. George Clinton was elected Vice-President.

Major Legislation During Presidency

Ohio was admitted to the Union on March 1, 1803, as the 17th state, the first state formed from the Northwest Territory.

On January 1, 1808, the abolition of the African slave trade bill became law.

The Embargo Act of 1807-1809, was passed in response to British and French attacks upon American ships. The act prevented American ships from docking at foreign ports and prevented foreign ships from docking in the United States. The embargo almost destroyed the United States shipping industry and caused havoc in northern manufacturing states. It was repealed in March, 1809. It was replaced by the Non-Intercource Act which would allow trade with Britain or France as soon as they respected the rights of the United States on the high seas.

Major Events During Presidency

In 1803, the Louisiana Purchase was purchased. It doubled the size of the United States and extended the country west to the Rocky Mountains. Napoleon was paid $15 million or about three cents an acre.

Between 1804-1807, Aaron Burr was tried for treason and acquitted. He had been accused of trying to separate the western lands from the Union and to form a separate nation.

Jefferson continued the executive privilege doctrine set by Washington, releasing only those papers he deemed important in the treason trial of Aaron Burr.[1]

In 1804, President Jefferson sent Meriwether Lewis and William Clark out to explore the Louisiana Purchase. They left St. Louis, Missouri, on May 14. They spent that winter with the Mandan Indians near what is now Bismarck, North Dakota. They continued across the Rockies, reaching the Pacific Ocean on November 7, 1805.

The U. S. population in 1800 was 5,308,000.

---

1 Op Cit. Messages p. 425; p. 438

James Madison
4th President (1809-1817)

James Madison was a slight man, only 5 feet, 4 inches tall, weighing about a 100 pounds. He, more than any other individual, embodies the ideals of our American democracy. His greatest service to the nation took place before his presidency. He earned the title of "Father of our Constitution" by his unstinting energy and direction in the writing of the Constitution of the United States. He was also the principal advocate of the Bill of Rights, the first ten amendments to the Constitution. Madison strongly urged the need for active executive leadership along with a centralized government. A diarist, Madison kept a precise record of the founding of the United States government.

Biography

Madison was born on March 16, 1751, at Port Conway, Virginia, to James Madison, a planter and Eleanor Rose Conway Madison. He was educated at home until the age of 11, and then attended a private boarding school. At a young age he displayed a genius for languages and mathematics, as well as an interest in government. He graduated from the College of New Jersey, now Princeton University, completing the four year course in two years. With the Revolutionary War looming, poor health prevented his serving in the army. However, in 1776 he was elected to the Virginia Revolutionary Council. He wrote a resolution asking for a Declaration of Independence. Later he was sent to the Continental Congress to represent Virginia .

When peace came, he urged the replacement of the Articles of Confederation with suggestions for a new and stronger Constitution that would centralize government. It would be made up of checks and balances between the legislative, executive, and judicial branches. He saw all levels of government as having some autonomy in their affairs, but at the same time being closely aligned so that they supported one another. He felt that this would prevent factions from ruling the country. Madison contributed to *The Federalist* papers, which argued for the ratification of the Constitution. Later as a member of Congress, his nine proposals to amend the Constitution, resulted in Congress creating the Bill of Rights.

On September 15, 1794, Madison, 43, married Dolley Dandridge Payne Todd, 26, a widow with a son. She had instituted a social climate in Washington by occasionally being the hostess for the widowed Thomas Jefferson. As First Lady she enlivened the social scene with many galas at the White House. During the War of 1812, she fled the capital with the Stuart portrait of Washington, thus saving it for posterity.

Madison became Secretary of State under President Thomas Jefferson from 1801 to 1809. He began the long task of dealing with Britain and France as they fought one another. It was a dispute that slowly involved the United States. Later this involvement resulted in the War of 1812 during Madison's presidency.

Madison was elected in 1808 and served two terms as president before retiring to his Virginia estate, Montpellier.

In 1826, he succeeded Jefferson as rector of the University of Virginia. He was an adviser to President Monroe, exchanging many letters dealing with the role of America in foreign affairs. His writings on the Constitution were prepared for publication by him and published posthumously.

James Madison died on June 28, 1836, at the age of 85.

Presidential Campaign-1808

Thomas Jefferson helped establish precedent by refusing to serve a third term. He urged the Democrat-Republicans to endorse Madison. Madison's vice-president was George Clinton of New York. The Federalists opposing Madison and George Clinton were Charles Pinckney of South Carolina for president and Rufus King of New York for vice-president.

The major issue was the embargo of British cargo that Madison as Secretary of State had imposed. The British were not hurt by it because Madison had overestimated the British dependence upon

American goods. However, it had caused serious economic problems for American businesses because Britain was their biggest customer. With few goods being shipped on American ships, hardship and failing seaport towns resulted.

Madison's political opposition was not strong because the Federalists were almost nonexistent after the Jeffersonian Republican victory in 1800.

Presidential Election-1808

James Madison, Democrat-Republican, won easily with 122 electoral votes from 12 states. Charles Pinckney, Federalist, received 47 electoral votes from 7 states. New York gave George Clinton 6 votes.

Presidential Campaign-1812

The only significant issue of the campaign was the War of 1812 and how it was being pursued. The Federalists made the slogan " Madison's War" into a rallying cry. Madison was attacked for getting into war and then for not pursuing it with enough vigor. His strongest opposition came from the New England states because their industries suffered most from the conflict. His opponent was Federalist De Witt Clinton of New York.

Presidential Election-1812

Madison defeated George Clinton winning 128 electoral votes from 11 states to Clinton's 89 votes from 7 states.

Major Legislation During Presidency

In 1810, Madison and Congress brought an end to the trade ban with the British and the French.

The shipping embargo of Britain was again instituted in 1811, prior to the war that was declared on Britain in 1812. The major issue was the stopping of American ships and forcing Americans sailors into the British navy.

Louisiana was admitted to the Union on April 30, 1812, as the 18th state.

On December 11, 1816, Indiana became the 19th state.

Major Events During Presidency

The War of 1812 produced major battles at Washington, D.C., Baltimore, and Fort McHenry, where Francis Scott Key penned the *Star Spangled Banner,* the future National anthem of the United States.

In August, 1814, a contingent of British troops landed near Washington and after a skirmish in which the American force retreated, proceeded to Washington where they looted and burned the Capitol and the White House. Dolley Madison fled the White House with what she could save. Only the charred walls of the building remained.

In 1814, John Quincy Adams led the American peace conference to end the War of 1812. The British and the United States signed the Treaty of Ghent on December 24, 1814. The basic agreement was to resume relationships as they were prior to hostilities. No mention was made of the stopping of ships.

The 1810 census found the United States population at 7,239, 881.

James Monroe
5th President (1817-1825)

The sturdily built 6 feet tall James Monroe spent his entire adult life in the service of his country beginning with his service in Washington's army during the Revolution and later as a member of the Continental Congress. A quiet, forceful man, who at times spoke his mind, Monroe envisioned a dominant world view of the American democracy. He was often overshadowed by his contemporaries from Virginia, George Washington, mentor Thomas Jefferson, and James Madison. He was the last of the Virginia dynasty of American presidents.

Biography

James Monroe was born in Westmoreland County in Virginia on April 28, 1758, to Spence and Elizabeth Jones Monroe. In 1774 at age 16, he attended William and Mary College, but after two years left in 1776 to join Washington's Continental Army after the start of the Revolution. During the war he fought in major battles at Brandywine, Germantown, Monmouth, and Trenton. He was wounded after crossing the Delaware River with Washington and then spent the winter with the Continental Army at Valley Forge.

After the war he returned to Virginia and studied law under Governor Thomas Jefferson. From 1783 to 1786, Monroe served in the Continental Congress. He was admitted to the bar in 1786. In the Virginia Ratification Convention, he spoke out against ratification of the proposed Constitution because there was no bill of rights. He felt that too much power was centered in the Federal government.

On February 16, 1786, Monroe, age 27, married Elizabeth Kortright, age 17, of New York City. They had two daughters and later a son who died in infancy. A Democratic-Republican, Monroe served as U. S. senator from 1790 to 1794. He was governor of Virginia four times.

In 1794, George Washington sent Monroe to Paris as minister to France. There he encountered the French Revolution and endorsed it wholeheartedly. Monroe was recalled because he did not openly support the Jay Treaty with Britain.

His greatest achievement occurred in 1803 when he served as a diplomat to France with the mission to negotiate with Napoleon for the purchase of the Louisiana territory. Jefferson later appointed Monroe to be minister to Great Britain from 1803 to 1807. He was unsuccessful in his negotiations with England in trying to stop their impressment of American seamen.

Monroe also tried to negotiate a treaty for the Florida territory from Spain but failed. Monroe returned to practice law, but was named Secretary of State by Madison He held the post from 1811 to 1817. During that time he was also appointed Secretary of War after the city of Washington was burned by the British in the War of 1812. He did both roles superbly and as a result became the natural successor to Madison.

In March, 1816, Monroe was chosen to run for president with Governor Daniel Tompkins of New York as vice-president.

James Monroe was elected and served two terms as president before retiring to his home at Oak Hill in Virginia. After the death of his wife in 1830, he moved to New York to live with his daughter. There he died on July 4, 1831, of heart failure.

Presidential Campaign-1816

Monroe's opponent was Federalist Rufus King of New York. After the failing Federalist party opposed the War of 1812, it was a foregone conclusion that Monroe would win. The Democratic-Republicans did little campaigning with King putting up only token opposition.

Election-1816

James Monroe easily won the election with 183 electoral votes from 16 states. Rufus King won 34 electoral votes from three states.

Election-1820

President Monroe and Vice-President Daniel D. Tompkins were such overwhelming choices that the Democratic-Republicans did not hold a nominating convention. The Federalists did not run anyone in opposition. Monroe won all 24 states with 230 electoral votes. New Hampshire cast one vote for Secretary of State John Quincy Adams to preserve the unanimous vote for George Washington in 1789.

Major Legislation During Presidency

Monroe's great popularity brought about a period in America known as the "Era of Good Feeling."

In 1817, Secretary Rush and British Minister Bagot agreed to demilitarize the Great Lakes. Ratified in 1818, it set the stage for the Convention of 1818 at which the Great Lakes were opened to American fishermen by Great Britain and the boundary between Canada and the United States was agreed upon.

Under the Adams-Onis Treaty of 1819, Spain ceded Florida to the United States for cancellation of their debt owed to U. S. citizens, renounced all claims to the Oregon territory, and agreed to a commission to set boundaries between the U. S. and Spanish lands at the Sabine River..

In 1820, Congress adopted the Missouri Compromise to quiet the slavery question. After great debate, Maine was admitted as a free state and Missouri was admitted as a slave state. In addition, the Missouri Compromise established 36°, 30" N. latitude as the line which separated southern slave territory from northern free soil territory.

The United States was expanding rapidly with several states admitted to the Union. They were Mississippi, December 10, 1817, the 20th state; Illinois, the 21st state, December 3, 1818; Alabama, December 14, 1819, the 22nd state; Maine, March 15, 1820, the 23rd state; and Missouri, August 10, 1821, the 24th state.

On December 2, 1823, Monroe declared a policy for the United States which became known as the Monroe Doctrine. It stated that the governments of the Americas were different from Europe, and therefore the North, Central, and South American countries would no longer be open to European colonization. While the U. S. would not interfere with existing European territories already in place, it would not tolerate any new interference by a European power.

In March, 1818, Congress established the permanent design of the U. S. flag. The flag would retain thirteen red and white stripes for the thirteen colonies, but a star would be added to the blue field for each state admitted.

Major Events During Presidency

In 1817-1818, Spanish Florida raided settlers in Georgia. Monroe sent an army under General Andrew Jackson. He defeated the Seminoles in the First Seminole War and captured the territory.

In 1819, the nation faced its first depression. Wild speculation in Western lands caused a panic. To add to the depression, the United States Bank foreclosed on borrowers who had overextended themselves because Congress in 1817, ordered that all land purchases be paid for in gold or silver coin.

The 1820 United States population was 9,638,453.

John Quincy Adams
6th President (1825-1829)

For a man who reached the pinnacle of political power as president of the United States, the 5 feet, 7 inch, 175 pound, rotund John Quincy Adams earned his reputation as a diplomat before he became president and later as a leader in the Congress. Considered one of our great Secretaries of State, Adams' very candid personality was fitted for his role as Secretary. An adamant negotiator, he helped obtain the Florida territory, settled the Oregon occupation dispute with England, and advised President James Monroe on the formation of the Monroe Doctrine.

As president, Adams can be viewed as a transition leader. He bridged the four years between James Monroe and Andrew Jackson when the U. S. was in a period of limited diplomacy and a great deal of political unrest. The Federalist party was no longer a political force and the Democrat-Republicans were in internal turmoil. Adams fit with neither group and thus accomplished little. He was called the "New England Independent."

45

He recognized this when he said, "I shall be as I have been, a solitary."

Biography

John Quincy Adams was born on July 11, 1767, in Braintree (now Quincy), Massachusetts, to President John Adams, and Abigail Smith Adams. From his early childhood John Quincy was nurtured by his father to be president. He grew up with the Revolutionary War around him and as a child he saw Boston's Battle of Bunker Hill from Penn's Hill. Because of the Revolution, local schools were not running so he was educated at home until he accompanied his father abroad at age ten, remaining there until 1785 when he was seventeen. He became a cultured and urbane young man in the schools of Paris and the court of Russia in St. Petersburg.

John Quincy became a master of languages, speaking French, Dutch and Russian fluently. He entered Harvard as a junior and graduated second out of 51 classmates in 1787. From 1787 to 1790, he studied law and was admitted to the bar in 1790. He practiced law until 1794, when President Washington appointed him Minister to the Netherlands because of his fluent Dutch. Later, his father appointed him Minister to Prussia for three years where he completed the Prussian-American Treaty of 1799.

Returning home, he served as a state senator and then won a U. S. Senate seat from 1803 until 1808 where, although a Federalist, he supported Thomas Jefferson, the Democratic-Republican. For this support he was defeated in the next senatorial election.

President Madison appointed him Minister to Russia where he convinced Czar Alexander to permit American ships access to Russian ports. From St. Petersburg, Adams sent vivid accounts of Napoleon's army in Russia. Adams wrote in his diary his entire life so we have detailed historical accounts of events in which he was involved.

John Quincy Adams' greatest achievement was his negotiations at the Treaty of Ghent in 1814, which ended the War of 1812. Following that success, he served as President Monroe's Secretary of State from 1817 to 1825, further establishing himself as a superb negotiator. He led a delegation at the Convention of 1818 with Britain which set Great Lakes fishing rights for the U. S. and established the border with Canada from Minnesota to the Rockies. With Spain he brought about the transfer of South Florida to the United States. Finally, his views of South American countries prevailed in the Monroe Doctrine.

After his one term as president, John Quincy became the only president to serve in the House of Representatives. He served seventeen years in the House, working for the abolition of slavery and citizens' personal freedoms. He never retired officially, but served in the House until his death on February 23, 1848, suffering a stroke at his desk. He died two days later.

Presidential Campaign-1824

The presidential campaign of 1824 was centered around sectional differences. Three candidates were nominated by state legislatures. John Quincy Adam was nominated by Massachusetts and represented the established East. Tennessee nominated Andrew Jackson, who was popular because of his war record and rugged individualism. The highly qualified Henry Clay, serving in the House of Representatives, was nominated by Kentucky. William Crawford, a noted senator from Georgia with a strong southern following, declared his candidacy. Crawford suffered a stroke during the campaign, but he remained an important figure. The only real campaign issue was protective tariffs. All four candidates supported the tariffs in some way. No candidate received the required majority thereby moving the election into the House of Representatives.

Election-1824

In 1824, a majority of the 261 electoral votes was needed to be elected president. The popular vote was 152,271 (41%) for Andrew Jackson; 113,122 (31%) for John Quincy Adams; 47,531 (13%) for Henry Clay, and 40,856 (11%) for William Crawford.

Therefore, the election was not decided by the popular vote because of the majority needed by a candidate. Jackson received 99 electoral votes from 11 states. Adams won 84 electoral votes in 7 states. Crawford won 41 electoral votes from 3 states . Clay won 3 states with 37 electoral votes.

The election went to the House of Representatives as required in the Twelfth Amendment. Here the election was decided among the top three candidates. Thus Henry Clay was dropped from consideration.

Because Clay was opposed to Jackson's politics, he gave his support to Adams thereby electing Adams president without a majority of popular votes. Adams' vice-president was John C. Calhoun

Major Legislation as President

John Quincy Adams attempted an ambitious program to enhance the culture and living conditions of the nation with projects such as a national university, a network of public roads and canals, and an astronomical observatory. Southern states' rights representatives opposed these governmental projects. With Congress not supporting Adams on these programs, little was done. Roads were built into Ohio and the Chesapeake and Ohio canal was completed. Congress, dominated by Jackson's followers, prevented any important legislation during Adams' administration.

With Adams' support, the New England states with their manufacturing were in favor of high tariffs while the southern states that depended upon exports, opposed it. The "Tariff of Abominations" passed in May, 1828, imposing high tariffs. This act marked the beginning of the tariff controversy that would continue into the 1900's.

Major Events During Presidency

The Erie Canal opened on February 9, 1825.

In February, 1827, the Baltimore and Ohio Railroad was chartered. It was the first railroad in the United States allowed to carry both passengers and freight.

Andrew Jackson
7th President (1829-1837)

A tall, raw-boned, 6 feet tall frontiersman, Andrew Jackson was a blunt, direct man who often brooked no nonsense, but went straight to the heart of things to get things done. He was a simple man, a fighter given to anger; however, he always showed passion for the common man and acted accordingly. He was a man for his time when the country was developing and expanding with an energy that was hard to control. He was a man of vision and action for the developing nation, directing all his energies to significantly advance and shape the American democracy. Jackson was the first president not from the original 13 colonies. He was the first president born in a log cabin.

Andrew Jackson involved himself in all aspects of government, showing compassion toward the Indians as they came in contact with settlers. His intense involvement in the military was mixed with empathy for his troops. It earned him the nickname of "Old Hickory."

Biography

The Scotch and Irish Andrew Jackson was born March 15, 1767, in the border area between North Carolina and South Carolina after his father died. His father, Andrew, and his mother, Elizabeth Hutchinson Jackson, were from Ireland. They had immigrated to America in 1765, where his father again turned to farming. His mother, Elizabeth, died when Andrew was 14.

Jackson grew up in a haphazard fashion. He had been well educated by private tutors until his mother died. Then he was cared for by two uncles until manhood. He fought as a 13 year old in the American Revolution and was captured and released. He had the red hair and dark eyes of his mother and grew to be a tall, raw-boned man, spending his early manhood in riotous living, never saving a cent for the future.

In 1784, he turned to the study of law and was admitted to the bar in 1787. While in Charleston, South Carolina, Jackson followed his favorite pastime, breeding and racing horses, managing fighting gamecocks, and card playing.

Then in 1788, he moved westward to the frontier settlement of Nashville, Tennessee. There he prospered in land speculation. In August, 1791, he married Rachel Donelson Robards and again on January 17, 1794, when it was learned that her divorce had not been final in 1791. They had no children. On the extensive acreage that he acquired in 1819, he built his great house, The Hermitage. He owned a store near his home and slowly became the most important person in his area, known as a lawyer with common sense and compassion for the common man.

When Tennessee became a state in 1796, Jackson became the state's first representative in Congress. It is said that Jackson gave the name Tennessee to the state from the name Tinnase, a Cherokee chief.[1]

Jackson was elected to the United States Senate in 1797, but resigned a year later because of business problems. He was appointed a major-general in the Tennessee militia in 1802. This prepared Jackson for his great adventure during the War of 1812. He was commander of the troops that defeated the Creek Indians in 1814. For this victory Jackson was commissioned a major general in the United States Army and led the defense of the city of New Orleans.

In the Battle of New Orleans in 1815, Jackson defended the city against a British force of 5,000 troops. His smaller army of Creoles, African-Americans, and pirates won a victory over the British. The British casualties were over 2,000 against just 21 American losses. For this victory, "Old Hickory", became America's greatest hero, saving the city and the area that became Louisiana. His later invasion of South Florida in pursuit of the Seminole Indians led to its purchase by the United States from Spain.

Following his victory, he retired to The Hermitage where friends convinced him to run for the Unit-

---

1 Robert V. Remini Andrew Jackson (New York: Twayne Publishers Inc., 1966,) p. 164

ed States Senate as well as voicing his name for the presidency.

In the election of 1824, Jackson received the most votes over John Quincy Adams and William H. Crawford, but because a majority of electors was needed to become president, the election among the three best vote getters was thrown into the House of Representatives which was dominated by followers of John Quincy Adams and Henry Clay, who had come in fourth. Clay threw his support to Adams and John Quincy Adams was elected.

Jackson was elected president four years later in 1828. He so dominated the national scene for the next eight years that the period of his presidency became known as the Age of Jackson. The Jackson led political approach to governing avowed the equality of men in their dealings with government and it asked that all citizens increase their participation in party politics.[2] This helped to bring about the rise of popular democracy.

After serving two terms as president, Jackson retired in 1837, to live out his life at The Hermitage. He died June 8, 1845, at the age of 79.

Presidential Campaign-1828

The campaign of 1828 matched two different personalities, Jackson, the rugged frontiersman and war hero, against the well-educated, learned John Quincy Adams. For his vice-president Jackson chose incumbent John C. Calhoun, vice-president under John Quincy Adams. Jackson's party became officially the Democratic party. Adams' followers were called the

2 Ibid., p. 164

National Republicans, forerunners of the Whigs and later the modern Republican party. Democrats charged that Adams had made a deal with Clay four years before when Clay gave his support to Adams for president in the House vote. They charged Adams with paying Clay off by making him Secretary of State.

Adams' Republicans brought Jackson's wife, Rachel, into the campaign, charging her with adultery before she and Jackson were married a second time. It is said that this contributed to her death shortly after Jackson's election to the presidency.

Presidential Election-1828

Andrew Jackson again received the majority of the popular vote. He easily defeated John Qunicy Adams, winning 15 states and 178 electoral votes to Adams' 83 electoral votes from 9 states. Jackson's popular vote was 642, 553 (56%) to President Adams' 500,897 (44%) votes.

Presidential Campaign-1832

The campaign of 1832 marks the first time that candidates were chosen by a national nominating convention. Both parties met in Baltimore to select their nominees for president. The Democrats nominated Jackson for president and Martin Van Buren of New York became Jackson's choice for vice-president. The Democrats passed a rule that a two-thirds majority was needed to nominate. This remained in their convention rules until 1936.

The National Republicans also met in Baltimore and nominated the anti-Jackson, Henry Clay with John Sergeant as vice-president. Clay's defense of the national bank that Jackson wished to abandon was the dominant topic of contention. The controversy continued into Jackson's second term when Jackson refused to recharter the Second National Bank and moved the government's deposits to state banks.

Presidential Election-1832

Again Jackson won easily over a new opponent, Henry Clay. The popular vote was Jackson, 701,780 (54%) to Clay's 484,205 (37%). The electoral vote gave Jackson 219 votes from 16 states to Clay's 49 electoral votes from 6 states. Other candidates gained 18 electoral votes. Van Buren received 189 votes for vice-president to 49 for Sergeant.

Major Legislation During Presidency

Jackson was one of the few early presidents to use the veto to regulate legislative policy

During Jackson's eight years as president the "spoils system" was firmly established. Until then government appointees often were carried over from one presidential administration to the next with only a few positions filled by presidential supporters. Jackson felt that "To the victors belong the spoils" and saw the present system as ingrained and incompetent. Wishing to make a more democratic government, he fired 15% of government workers and put persons loyal to him in the posts. It was done so abruptly that he was criticized for it. Jackson saw the Federal bank as a tool of the eastern establishment for favoring the eastern manufacturers at the expense of the working class.[3]

Jackson vetoed a new charter for the Bank of the United States and withdrew $10 million in federal deposits from the bank, putting funds in state banks, thus putting the national bank out of existence.

The Indian Removal Act of 1830 moved Cherokee Indians from Georgia, westward into what is now Oklahoma. The forced march was called the Trail of Tears.

Throughout the second term, Jackson's administration was concerned about moving Indian tribes westward beyond the Mississippi River. His government fashioned treaties at the time favorable to the Indians as well as the settlers moving westward. He laid this policy out in his Second Annual address on December 6, 1830.[4]

In 1835, Jackson accomplished a goal he had set for his administration when the government made the final payment on the national debt. He was the only president to get the United States out of debt.

In 1836, Jackson issued the Specie Circular which stated that After August 15, 1836, all purchasers of federal lands must pay for them in gold or silver. Jackson defended the Circular saying it ended the wild speculation on western lands by halting the extension of credit. Local state banks suffered. This policy eventually brought about a six year depression that lasted through Martin Van Buren's term.

3 Op cit. Messages pp. 1224-1238
4 Ibid., pp.1103-1105

Major Events During Presidency

The issue of states' rights versus the federal government continued during Jackson's terms. The issue peaked when Jackson signed a law for a moderate tariff increase in 1828. South Carolina again objected to the higher import tariff and following John Calhoun's earlier declaration against the Tariff of Abominations of 1828, that states should have the right to nullify federal laws they disagreed with. South Carolina proceeded to nullify the new tariff. Jackson declared that it was treasonous and threatened federal troops to enforce the tariff. Henry Clay brought about a compromise that the tariffs would slowly be lowered and the crisis was over.

In 1832, the Black Hawk War occurred in Illinois and Wisconsin. General Henry Atkinson defeated Chief Black Hawk, leader of the Sac and Fox Indians. . Future president, Abraham Lincoln was in the army that pursued Chief Black Hawk.

On January 30, 1835, Richard Lawrence attempted to assassinate President Jackson first by firing a pistol, then a second derringer. Neither worked and Jackson struck him with a cane. Lawrence was found not guilty by reason of insanity and sentenced to life in a mental institution. .

In 1836, Texans sought freedom from Mexico. Mexican leader Santa Anna invaded Texas territory and was met by 188 Texans led by Sam Houston. They fought the 3,000 Mexicans, but were overrun and killed on March 6th at the Alamo in San Antonio.

The 1830 census showed a 33% rise in population since 1820. The 1830 population of the United States was 12,866,020, an increase of 3,227,567 in a decade.

The Hermitage of Andrew Jackson

Martin Van Buren
8th President (1837-1841)

Seldom does a president come into the highest office in the United States with more experience and knowledge of government than Martin Van Buren. He had been Secretary of State and then vice-president under his friend and predecessor, Andrew Jackson. Because of his experience, Van Buren was the first true politician to become president. However, after he took office, occurrences show that often a country's leader has no control over events regardless of experience.

Van Buren's sandy-colored hair and his ability to negotiate and to solve problems earned him the nickname "Red Fox." The 5 feet, 6 inch affable, cheerful people-person and gentleman was highly respected by his associates.

Biography

Martin Van Buren was born December 5, 1782, in Kinderhook, New York, to a farmer and tavern keeper, Abraham Van Buren and Maria Hoes Van Buren. He was the first president born a American citizen. He grew up attending Kinderhook schools. The atmosphere of politics was all around him. His father's tavern was a favorite stopping place for lawyers and politicians as well as a polling place at election time.

At age 14 he began studying law with a local lawyer and argued his first case before a jury when he was 15 years old. At 18, Van Buren became a delegate to the Republican state congressional caucus. He was admitted to the bar in 1803, at the age of 21.

Van Buren 24, married his childhood sweetheart, Hannah Hoes, from Kinderhook on February 21, 1807. They had three children. She died ten years later and Van Buren never remarried.

Following his marriage, Van Buren served as New York state senator from 1812 until 1820, when he ran successfully for the United States Senate, serving in the Senate from 1821 to 1828. There he became a prominent leader and architect of the Democratic party that evolved from the Jeffersonian Republicans.

In 1829, Van Buren served three months as Governor of New York before becoming Secretary of State under Andrew Jackson. As Secretary he developed trade agreements with Turkey and Great Britain and won war reparations from France for American loses during the Napoleonic Wars.

In 1831, he led a general cabinet resignation so that President Jackson could reform the cabinet. Jackson appointed him Ambassador to Great Britain immediately after his resignation, but the Senate refused to confirm him.

At the 1832 Democratic convention there was much opposition to Jackson's choice of Van Buren as vice-president. In a political move, Jackson got the two-thirds rule passed certain that Van Buren was the only candidate that could get that number of delegates. The rule continued in effect until 1932.

Van Buren was elected president in 1836, and after a four year term was defeated for reelection in 1840 by William Henry Harrison. He remained an active party member and was nominated for president at the 1844 at the Democratic convention. He eventually lost the 1844 nomination to James K. Polk.

After moving away from the Democrats to an anti-slavery position and Free Soil interests, Van Buren made one last try for president in 1848. His candidacy drew enough votes away from the Democrats allowing the Whig candidate, Zackery Taylor, to be elected.

Van Buren retired at 66 to his home at Lindenwald in Kinderhook, New York. He remained politically active, returning to the Democratic party. He was an elector for Franklin Pierce in 1852 and James Buchanan in 1856. With the outbreak of the Civil War, he backed Lincoln and the Union.

Van Buren died on July 24, 1862.

Presidential Campaign-1836

Van Buren was vice-president from 1833-1837, when he ran for president with Richard M. Johnson, as his running mate. Opposition in 1834 to Jackson among the Democrats caused a break in the party. From this opposition the Whig Party formed. In order to deny Van-Buren the presidency, the Whigs nominated various men for president in the geographic area of their known strength with the hope that they could deny Van Buren a majority and thus throw the election into the House of Representatives. Future president, William Henry Harrison of Ohio, Hugh White of Tennessee, Daniel Webster of Massachusetts opposed Van Buren. The strategy failed.

Presidential Election-1836

Martin Van Buren was elected with 764,176 votes (51%) and 170 electoral votes from 15 states to 550,816 votes (37%) and 73 electoral votes from 7 states for Harrison; Hugh White received 146,107 votes (10%) and 26 electoral votes from 2 states; Daniel Webster had 4,201 votes (3%) from 1 state and 14 electors; non-candidate Willie Mangum received 11 electoral votes from 1 state. Vice-President Richard Johnson of Kentucky did not receive a majority. His election occurred in the Senate by a vote of 33 to 16 for Francis Granger of New York. It is the only time that the vice-presidency has been decided in the Senate. In this campaign the donkey became a symbol for the Democratic party.

Major Events During Presidency

After Texas won independence in 1836, the question was when and whether it should be annexed and admitted to the Union as a slave or free state? Van Buren had always sided with the South on the slavery question, but with Texas he felt that it should be a free state, and thus he sided with the North against adding a slave state.

The Panic of 1837 was the major event of Buchanan's term. Over 900 banks across the nation collapsed because of poor balance of trade with England and the Jacksonian money policy The policy was called the Specie Circular in which gold and silver had to be used to pay for public lands.

Relations with Canada were poor because of border disputes. The Caroline Affair of 1837 resulted in a ship being seized by Canadian authorities who sent it over the Niagara Falls.

The so-called Aroostock War of 1839 occurred over the boundary line between Maine and Canada. It was peacefully resolved when Van Buren, amid cries for war, sent General Winfield Scott to pacify the opponents and resolve the problem. General Scott arranged for a truce and further study of the dispute. It was eventually solved in the John Tyler administration in 1842 by the Webster-Ashburton Treaty.

The Second Seminole War in Florida had begun during Jackson's last term. Van Buren continued Jackson's policy toward the Indians, continuing to enforce the Indian Removal Act of 1830, that forced the Indians living in Georgia, Alabama, Mississippi, and western Florida to move to Indian territory west of the Mississippi in what is today Oklahoma and parts of Kansas and Nebraska. By 1842, the final Indian resistance was eliminated.

Texas was admitted to the Union on December 29, 1845, as a slave state.

The 1840 Census showed a population of 17,069,453.

William H. Harrison
9th President (1841)

The tall, slim 68 year old William Henry Harrison was the last president who had been born a British subject. He was an active man all his life with major service to his country in the army where he rose to brigadier general. As a boy he personally experienced the Revolution when his family had to flee Loyalist and Hessian troops under Benedict Arnold.

Biography

Harrison was born on February 9, 1773, to Benjamin Harrison V and Elizabeth Basset Harrison at Berkeley plantation in Virginia. His father, a signer of the Declaration of Independence, was a member of the Virginia House of Burgesses, the Continental Congress, and later became the governor of Virginia.

Until age 14, young Harrison's education was by local tutors. At 14 he enrolled in a college pre-med program serving as a medical apprentice. He enrolled at the University of Pennsylvania Medical School in Philadelphia to become a medical doctor.

In 1791, the 18 year old Harrison joined the army to become a professional soldier. He resigned in 1798 to become secretary of the Northwest Territory under President John Adams.

In 1795, while on active duty at Fort Washington, which today is Cincinnati, he married 20 year old Anna Tuthill Symmes. They had ten children with only four living to see him president. Their son, John Scott Harrison, was the father of Benjamin Harrison, who became the 23rd president.

In 1799, William Henry Harrison was elected to Congress representing the Northwest Territory. Later in 1800, when the Territory was divided into Indiana and Ohio, he was appointed governor of Indiana, serving from 1800 until 1812. Over time the Indians slowly gave up territory and in 1809, Harrison made the Treaty of Fort Wayne with four Indian tribes, adding three million acres to the United States. Indians under Chief Tecumseh and the Prophet protested the treaty. In 1811, Harrison led an army and defeated them at the Battle of Tippecanoe in the Indiana territory.

During the War of 1812, Harrison again joined the army and was commander of the Army of the Northwest. In 1813, he won a major victory over the British and Indians when he retook Detroit at the Battle of the Thames in Ontario.

After he again resigned from the army, he entered politics and in 1816, was elected to Congress. In 1819, he was elected to the Ohio Senate, and then in 1825, to the U. S. Senate. In 1828, Harrison served as minister to Columbia before President Jackson called him home. He had retired but ran for president as a Whig in 1836. He lost to Martin Van Buren.

In 1840, he again opposed Van Buren and defeated him decisively. He caught cold at the Inauguration and developed pneumonia. He died on April 4, 1841, after a month as president. He was the first president to die in office.

Presidential Campaign-1840

The 1840 campaign was the first all out attempt to sell the candidates. Both sides carried on with songs, slogans, and speeches. A newspaper backing Van Buren tried to depict Harrison as a backwoods, ignorant dweller of a log cabin and drinker of hard cider. The Whigs picked this theme up and held pro-Harrison rallies in log cabins, serving up hard cider to go along with the campaign. Consequently, he was seen as a frontier man of the people. One of the most important elements against Van Buran was the depression of 1837. The telling part of the campaign was the Whigs' emphasis on Harrison as a war hero in the Northwest Territory. They succeeded with the slogan "Tippecanoe and Tyler too," emphasizing his victory over Tecumseh and the Prophet in the Indiana territory. John Tyler was his vice-presidential running mate.

Presidential Election-1840

Harrison was elected with a popular vote of 1,275,390 (53%), and 234 electoral votes from 19 states. Van Buren had 1,128,854 votes (47%) and 60 electoral votes from 7 states.

John Tyler
10th President (1841-1845)

The 6 feet tall John Tyler appears to have been a rather reluctant president who was thrust into the role by the death of William Henry Harrison in 1841. Tyler was the first vice-president to succeed a president. He was a benevolent, dignified man with the charm of a well-bred Southern gentleman who had a good sense of who he was and what he felt his role should be. His persistence in the face of personal vendettas and his defense of states' rights presents a view of his strong character and determination to carry out his duties as president regardless of the political consequences.

Biography

John Tyler was born March 29, 1790, to John Tyler and Mary Armistead Tyler in Charles City County, Virginia. His father, a devotee of Jefferson and a strong believer in states' rights, was a plantation owner with a great number of slaves. Because of this belief his father opposed the Constitution. He did serve as Virginia's governor, so young Tyler came to learn about politics early in his life.

Tyler's education began at age 12 in the William and Mary prep school. It continued until he graduated in 1807 at age 17 from William and Mary College in Williamsburg, Virginia. At college he enjoyed ancient history, music, poetry and played the violin. Following graduation he returned home and studied law, first with his father and then in a Richmond law office. He was admitted to the bar in 1809.

On March 29, 1813, Tyler, 23, married Letitia Christian, 22. From this union they had four daughters and three sons who lived to maturity. That same year, 1813, Tyler joined the militia as a captain to help defend Richmond during the War of 1812, but saw no action.

Tyler began his political service with his election to the Virginia House of Delegates as a Jeffersonian Democrat. In 1816, he was elected to the House of Representative as a supporter of states' rights and opposed the Bank of the United States that took funds belonging to the states. He opposed Federal tariffs as inhibiting the states' right to trade as they wished. He was opposed to the Missouri Compromise of 1820 because he felt that the Compromise would only lead to open opposition. He believed th3 new western states should not be slave holding if the climate could not support agriculture. He did support the Kansas-Nebraska bill and recognized the legal equality of Southern and Northern institution in unorganized territories.

Poor health, which plagued Tyler all his life, forced his resignation from the Congress in 1821. His health improved and he was elected and served in the Virginia legislature until he became governor of Virginia in 1825. He served two years as governor and then was elected to the United States Senate. It was in the second campaign of Andrew Jackson that Tyler attempted to take a middle ground between Jackson's anti-nullification stand and actual secession by states. However, he did take a firm stand for secession when the rights of the states were not granted by the Federal government. By then he had joined Henry Clay's Whig party which opposed Andrew Jackson. Because of his views on states' rights, the Whigs nominated and elected Tyler for vice-president in 1840. Following Harrison's death, Tyler became the first vice-president to assume the presidency and the youngest president to take office.

As the first vice-president to became president, Tyler established the actual assumption of the role as president and set the precedent for future transfers of powers. Many people such as Henry Clay had interpreted the Constitution more narrowly, saying that he was merely an acting president, not the president. From the beginning, Tyler would have nothing to do with this interpretation. He took the oath in Washington on April 6, 1841, and issued an inaugural message on April 9th.

Tyler differed on the banking question with Clay and vetoed the Whig passed bill proposing a National bank in states' hands. Later he vetoed two Whig passed tariff bills and an impeachment resolution was introduced but failed.

Because Tyler had now broken with the Whigs and failed to support Whig legislation, he became a president without a party. The Whigs voted him out of the party in September, 1841.

On June 26, 1844, Tyler married Julia Gardiner at New York City, two years after the death of his wife, Letitia. They had seven children.

Following his presidential term, Tyler retired in 1845 to his plantation of Sherwood Forest near Richmond, Virginia. Instead of forming a third party to run for the presidency, Tyler withdrew from consideration and gave his support to Democrat James K. Polk. He remained active in the Southern states' rights movement. By 1861, the secession movement had begun. A moderate, Tyler was elected President of the 1861 Peace Conference that tried for a compromise. Its efforts to stave off Civil War failed. Tyler then helped to form the Confederacy.

Tyler died on January 18, 1862, in Richmond before he could take his seat as an elected member of the Confederate legislature.

Major Legislation During Presidency

The Distribution-Preemption Act of 1841 gave occupiers of unsurveyed public lands first choice in purchasing up to 160 acres of Federal land for $1.25 an acre.

In 1842, the Senate ratified the Webster-Ashburton Treaty with England. It set the boundary between Canada and the state of Maine and the boundary from the East Coast to the Rocky Mountains. This settled the dispute that had errupted during Van Buren's presidency with the Aroostook War.

Tyler wanted his crowning achievement to be the annexation of Texas, first as a territory, and then as a state. With Polk's election on a pro-Texas platform, Congress approved the annexation. In one of his final pieces of legislation, Tyler signed the Texas annexation on March 1, 1845, three days before leaving office. Texas became a state on December 29, 1845.

On January 23, 1845, Congress passed the act setting the Tuesday following the first Monday in November as the election day for the presidency.

On March 3, 1845, the final day of Tyler's presidency, Florida became the 27th state.

Major Events During Presidency

In 1841, from May 1 to November 4, the first settlers to California completed a six months journey by wagon train using the overland route from Independence, Missouri.

In 1842, the Second Seminole War ended in Florida. The last of the Seminole Indians were moved west of the Mississippi River.

The 2,000 mile Oregon Trail was established when the first group of 1,000 settlers left Independence, Missouri, on May 22, 1843, and arrived in Oregon in November, 1843. It opened the way for Northwest settlement.

Samuel F. B. Morse built the first telegraph line and sent the message, "What hath God Wrought?" from Baltimore, to Washington, D. C. on May 24, 1844.

Caleb Cushing negotiated the 1844 Treaty of Wanghia that gave the U. S. access to Chinese ports.

James K. Polk
11th President (1845-1849)

James K. Polk, a trim 5 feet 7 inches tall man, could be called the president of the western expansion movement in the United States. Polk was a strong believer in America's "Manifest Destiny," the expansion of the nation to the Pacific Ocean. While the United States had been adding territory, it was during Polk's administration that the vast territory from the Rocky Mountains to the Pacific was added as territory, reflecting the peoples' desire to expand the country.

A tireless worker with a planned program worked out when he became president, Polk was the last of the Jacksonian Democrats and the first truly "dark horse" to win the presidency. At age 51, he was at that time the youngest man to be elected president.

Biography

James Knox Polk was born in Mecklenburg County, North Carolina on November 2, 1795. He was the eldest son of ten children born to Samuel and Jane Knox Polk. While his father was a farmer, the young, sickly Polk never cared for the farm.

Polk was educated at home by local tutors. In 1818, he later graduated with honors from the University of North Carolina and delivered the Latin salutatory, He studied law and was admitted to the bar in 1820, setting up practice in Columbia, Tennessee. As a young man newly elected to the state legislature of Tennessee, he met Senator Andrew Jackson and became an ardent follower.

On January 1, 1824, Polk, 28, married Sarah Childress, 20. A year later, 1825, he was elected to the House of Representatives and his political career was assured as he pushed Jackson's ideas and wishes in the House after John Quincy Adams had defeated Jackson. Later when Jackson was elected president in 1828, Polk became a leader for his policies. Twice he was elected Speaker of the House of Representatives, wielding great political power.

A short hiatus from national politics occurred in 1839 when the Democrats asked him to run for governor of Tennessee. He was elected with a 2,500 majority and served as governor for two years before returning to national politics.

Polk's reentrance into politics occurred at the Democratic Convention in Baltimore in 1844, on the question of the annexation of Texas. This move for annexation had been brewing since 1836 when the Mexicans under Santa Anna had defeated the Texans at the Alamo in San Antonio. Later when Mexico had tried to dictate policy to the Texans who were still part of Mexico, rebellion flared anew and the Tex-ans declared their independence. The Texans wished to be annexed to the United States. President Van Buren was opposed to this because Texas was below the line drawn for slavery and non-slavery states in the 1820 Missouri Compromise. Hence, Texas would become a slave state upsetting the balance between slave and non-slave states.

Polk reflected the general public's wishes that Texas should become a part of the United States as part of the "manifest destiny" of the country in its expansion to the Pacific. He was nominated to run for president and was elected on this platform. Polk was president from 1845 to 1849, retiring in March, 1849, happy to be free of the office. He died three months later in Nashville, Tennessee, on June 15, 1849, at the age of 53.

Presidential Campaign-1844

At the start of the campaign of 1844, Henry Clay, the Whig candidate from Kentucky, was well known because he had been on the presidential scene since 1824. In 1844 he was considered the front runner to easily beat the "dark horse" Polk who had been nominated by the Democrats because Martin Van Buren had come out against Texas' annexation and lost supporters. Henry Clay could not gain the two-thirds majority needed so the convention finally nominated Polk on the ninth ballot.

For the first time the Abolitionist party organized and put a candidate in the race. He was James Birney of Michigan. His candidacy hurt Clay in the northeast even though he was against the annexation of Texas, fearing a war with Mexico. Polk had received Tyler's support when Tyler dropped out and in return Polk made one of Tyler's objectives his own, the annexation of Texas. He also stated that he would not seek a second term.

Presidential Election 1844

James K. Polk, Democrat, defeated Henry Clay, Whig, with a popular vote of 1,339,494 (49%) to 1,300,004 (48%). The Abolitionist, James Birney, received 62,103 (2%). The electoral vote for Polk was 170 votes from 15 states to Clay's 105 electoral votes from 11 states. Polk's vice-president was George Mifflin Dallas of Pennsylvania.

Major Legislation During Presidency

The Oregon territory had been a point of contention with Great Britain. Polk wanted the entire area of land between the United States and Canada to be between 40°and 54°40' latitude. The Democrats' slogan was "Fifty-four, Forty or Fight." Polk compromised and the Oregon Treaty of 1846, set the dividing line at the 49th parallel. Vancouver Island south of the 49th parallel went to Britain.

The Treaty of Guadalupe Hidalgo, 1848, ended the Mexican War. Terms were that the Rio Grande would be the border between Mexico and the United States. Mexico gave up the territory which today includes the states of California, Utah, Nevada, Wyoming, Colorado, Texas, New Mexico, and Arizona. The United States paid Mexico $15 million for this territory. Mexican citizens could remain or return to Mexico.

Polk set forth the Polk Doctrine which extended the Monroe Doctrine and stated that no European country could interfere with any country or territory in the Americas. This applied primarily to the Oregon Territory where Polk's administration was faced by Britain over the joint occupation of the territory. Polk wanted it to end.

On December 28, 1846, Iowa became the 29th state. Wisconsin became the 30th state on May 29, 1848. Oregon became a federal territory on August 2, 1848. The bill also prohibited slavery in the territory.

Major Events During Presidency

The Mexican War began in 1845 with a Mexican raid across the Rio Grande against General Zackery Taylor's forces. Polk announced that Mexico had invaded and shed American blood. Congress declared war on May 13, 1846. The conflict lasted a year and a half with General Winfield Scott penetrating Mexico and capturing Mexico City. In 1848, the war ended with the Treaty of Guadalupe Hidalgo.

In 1846, the Irish potato famine in Ireland occurred, sending a wave of Irish immigrants to the United States. From 1841 to 1850, nearly 49% of immigrants were Irish.

Nine days before the signing of the treaty with Mexico, gold was discovered at Sutter's Mill in California. The great gold rush began with 100,000 of the "Forty-niners" streaming westward.

For the first time on November 7, 1848, the presidential election was held in all states on the same day.

Zackery Taylor
12th President (1849-1850)

Zachary Taylor known as "Old Rough and Ready" was a life-long career soldier who spent most of his life out of the arena of politics. In fact, he didn't vote until he was 62. Taylor was a short, squat, 5 feet, 8 inches tall man with gracious, gentlemanly manners as well as an iron will that brooked no pomp and ceremony. He conducted his armies on the battlefield in comfortable clothes rather than in uniform. The aura of command carried over to his conduct during his short presidency. Even though he was a slave owner from Virginia, the preservation of the Union was more important. To Southerners who came to protest and threaten secession, Taylor's reply was that he would head the army against them and hang each and every one who led the secession.

Biography

Zachary Taylor's ancestry goes back to the Pilgrims and the *Mayflower*. President James Madison was a second cousin and General Robert E. Lee a relative. Franklin D.

Roosevelt was a distant cousin.

Taylor was born November 24, 1784, in Orange County, Virginia, to Richard Taylor and Sarah Dabney Strother Taylor. His father owned a plantation and had served in the Continental Army during the Revolution so Taylor grew up hearing stories of army life. The family moved to Kentucky when Zachary was an infant. He grew up on the fringe of the western frontier and was educated at home.

In 1808, at the age of 24, Taylor joined the army as a first lieutenant. This would be his career until 1848.

On June 21, 1810, Taylor, 25, married Margaret Mackall Smith, 21, from near Louisville, Kentucky. They had three daughters and a son, Richard, who became his father's aide during the Mexican War.

The Taylor family illustrates the divisiveness of the Civil War. His son, Richard, later became a Confederate general and was the last general to surrender at the war's end.

During his army career, Zachary Taylor achieved an impressive war record. He spent most of his military life on the western frontier in such places as Fort Crawford which is now Prairie du Chien, Wisconsin. He helped to defeat Blackhawk during the Blackhawk War at the Battle of Bad Axe in Wisconsin. Later in 1837 to 1840, he led forces in Florida during the Second Seminole War.

"Old Rough and Ready" as his troops called Taylor had his final service in the Mexican War where he became a national hero, leading outnumbered troops and defeating Santa Anna in the Battle of Buena Vista. This opened the route for General Winfield Scott to move on Mexico City which he captured, setting the stage for the Treaty of Guadalupe Hidalgo, ending the Mexican War.

Taylor was elected president in 1848 and served a year as president before becoming ill apparently from food poisoning caused by the summer heat. He died at the age of 65 on July 9, 1850. Taylor's wife survived him by two years. Both are buried near Louisville, Kentucky.

Presidential Campaign-1848

Zachary Taylor won the Whig nomination on the fourth ballot of the Whig convention in 1848. His closest rivals were 70 year old Henry Clay, General Winfield Scott, and Daniel Webster. He had not attended the convention and because of mail service, did not find out about his nomination for several weeks. His running mate for vice-president was Millard Fillmore of New York. Taylor's Democratic opponent was the governor of Michigan, General Lewis Cass, who had lost out to James Polk four years earlier.

The slavery question was the dominant theme of the campaign with the major debate over support or non-support of the Wilmot Proviso which stated that no slavery could exist in any territory received from Mexico because of the Mexican War.

Lewis Cass and the Democrats were against the Proviso. He suggested a policy whereby the residents of the territory could vote to be slave or non-slave, making it a basic states' right issue .

Former President Martin Van Buren also entered the race for president as a nominee of the Free Soil party, an anti-slavery group of Democrats that did not like Cass' stand.

While the Free Soilers and Martin Van Buren did not receive many votes, their party did take enough New York state votes away from Cass to assure Taylor's election. With Taylor the voter's elected a president they hardly knew.

Presidential Election-1848

The 1848 presidential election was the first national election held on the same day nationwide. Zachary Taylor, Whig, received 1,361,393 (47%) popular votes and 163 electoral votes from 15 states. Lewis Cass polled 1,223,460 (43%) popular votes and 127 electoral votes from 15 states. Free Soiler Martin Van Buren received 291,501 (10%) popular votes.

Major Legislation During Presidency

The only legislation that occurred during Taylor's short tenure as president was an agreement between the United States and Great Britain regarding the future building of a canal in Central America. The Clayton-Bulwer Treaty of 1850 stated that both countries agreed to exercise no control over any canal that might be constructed across Central America. It also stated that no fortification could be constructed by either government on Central American soil. This agreement would become a negotiating point with Britain under President Theodore Roosevelt in 1901 when the Hay-Pauncefote Treaty of 1901 was signed. In it Britain ceded to the United States the right to build and operate a canal across Central America with the provision that the canal stay open to the vessels of all nations.

Major Events During Presidency

With the discovery of gold at Sutter's Mill in California on January 24, 1848, the great Gold Rush was on, bringing over 80 thousand "Forty-niners" to the territory. It set the stage for California to eventually become a state.

Taylor did not approve of Henry Clay's proposed Compromise of 1850 which attempted to deal with new areas entering the Union as free or slave states. Clay was hopeful that the Compromise would stave off a civil war over the issue.

Taylor wanted California to come into the Union as a free state, but with Taylor's death on July 9, 1850, the debate continued into Willard Fillmore's presidency with Fillmore more approving of the Compromise.

The slavery question for new states had been addressed in 1846 in the Wilmot Proviso which stated that there be no slavery in new territory gained from the Mexican War. However, the Southern view articulated by John Calhoun for the southern states' rights followers stated that the Federal government had no right to interfere with a state's determination to permit or not permit slavery within its borders.

Census-1850

In the past decade the United States population increased by over 6 million. The 1850 census set the population at 23,191,876.

Millard Fillmore
13th President (1850-1853)

In appearance and dress, Millard Fillmore was the complete opposite of his predecessor, Zachary Taylor. He was 6 feet tall and a careful dresser, handsome rather than rugged. He and Taylor did not meet until after he was president.

Fillmore was a statesman and diplomat. In his many years as a congressman, he used his persuasive skills and common sense to guide legislation through the Congress. Almost a self-taught man who became a vociferous reader, he possessed a large library, establish-ing the White House library when he became president. The presidency was thrust upon him, and as he did all his life, Fillmore attempted to fulfill his duties. His efforts prevented civil war for over ten years.

Biography

Millard Fillmore was born on January 7, 1800, to Nathaniel Fillmore and Phoebe Millard Fillmore in the village of Locke in the New York state Finger Lakes area. His family were tenant farmers and as a child, Millard learned to work hard on the small farm that produced meager crops.

At age 15, Fillmore became an apprentice to a clothmaker. During his early youth, he was mostly self taught and it wasn't until the age of nineteen that he received formal schooling when he went to an academy in New Hope, New York. With the training he received, he taught in an elementary school and began the study of law at a county judge's office near Buffalo, New York. He was admitted to the bar in 1823, and opened a practice in East Aurora, New York, located near Buffalo.

When he was 19, he had met Abigail Powers. After Fillmore had established himself in his law practice, they were married on February 5, 1826, They had a son and a daughter.

In the years following, Fillmore became involved in state and national politics. As an established lawyer, Fillmore's first involvement was as an Anti-Mason, supporting John Quincy Adams in 1824. Later as the Anti-Mason movement subsided, he followed the Whig leaders. As a Whig, he was elected to the House of Representatives and spent four terms in Congress backing William Henry Harrison for president. He became chairman of the powerful Ways and Means Committee from 1841-1843 and was instrumental in getting the Tariff Act of 1842 passed.

In 1844 Fillmore was a candidate for the vice-presidential nomination for the Whig party and for the New York governorship. He won neither.

In 1848-1849, Fillmore was comptroller for New York State. He helped in the expansion of the Erie Canal and with the establishment of a state currency system.

The anti-slavery Whig party wanted a balanced ticket. Fillmore was nominated for the vice-presidency as a running mate with Zachary Taylor, a slave owner. Taylor and Fillmore were elected. With the early death of Taylor, Fillmore assumed the presidency at a crucial time on the slavery question. A balance had to be maintained between slave and free states in order to prevent a civil war. Fillmore supported the 1850 Compromise which maintained for a time the balance between slave and free states.

After serving out the term of Taylor, Fillmore was not renominated because of his support of the Compromise. He retired to Buffalo and returned to the practice of law.

Fillmore's wife caught pneumonia at the inaugural of Fillmore's successor, Franklin Pierce in 1853, and died on March 30, 1853. After her death, Fillmore traveled for a time in the United States and across Europe, returning home to immerse himself in civic affairs.

In 1856, while still in Europe, Fillmore was notified that he had been nominated the presidential candidate for the American or Know-Nothing party which wanted only white American Protestants to hold public office. They gained that name because of their opposition to the tremendous immigration from Europe, especially the Catholic immigrants from Ireland who were fleeing that country during the potato famine. Fillmore ran third in the election.

On February 10, 1858, he married Mrs. Caroline Carmichael McIntosh, a wealthy widow from Albany. They had no children.

During the years following his marriage, Fillmore was active in Buffalo, New York, civic affairs.

During his lifetime he was instrumental in establishing the city's first high school, a fire insurance company, the Young Man's Christian Association, the Buffalo Historical Society, a fine arts school, a hospital, and the University of Buffalo. In February, 1861, Fillmore was host to a visit by Abraham Lincoln as Lincoln journeyed to Washington to be inaugurated as the 16th president.

Millard Fillmore died of a stroke on March 8, 1874, in Buffalo, New York

Major Legislation During Presidency

Congress passed the Compromise of 1850. It was a series of resolutions to set a format for dealing with new territory. The Compromise put off for some time the eventual conflict between the Union and secession states.

The Compromise of 1850 admitted California as a free state, organized Utah and New Mexico into territories where the residents could vote on the slavery question. It maintained for a time the balance between slave and free states. The Compromise abolished slavery in the District of Columbia and strengthened the fugitive slave law that required free states to return escaped slaves. The debate over the Compromise was the last great debate involving Henry Clay, Daniel Webster, and John J. Calhoun.

The Texas and New Mexico Act, 1850, using the Compromise provisions, organized New Mexico as a territory without a reference to slavery, and adopting the "popular sovereignty" concept that allowed the citizens of an area or territory to decide the issue of slavery. It also provided for the payment of $10 million to Texas for it to abandon all claims to New Mexico territory.

The Utah Act, 1850, had similar provisions when Utah was made a territory.

On September 9, 1850, California became the 32nd state. It entered the Union as a free state.

Major Events During Presidency

The opening of Japanese ports was one of the Fillmore administration's more important accomplishments. In 1852-3, he sent Commodore Matthew C. Perry with a naval fleet to Japan to attempt through diplomacy to open their ports to American ships. The Treaty of Kanagawa, signed in 1854, after Fillmore left office, opened two ports to American ships.

The Underground Railroad aided thousands of black slaves to escape to freedom in the North. .

Harriet Beecher Stowe's novel *Uncle Tom's Cabin or Life Among the Lowly* was published in book form in 1852. A best seller that illustrated the differences between North and South. It pointed out the unfairness of the Fugitive Slave Law bringing the debate over slavery and its abolishment into the main stream of American life.

Franklin Pierce
14th President (1853-1857)

The handsome, affable 5 feet, 10 inches tall Franklin Pierce was a man whose leadership qualities were overshadowed by the inability of the country to solve the slavery question. As a young man he was not as punctual and persevering as he was as an adult. A gregarious, social man, given to heavy drinking at times, Pierce was at first popular in Washington but later he was deserted by friends when he deplored the policies of Lincoln after he saw the loss of life from the Civil War.

As president and in retirement, he had to face family tragedy with the loss of children and later his wife. Almost a recluse late in life, he gave in to his drinking. He was a man ill-fitted to the responsibilities of the presidency.

Biography

Franklin Pierce was born on a frontier farm near Hillsborough (now Hillsboro), New Hampshire on November 23, 1804, to Benjamin and Anna Kendrick Pierce. His father had served in the Revolutionary War; his brothers had fought in the War of 1812. Later his father was elected governor of New Hampshire.

As a child, Pierce attended local schools and a nearby boarding school. In 1820, he entered Bowdoin College in Maine and there met the future novelist, Nathaniel Hawthorne. Pierce was not a good student, but he continued to apply himself, and he ended up fifth in his graduating class in 1824.

Pierce studied law under several lawyers. After his admission to the bar in 1827, he decided to enter politics when his father was elected governor of New Hampshire for the second time. Franklin was elected to the state legislature at age 24 and two years later became Speaker of the house.

On November 19, 1834, Pierce, 29, married Jane Means Appleton, 28, a shy withdrawn woman. Over the years she did not care for Pierce's involvement in politics nor his drinking.

In 1833, he was elected to the House of Representatives and spent four years there before his election to the Senate in 1837. He remained in the Senate until 1842, resigning because of his wife's health. After his resignation from the Senate, he practiced law in Concord, New Hampshire

A Democratic follower of Jackson, Van Buren, and finally, Polk, Pierce stayed active in politics, directing Polk's election in New Hampshire. In the years while he was in politics, the Pierces lost three sons, two while very young. The third child, Benjamin, 12, was killed in a train accident two months before Pierce's inauguration as president. A sickly woman all her life, Pierce's wife never recovered from these tragedies and became a recluse in the White House.

Pierce served in the militia in the Mexican War, 1846-1848, reaching the rank of brigadier general. After service in Mexico, he resigned from the army in 1848. At age 48, Pierce won the Democratic nomination for president. Pierce easily won the election in 1852, and served a single term. He retired and watched in disbelief at the mounting tide toward civil war as "Bleeding Kansas" erupted in violence near the end of his term. He lived to see the destruction and lamented the terrible human waste that the war cost.

On October 8, 1869, Franklin Pierce died in Concord, New Hampshire, where he is buried.

Presidential Campaign-1852

In 1852, Pierce was almost unanimously nominated to be the Democratic nominee for president on the forty-ninth ballot of the convention. Pierce was not even considered at the start because the party had four viable names: Lewis Cass of Michigan, supporter of the Compromise of 1850; James Buchanan of Pennsylvania; Stephen Douglas of Illinois; and William Marcy of New York. Pierce's vice-president was Senator William Rufus King of Alabama. It was an ideal ticket with Pierce, a Northerner who supported the Compromise of 1850, and King, a Southerner, for vice-president.

Pierce's opponent in the election was General Winfield Scott, a Whig from New Jersey, who defeated Millard Fillmore for the nomination on an anti-slavery platform. The Whigs made much of Scott's war record, but it was the slavery question that decided the voters. The Democrats came up with the clever slogan, "We Polked you in 1844; we will Pierce you in 1852!"

The Whig party became divided between those who wished to compromise on the slavery question and those who were totally against slavery. This division helped bring about the end of the Whig party .

Presidential Election-1852

The voters saw in Pierce, who supported the Compromise of 1850, a candidate who might maintain the status quo and avoid conflict. It was a highly negative campaign with charges being leveled by both candidates.

Franklin Pierce won the election easily, winning all but four states. His popular vote total was 1,607,510 (51%) to Winfield Scott's 1,386,942 (44%). Pierce received 254 electoral votes from 27 states to Scott's 42 electoral votes from 4 states. William Rufus DeVane King was Pierce's vice-president.

Major Legislation During Presidency

The Gadsden Purchase, 1853, was an addition that further refined the southwest boundary of the United States. In the Purchase Mexico ceded to the United States a strip of land south of the Gila River for $10 million dollars.

After months of debate the Kansas-Nebraska Act of 1854 literally repealed the 1820 Missouri Compromise. The Act put into law the principle of allowing state residents to construct their constitutions as they wished. This concept of "popular sovereignty" allowed them to decide whether to allow slavery or to prohibit slavery in their state.

Major Events During Presidency

The opening of two Japan ports to United States ships was brought about by Commodore Matthew Perry's successful peace mission with the signing of the Treaty of Kanagawa in 1854.

The Kansas-Nebraska Act of 1854 caused political dissatisfaction. A meeting of political forces opposed to extending slavery in new territories brought together Whigs, Free-Soilers, and the anti-slavery Democrats to form the Republican Party in Ripon, Wisconsin, in July, 1854,

In October, 1854, Abraham Lincoln gave a speech in Peoria, Illinois, in which he condemned the Kansas-Nebraska Act. It was his first public condemnation of slavery and laid the foundation for his eventual run for the presidency.

The final two years of the Pierce administration were almost predictable. The slavery question and its settlement in favor of the north or the south had been brewing toward a climatic moment for the past fifteen to twenty years. In 1856, despite Pierce's admonitions, conflict between Free State forces and pro-slavery forces broke out in Kansas territory. Pierce had supported the pro-slavery assembly. The conflict in "Bleeding Kansas" began with a pro-slavery attack and killing in Lawrence, Kansas. Anti-slavery leader, John Brown, retaliated. The conflict eventually spread into a full scale civil war in 1861.

James Buchanan
15th President (1857-1861)

James Buchanan embodied the ideal of a good and humane individual. He was a dignified, gracious, 6 feet tall, handsome man who demonstrated a scrupulous regard for social understanding and good will toward his family and others. Of all our presidents perhaps none was more unfortunate to be placed in the cauldron of history at a point where events seemed to control decisions. Before he became president, Buchanan had proven himself a shrewd negotiator in the world and in national politics.

Buchanan had negotiated a trade agreement with Russia, he was involved in gaining the Treaty of Guadalupe Hidalgo ending the Mexican War, and he successfully compromised an agreement with Great Britain in the Oregon Treaty of 1846, thus avoiding a war.

By 1850, the North and South had taken almost irreconcilable positions on slavery. The civil strife in "Bleeding Kansas" illustrated the differences. Because of his strong southern views, Buchanan wished to bring about a tolerance of slavery.

Biography

James Buchanan was born in a log cabin in Cove Gap, Pennsylvania, on April 23, 1791. His parents, James Buchanan, Sr. and Elizabeth Speer Buchanan, were merchants. He grew up in Mercersburg, Pennsylvania, where his family had moved in 1796. Buchanan had a public school education and followed this with graduation from Dickinson College in 1809. After studying law, he was admitted to the bar in 1812.

Despite an eye disorder, Buchanan was a great reader. He had what is known as a wryneck. He would cock his head to one side in order to use one eye that was far-sighted or the other eye that was near-sighted. He would close the eye he wished to use and cock his head to the left. The condition was never corrected with eye glasses until he was very old.

In 1819, Buchanan fell in love and was engaged to Anne Coleman of Lancaster. After a quarrel, she broke off the engagement. She died later that year, and the heart-broken Buchanan vowed never to marry. He was the only president who never married.

Buchanan's political career began when elected to the Pennsylvania Legislature in 1814 as a Federalist. He was against a conscription bill for the War of 1812. After two legislative terms, he was defeated. He returned to his law practice in Lancaster.

In 1821, he was elected to the House of Representatives as a Federalist where he served for the next ten years. The Federalist party decl-ined and Buchanan became a Jacksonian Democrat and supported Andrew Jackson's programs in Congress. He left Congress in 1830, but almost immediately upon his retirement, Jackson made him Minister to Russia until 1833. The next eleven years from 1834 to 1845 were spent as a Democrat in the United States Senate representing the state of Pennsylvania.

As a Senator he supported Jackson's programs of national defense and supported him in his attacks upon the Bank of the United States, firmly aligning himself with the states' rights Democrats.

From 1845 to 1849, Buchanan served as Secretary of State under President Polk. It was Buchanan who brought about the annexation of Texas and negotiated the Oregon Treaty with Great Britain. Twice he was a candidate for the Democratic nomination for president, but lost first to Lewis Cass in 1848, and then in 1852, to Franklin Pierce. In 1849, he had purchased the Wheatland estate near Lancaster, Pennsylvania, and retired to it at the end of Polk's term to care for his family of nephews and nieces.

Probably the most interesting assignment for Buchanan was his service as Minister to Great Britain in 1853. He was part of the United States delegation that drew up the Ostend Manifesto (1855) that set down the terms for the United States to acquire Cuba by any means, including force, in order to further slavery. President Pierce rejected the idea, but it increased Buchanan's reputation in the South.

Buchanan was nominated over President Pierce by the Democratic party. They wanted someone who was least known in the South. Pierce and Senator Stephen Douglas were known to uphold slavery, but Buchanan had gained popularity because he had gone against Pierce by supporting the Ostend Manifesto It took sixteen ballots before Buchanan was nominated.

Buchanan was elected and served a single term, declining to run again because of the growing tension over slavery and his loss of favor with the northern Democrats. He was faced with many untenable positions on the slavery question. He understood the Southern anger, but at the same time maintained that secession was not the solution.

After the 1860 election of Lincoln, Buchanan tried many tactics to prevent secession before he left office. He reinforced Union forts in the south and tried diplomacy to discourage the southern secessionists. When the day for the inauguration of Lincoln came, a tired and relieved Buchanan turned the troubles over to Lincoln who was determined to preserve the Union.

After a quiet retirement in which he did support Abraham Lincoln during the Civil War, and later Andrew Johnson during the Reconstruction, Buchanan died of pneumonia at his Wheatland estate. His death on June 1, 1868, brought to a close a life of dedicated service to the nation.

Presidential Campaign-1856

The presidential campaign of 1856 was a precursor of the civil strife that was to come. Opponents of Buchanan were Republican John C. Fremont, who spoke out against the Pierce administration for the tragedy of Bleeding Kansas. Fremont opposed extending slavery to new territories, denounced the Ostend Manifesto, and supported the building of a transcontinental railroad.

Buchanan's other opponent was former president Millard Fillmore who was nominated by the American or Know Nothing party that opposed foreign immigration.

It was a spirited campaign with the Republicans shouting their slogan of "Free Speech, Free Press, Free Soil, Free Men, Fremont and Victory" with Buchanan followers adding "And Free Love" to remind voters of Fremont's illegitimacy.

The Democratic campaign for Buchanan was to create the fear that if a Republican became president, the South would rise in rebellion. The Republicans retorted that the unrest would persist as long as the Democrats courted the South by appeasing them on the slavery question.

Presidential Election-1856

In the 1856 election, James Buchanan, Democrat, easily defeated John Fremont, candidate of the newly formed Republican Party and Millard Fillmore, of the American Know Nothing and Whig party.

Buchanan's popular vote was 1,836,072 (45%) to Fremont's 1,342,345 (33%) and Fillmore's 873,053 (22%) votes.

Buchanan won 174 electoral votes from 19 states. Fremont won 114 electoral votes from 11 states. Fillmore won the 8 votes of Maryland.

Major Legislation During Presidency

Three states: Minnesota on May 11, 1858, the 32nd state; Oregon on February 14, 1859, the 33rd state and Kansas on January 29, 1861, the 34th state were admitted to the Union.

Major Events During Presidency

James Buchanan's term was dominated by the slavery question and the struggle in Kansas over its becoming a free or slave state. Buchanan endorsed the admission of Kansas as a slave state, but the Congress rejected the Kansas constitution. In 1858, Republican anti-slavery forces won both houses of Congress and opposed Buchanan.

With the Whig party loss of influence because its congressional members accepted the southern "popular sovereignty" views, its remnants were involved with the formation of the Republican Party in 1854 in Ripon, Wisconsin, where all the parties that opposed the spread of slavery into new territories, united.

The Panic of 1857 and the depression that followed were brought about by events. Banks failed because the Gold Rush of 1849 sent the price of gold down, the end of European wars brought about the purchase of fewer United States goods, and the over extension of the nation's railroads into sparsely settled lands in central United States resulted in loss of public confidence. This occurred especially where the railroads fought one another for cheap European labor in order to extend the railroad lines into Illinois and Wisconsin.

In 1857, the Dred Scott decision was made shortly after Buchanan was inaugurated president. Scott had sued Missouri for his freedom based upon his having worked in the free states of Wisconsin and Illinois before returning to Missouri, a slave state. The Supreme Court ruled that Negroes were not citizens and could not sue, and that his having been in free territory did not make him free. It invalidated the 1820 Missouri Compromise.

In 1858, Abraham Lincoln and Stephen Douglas debated the slavery issue. Lincoln lost the senate race, but established himself as a future presidential candidate.

In 1859, John Brown, who led a rebellion of slaves in Kansas, was captured at Harper's Ferry, Virginia, after he had seized the Federal armory along with hostages. He was tried for treason and hanged.

The Secession Movement began after the election of Abraham Lincoln in 1860 and before Buchanan left office. On December 20, 1860, South Carolina elected to dissolve the Union between the state and the federal government. Alabama, Florida, Georgia, Louisiana, Mississippi, and Texas followed South Carolina. Together they formed the Confederate States of America with Virginia, Arkansas, Tennessee, and North Carolina joining later. They elected Jefferson Davis, president. Buchanan conceded that the secession was an illegal act, but that the federal government did not have the legal authority to force states to remain in the Union.

The 1860 census showed that the United States population was 31,443,321 up 8,251,445 from 1850.

Abraham Lincoln
16th President (1861-1865)

When Abraham Lincoln stated, "With malice toward none," he was describing himself. The gaunt, 6 feet, 4 inches tall Lincoln was an unpretentious, strong willed, plain speaking and at times, morose man. A deep natural wit was shown in the anecdotal stories filled with humor and humanity that he told to illustrate a point he wished to make.

With his election this awkward, backwoods politician faced the enormous task of preserving the Union, giving direction to the Union cause, and stating the need for its preservation in clear, elegant language.

Mostly self-taught, Lincoln's thoughts about events such as the Battle of Gettysburg were expressed in a clarity of words and in a style that have immortalized his speech.

Biography

Abraham Lincoln was born on February 12, 1809, near Hodgenville, Kentucky. His father, Thomas Lincoln, was an illiterate carpenter who moved around the frontier, seeking work. His mother, Nancy Hanks

Lincoln, died in 1818, age 34, when he was nine years old. His father remarried and it was his stepmother who saw to it that Lincoln was occasionally sent to school. He was primarily self-taught, spending his nights before the fireplace reading books that he bought or found.

Lincoln grew up on the farm helping with the farm work. He even hired out to other farmers. At 17, he worked the Mississippi River boats transporting goods. As he grew and learned to read and do math, he began to read Shakespeare, Poe, the English poets and the Bible. He became an entrancing story teller and would continue to use stories all his life to illustrate his ideas.

Lincoln moved to New Salem, Illinois, in 1831. There he fell in love with Ann Rutledge. Before the courtship could mature, she died of malaria and Lincoln was inconsolable for long periods of time. In 1842, he enlisted in the militia for a part of a year and took part in the pursuit of Chief Black Hawk in southern Wisconsin during the Black Hawk War.

Lincoln spent the next several years running a grocery store in New Salem, Illinois, running for state assembly, journeying down the Mississippi to New Orleans, and from 1833 to 1836, serving as postmaster in New Salem.

He was elected to the Illinois state legislature as a Whig candidate and served in the assembly from 1834 until 1842. In 1836 he was admitted to the bar.

On November 4, 1842, Lincoln, 33, married Mary Todd, 23. They had four boys, with only Robert living to adulthood. Edward lived un-til age 4, William died at 12, the only child to die in the White House. Thomas died at age 18.

After Lincoln's successful legislative terms, he moved to Springfield, Illinois, and there began the road to the presidency. In 1847, he was elected as a Whig to the House of Representatives for a two year term.

In 1849, Lincoln decided to return to Springfield and continue his law practice. Because of his disagreement with the Whig position on allowing slavery in the territories, Lincoln joined the new radical Republican party in 1856.

In 1858, Lincoln was nominated by the Illinois Republicans to be their candidate for the United States Senate. At the state convention, Lincoln gave his radical view of the slavery situation. He stated in his speech, "that a house divided against itself cannot stand." Further that a government half-slave and half-free could not endure; it would have to be either one or the other, not both.

In the months before the election, he and Stephen Douglas debated seven times on the issue. The most famous was the Freeport, Illinois, debate where Lincoln challenged Douglas to equate local decision of the slavery question with the Dred Scott decision. It differentiated Lincoln, who viewed slavery as a moral, social, and political wrong, from Douglas who did not view slavery as a moral problem. Douglas defended his belief in "popular sovereignty" that the Kansas-Nebraska Act stated and one that he had been instrumental in getting passed. In a close vote, Lincoln lost the Senate race to Douglas.

Later Douglas would lose the presidential nomination to Lincoln.

In 1860, Lincoln was chosen by the Republicans to run for president on their anti-slavery platform. Hannibal Hamlin of Maine was selected for vice-president.

Lincoln won election over the divided Democrats. After the secession of the Southern states just prior to Lincoln assuming the presidency, war erupted with the shelling of Fort Sumter, South Carolina.

At the beginning of his term as president, Lincoln relied on General McClellan to organize the army. However, Lincoln began learning the conduct of war almost immediately.

The year, 1862, was a momentous one for Lincoln. On February 20, his son, Willie, died at age 12. It plunged Lincoln in extreme grief that lasted for weeks. His wife, Mary, had been accused of having Southern sympathies because her brother and three half brothers were in the Confederate army. Willie's death and Lincoln's grief began her eventual breakdown.

On March 6, 1862, Lincoln put into words his proposal to the Congress to compensate any state that would gradually eliminate slavery.[1] This proposal was given substance on September 22, 1862, when Lincoln issued the Emancipation Proclamation. It became effective January 1, 1863.

Lincoln was reelected president in November, 1864, along with Andrew Johnson, a Southern Democrat, his choice for vice-president.

The compassion and the resolve of Lincoln to pursue and overcome the rebellion is stated in his short Second Inaugural Address which concludes with the words, "With malice toward none, with charity for all, with firmness in the right as God gives us to see the right, let us strive on to finish the work we are in, to bind up the nation's wounds, to care for him who shall have borne the battle...to do all which may achieve and cherish a just and lasting peace among ourselves and with all nations."[2]

One of Lincoln's greatest needs for pursuing the war was a reliable general. George McClellan did not pursue Robert E. Lee's defeated army at Antietam. This might have ended the rebellion. Lincoln replaced McClellan with a succession of generals: Generals Ambrose Burnside, Joseph Hooker and George Meade, the victor at Gettysburg, who again let Lee escape. Finally, he settled on Ulysses S. Grant, the victor of the siege of Vicksburg. With General Grant, Lincoln found a general who would pursue the enemy and destroy their army. Grant pursued General Lee and finally cornered him at Appomattox Courthouse,Virginia, where on April 9, 1865, four days after Lincoln's second inaugural, General Ulysses S. Grant accepted General Robert E. Lee's surrender of Confederate forces at the McCean house. The Civil War was over.

Five days later, on April 14, 1865, John Wilkes Booth, shot Lincoln at Ford's Theater. Lincoln died at 7:22 the next morning. The Lincoln Funeral Train carrying "Honest Abe" to Springfield was met along the way by thousands of mourners

---

[1] Messages, Vol. 5, pp.3269-70

[2] Messages, Vol. 5, pp. 3477-78

as it journeyed across the land. Burial was at Springfield, Illinois, on May 4, 1865.

The surrender of the final major Southern army occurred near Durham Station, North Carolina, on April 26, 1865.

Presidential Campaign-1860

Threats of secession were the major theme of the 1860 campaign. Abraham Lincoln, Republican, was opposed in the campaign by several other party candidates. The Democrats ran Stephen Douglas, the National Democratic party ran John C. Breckenridge of Kentucky, and the Constitutional Union party ran John Bell of Tennessee. The several candidates for the Democrats caused a splintering of their party. The united Republicans were triumphant when Lincoln was elected.

Presidential Election-1860

Lincoln was elected with only 40% of the vote. His popular vote total was 1,865,908. Douglas' popular vote was 1,380,202 (29%). Breckenridge received 848,019 (18%) popular votes, and Bell received 590,901 (13%) votes. Lincoln's electoral vote count was 180 votes from 18 states to Breckenridge's electoral count of 72 from 11 states. Douglas won the state of Missouri with 9 votes and 3 votes from a New Jersey split vote. John Bell, Constitutional Union, 39 votes.

Presidential Campaign-1864

Once again Lincoln was nominnated by the Republicans who took on the National Union party label to bring in Democrats who had supported Lincoln and the Union in the war. Lincoln wanted and got Andrew Johnson of Tennessee as his running mate. Lincoln's opponent in the 1864 election was former Union commander-in-chief, George B. McClellan of New Jersey whom Lincoln had relieved of command.

The major issue was the conduct of the war and whether it was thought that Lincoln could lead the Union to victory. With McClellan in the lead in the presidential race, Union forces led by General William Sherman's captured Atlanta. Later successes by Grant indicate that the war was turning in the Union's favor. In the campaign the Republicans stated that the Union must not change commanders in the midst of war and therefore Lincoln should be reelected.

Presidential Election-1864

Lincoln received 2,218,388 (55%) popular votes, the first time any presidential candidate had reached two million votes. McClellan received 1,812,807 (45%) votes. In the electoral vote Lincoln received 212 votes from 22 states. McClellan had 21 electoral votes from 3 states The Confederate states did not vote.

Major Legislation During Presidency

Abraham Lincoln's greatest accomplishment was the preservation of the Union, not the abolition of slavery. The enormous difficulties he faced could only have been handled by a man with a strong will and the determination to achieve a strongly held goal. He knew that if the Confederacy could defend itself and force a stalemate, the Union's cause would be lost. Because of the Union's superior number of troops, Lincoln resolved to carry the battle to the Confederacy on all fronts and destroy their army.

During his first term, his Preliminary Emancipation Proclamation[3] was issued on September 23, 1862, to take effect on January 1, 1863. It freed all slaves in Confederate territory. The Proclamation was the basis for the 13th Amendment that was ratified by 27 states and took effect on December 18, 1865.

The Homestead Act of 1862, gave free title of 160 acres of public lands to citizens who occupied government land for a period of five years. This act helped to settle the West after the war.

The Morrell Act of 1862, was sponsored by Republican Justin Morrell of Vermont. It allowed the government to grant to each state 30,000 acres of land which in turn they could sell to help pay for agricultural and mechanical arts colleges. Over the years, sixty-nine land-grant colleges were established from the sale of these lands.

In 1862-64, the Pacific Railway Acts were enacted to begin the building a transcontinental railroad. The Northern Pacific Railroad was chartered in Congress in 1864.

West Virginia was admitted to the Union on June 20, 1863 as the 35th state. The new state of West Virginia was a direct result of the division that the Civil War created. The residents of the uplands were Union sympathizers while the flatlands or coastal residents were Confederates. The northwestern counties organized the state of West Virginia.

Nevada became the 36th state on October 31, 1864.

Major Events During Presidency

In the Civil War, 1861-1865, the 23 Union states fought the 11 states that had seceded from the Union. The Confederate States of America chose Richmond, Virginia, as the new capital of the Confederacy.

Many of the Union states were divided in their loyalty. Maryland was torn by Unionists and other states wished to remain neutral or side with the South. Missouri was a divided armed camp, reflecting the divisions in the United States.

On April 3, 1860, the first pony express rider left St. Joseph, Missouri, to carry mail to Sacramento, California. Each rider rode about 75 miles from station to station. The Pony Express lasted nineteen months until the telegraph line between East and West was connected on October 24, 1861.

On March 3, 1863, Congress passed the first conscription act. This was followed by Lincoln's proclamation to call up state militia

In a proclamation, Lincoln called up 100,000 conscripts to be drafted into the army on June 15, 1863, with 30,000 coming from Ohio and 50,000 from Pennsylvania.[4]

On April 11, 1865, Lincoln made his last public address. He expressed the hope that the Southern secessionist states would soon return to the Union. He urged a policy of conciliation toward the Confederate states.

---

3 Messages, Vol. V, pp. 3358-60

4 Messages, Vol. V, p.3370

Andrew Johnson
17th President (1865-1869)

The robust 5 feet 10 inches tall Andrew Johnson was thrust into the center of Reconstruction by the assassination of Lincoln. Lincoln had given much thought to the problems facing the United States in the post-war era. Johnson was determined to carry out Lincoln's flexible plan for Reconstruction, but the situation that Johnson was placed in needed someone who was better able to work with the diverse forces in the bitterness that followed the ending of the Civil War. He attempted to meet the problems and solve them but the difficulties of Reconstruction were too great. He was a Southern Jacksonian Democrat who favored states' rights. He faced a Congress led by a majority of Radical, Moderate, and Conservative Republicans, who wanted to punish the South for seceding rather than bring them back into the Union without penalty as Lincoln had planned.

An accomplished orator, Johnson used his direct approach to Reconstruction to try to bring the South back into the Union.

Biography

Andrew Johnson portrays the American dream that any child can grow up to be president. Johnson was born on December 29, 1808, in Raleigh, North Carolina, to Jacob and Mary "Polly" McDonough Johnson. His father died when he was three, and his mother barely managed to raise Andrew and his brother, William. Johnson spent most of his childhood in poverty trying to help his mother earn a living.

At age 14, Johnson was sent as an indentured worker to learn a trade from the village tailor. At age 17, he and his mother along with William, moved to Greeneville, Tennessee, where he set up a successful tailoring business.

On May 17, 1827, when he was 18, he married Eliza McCardle, 16, whose father was the town shoemaker. They were to spend over 48 years together and have five children. Johnson never went to school so he was self-taught in reading. His wife, Eliza, taught him to write.

At 21, Johnson became a town alderman and several years later, mayor of Greenville. A state legislator, he was elected to the House of Representative in 1842 where he remained for five terms. By 1853, he was well known and was elected governor of Tennessee. Four years later he was elected to the United States Senate and served from 1857 to 1862.

After the Civil War began, Johnson remained in the Senate even after Tennessee withdrew from the Union. He spoke often to people in Tennessee on the need to preserve the Union, urging them not to secede. He had come to the attention of Abraham Lincoln after the Union army captured Tennessee. Lincoln asked him to serve as occupation governor. Johnson served for three years.

When Lincoln ran for reelection in 1864, he chose Johnson to be his vice-president on the National Union Republican ticket.

Johnson, a former Democrat, was elected vice-president when Lincoln won reelection. After Lincoln's death on April 15, 1865, he assumed the office of president and attempted to carry on Lincoln's program for Reconstruction of the eleven states of the Confederacy.

Andrew Johnson immediately became involved in a power struggle with the Republican Congress most of whom were Radical Republicans. He attempted to help the Southern states to form new governments, but was stopped by the Radical Republican Congress' moves to punish the South. Moderate Republicans would pass bills dealing with the Reconstruction that they thought Johnson approved, but Johnson would veto them. This turned Congressional support against him. Finally, the Republican Congress found that they could override his vetoes and Johnson's ability to lead was gone.

As a result of his constant opposition to Congress, Congress passed the Tenure of Office Act which Johnson defied. This resulted in eleven articles of impeachment against him and a Senate trial occurred. He was acquitted by one vote short of the two-thirds needed to impeach.

After his term, Johnson was denied the party's renomination, and returned to Greeneville, Tennessee. He remained active in politics. In 1874, he was elected a senator for Tennessee, becoming the only former president to serve in the United States Senate. Shortly after taking office, he suffered a series of strokes and died on July 31, 1875, at the age of 66. He had asked that his body be wrapped in the American flag and his head placed on a copy of the Constitution.

Major Legislation During Presidency

Most legislation was concerned with the Reconstruction of the South following the Civil War.

On March 29, 1865, Johnson issued a Amnesty Proclamation that pardoned all Confederates except those whose property totaled more than $20,000. Some Confederate leaders were not given pardons. Those pardoned had to sign an oath to uphold the Union.

On December 18, 1865, the Thirteenth Amendment abolishing slavery or involuntary servitude was ratified.

In 1866, Johnson felt that the congressional elections were a referendum on his Reconstruction plan. He was the first president to travel across the country selling his program. There were riots in the South and in the election, Republicans gained seats in spite of Johnson's efforts.

On March 2, 1867, Nebraska became the 37th state in the Union.

On March 2, 1867, the Tenure of Office Act passed, preventing the president from removing without Senate approval, government offic-ers that had been given tenure by the Senate. The act was the basis for impeachment when Johnson tried to remove Secretary of War Edwin Stanton, a Radical Republican who opposed his policies. After hearings were held, the House of Representatives brought eleven articles of impeachment against Johnson, citing "high crimes and misdemeanors" against the Tenure of Office Act. He asked for a month to prepare a defense. The Senate gave him ten days.

At the trial, evidence was presented that showed that the Tenure of Office Act could not be applied to Stanton because he had been in Lincoln's cabinet. Johnson was acquitted by one vote.

The Civil Rights Act of 1866 prevented states from passing and enforcing Black Codes that prevented freed slaves from exercising their citizen rights.

Congress extended the Freedman's Bureau Act, 1866. It gave land, jobs, and education to blacks. Congress overrode Johnson's veto.

March 30, 1867, Russia ceded the Territory of Alaska to the United States for $7.2 million.

On July 28, 1868, the Fourteenth Amendment to the Constitution established the federal rights of citizens. No state could make laws that were not consistent with federal law as to citizens' rights and privileges; nor could the states deprive citizens' of life, liberty, or property without due process of the law. They could not deprive citizens protection under the law. The amendment was intended to stop the southern states from preventing blacks the right to vote.

Ulysses S. Grant
18th President (1869-1877)

The short 5 feet 7 inches tall Ulysses Grant was a dynamo in the military service of his country.

A modest, mild man who achieved greatness because of his ability to conduct an army at war, Grant reluctantly became president. As he stated, "It was my fortune or misfortune to be called to the office without prior political training."

At times the honest, politically naive president could not seem to understand that others were not honest and so his presidency was filled with scandal.

His popularity carried him through two quiet almost uneventful terms without any great fanfare or show. However, he did try to continue the Reconstruction of the South.

As a Republican, he allowed the Reconstruction of the South to run its course, often using military force to bend the South in the direction the congressional Radicals wanted it to go. It was a period when the Congress controlled the country led by a president who neither led nor opposed their actions.

Biography

Ulysses S. Grant was born April 27, 1822, in Point Pleasant, Ohio, to Jesse Root Grant, a tanner of hides, and Hannah Simpson Grant.

Grant's first name was Hiram, but he preferred Ulysses. He was given the middle name of Simpson by the Congressman who appointed him to West Point

Grant's early schooling was in private schools. At the age of 17 he entered West Point where he became an expert horseman. Upon graduation he asked to join the cavalry, but he was assigned to the infantry because of his average grades.

On August 22, 1846, Grant, 26, married Julia Boggs, 22, in a marriage which neither of the parents approved. Grant's parents refused to attend the wedding. The Grants had four children.

Grant was in Texas in 1846 when the Mexican War started. He served under General Zachary Taylor and General Winfield Scott. He fought in most of the battles and was with the Scott forces that occupied Mexico City. He remained in the army until 1854, then left the army and moved his family to Missouri. For three years, he farmed unsuccessfully. He failed as a real estate salesman; then clerked in a leather goods for a brother who had a store in Galena, Illinois.

At the beginning of the Civil War, Grant was appointed by the Illinois governor to command a volunteer militia. Grant did the training so successfully that he was made a brigadier general and put in command of the southeast Missouri district. His first encounter of the war took place at Belmont, Missouri, where his forces overran a Confederate camp. However, on a counterattack, Grant's forces had to retreat. It was a lesson he never forgot.

In 1862, Grant gained his first fame in the North by capturing Fort Donelson in Tennessee, an important Confederate stronghold and the first Union victory. For this Lincoln promoted him to major general of volunteers.

Grant successfully led Union forces at Shiloh in Tennessee and helped drive the Confederates from the state. His siege of Vicksburg in 1863, was so successful that it cut the Confederacy in half.

By 1864, Grant was made lieutenant general and commander of all Union forces after he scored victories at Lookout Mountain and Missionary Ridge in Tennessee. Grant's superior forces pursued General Robert E. Lee relentlessly through the Wilderness Campaign which led eventually to Lee's surrender to Grant at Appomattox Courthouse, Virginia, on April 9, 1865. In July, 1866, Grant was made a full general of the army, the first man since General Washington to hold that rank.

Because of Grant's great popularity, he was nominated for the presidency on the first ballot by the Republican convention that met in Chicago in 1868. Speaker of the House Schuyler Colfax of Indiana ran as vice-president with Grant .

Grant retired in 1877 after serving two terms as president. He and his wife took a two year tour around the world and then retired to Galena, Illinois, for a year until 1881, when they moved to New York city. His brokerage firm went bankrupt, and the last years of his life were spent working on his memoirs. Mark Twain, part owner of a publishing firm, offered $25,000 for their publication.

Just prior to Grant's death from throat cancer, undoubtedly brought on by his smoking twenty cigars a day, the Congress restored him to his general's rank with pay. He died on July 23, 1885, a week after completing his memoirs.

Presidential Campaign-1868

Grant's Democratic opponent in the campaign was Horatio Seymour, former governor of New York. Grant took no active part in campaigning, but in his acceptance speech said, "Let us have peace." The dominant issue in the campaign was how Reconstruction should be conducted. The Republicans said that they would continue the hard line that they had been following, while the Democrats wanted an easing of the tough policies by extending the vote to freed blacks as well as getting the seceding Southern states back into the Union as soon as possible.

Presidential Election-1868

In the popular voting Grant outdistanced Seymour, receiving 3,013,650 (53%) to Seymour's 2,708,744 (47%). In the electoral vote Grant won 214 electoral votes from 26 states to Seymour's 80 votes from 8 states. Three former Confederate states of Mississippi, Texas, and Virginia could not vote because they had not been readmitted to the Union.

Presidential Campaign-1872

President Grant was assured the nomination, but he had a new vice-presidential nominee, Senator Henry Wilson of Massachusetts. Grant's opponent was Horace Greeley of New York, a Liberal Republican who was endorsed by the Democrats. The main issues of the 1872 campaign were the scandals that had run rampant through Grant's first term. Examples are James Fisk and Jay Gould's attempt to corner the gold market and the Credit Mobilier officers who skimmed profits from the federal subsidization of the Union Pacific Railroad.

Greeley called for a cleaner, honest government. Grant's war hero status and the fact that many thought that Grant had nothing to do with the scandals, won him the election. Prosperity and good times in Grant's first term also helped to reelect him.

Presidential Election -1872

Grant received 3,598,235 (56%) popular votes and 286 electoral votes from 29 states. Greeley received 2,834,761 (44%) popular votes. Greeley died before the electoral votes were cast and the 66 that he had won were divided among several states' with the largest block of 42 going to Thomas Hendricks of Illinois and 18 votes going to B. Gatz Brown of Missouri.

Major Legislation During Presidency

On March 30, 1870, a year into Grant's presidency, the Fifteenth Amendment to the Constitution was ratified. The amendment forbid any state from depriving the vote to a citizen due to race, color, or previous servitude.

May 8, 1871, The Treaty of Washington brought about Great Britain's settling the United States suit for damages that the Confederate frigate "Alabama" built by Great Britain did during the war. Great Britain settled for $15.5 million.

May 31, 1870 and April 20, 1871, Congress enacted the Ku Klux Klan Acts in order to enforce the 14th and 15th Amendments. Parts of the Acts were later declared unconstitutional. It gave sweeping powers to the president. If he felt that it was necessary, he could suspend the Writ of Habius Corpus and declare martial law in affected areas. The act was to guarantee rights for freed slaves in the South.

The Civil Rights Act passed March 1, 1875, giving African-Americans the equal rights in public places and the right to serve on juries.

January 14, 1875, Congress passed the Specie Redemption Act which limited the amount of paper money in circulation and required hard money in certain transactions. It made gold the standard.

On August 1, 1876, Colorado became the 38th state.

Major Events During Presidency

The Central Pacific and the Union Pacific met at Promontory Point, Utah, May 10, 1869, where a golden spike was driven, marking the completion of the transcontinental railroad.

September 24, 1869, was named Black Friday when the scandal broke about Jay Gould and Jim Fisk trying to corner the market on gold. They had urged a naive President Grant to stop the sale of gold thus driving up the price. When Grant realized what was happening, he ordered the sale of $4 million of United States gold deposits, driving the price down, causing panic and ruin to businesses.

In 1870, John D. Rockefeller formed Standard Oil Company. In ten years Standard Oil gained control of 90% of the nation's oil.

On February 24, 1871, Georgia became the final Confederate state to comply with Reconstruction legislation and return to the Union. Fires broke out in the Midwest. The Chicago Fire occurred on October 8-9, 1871, killing more than 300 people, leaving thousands without shelter, and destroying over 17,000 buildings.

In 1872, members of Congress and government were involved in the Credit Mobilier stock scandal. Vice-President Schuyler Colfax, who was not renominated and his replacement, Henry Wilson, were accused of buying stock at less than value from officers who had skimmed huge profits from the federally subsidized Union Pacific Railroad. An agreement was reached and Congress did not investigate.

A recession, the Panic of 1873, brought on a five year depression and bankrupted more than 10,000 businesses. It occurred with the failure of Jay Cooke and Company, a bank that had overextended investments in the railroads.

The 1870 census showed the United States population to be 39,818,449, a gain of 8,375,128 since 1860.

Rutherford B. Hayes
19th President (1877-1881)

Known for his high regard for principles, Rutherford B. Hayes brought integrity and honesty to the presidency that the office demands. He was a medium height, 5 feet, 8 1/2 inches tall, robust, full-bearded man who enjoyed people, a good conversation, and possessed a memory for names and people. Hayes was a man who had a deep sense of social justice, serving society well in his retirement. He believed that his role in life was to be a good public servant. His reputation for honesty and integrity, won him followers in war and in peace. His election was the most closely contested election in our history until the 2000 election. It marked the beginning of our industrial expansion.

Biography

Rutherford B. Hayes was born in Delaware, Ohio, on October 4, 1822, to Rutherford and Sophia Birchard Hayes. His father was a farmer and storekeeper who died several months before Hayes was born. Hayes was generally educated at home and in several private schools before attending Kenyon College at age 16. He graduated in 1842 and decided to study law. The biggest influence on Hayes besides his mother and sister, was his uncle, Sardis Birchard, from whom his middle name was taken. He studied at a law firm in Columbus, Ohio, and later attended Harvard Law School, graduating in 1845. He was admitted to the bar in 1845.

Hayes set up a practice in Lower Sandusky, Ohio, and a few years later moved to Cincinnati, Ohio, and created a successful practice.

On December 30, 1852, Hayes, 30, married Lucy Ware Webb, 21. She attended Wesleyan Woman's College. Later she would be the first First Lady to be a college graduate. She was dedicated to the temperance movement and did not allow alcohol in the White House when she became First Lady. She was nicknamed,"Lemonade Lucy." It was Lucy who started the Easter egg roll tradition on the White House lawn.

Hayes became politically active in Cincinnati, first as a Whig and then with the decline of the party, as an anti-slavery Republican.

Hayes' Union army service from 1861-1865 in the Civil War was exemplary. He was in over fifty engagements, wounded several times, and had four horses shot out from under him. By the end of the Civil War, he had risen to major general. While still in service, he was elected to the House of Representatives in 1865 as a Radical Republican. He voted to impeach Andrew Johnson.

Hayes became Governor of Ohio in 1868-72 and again in 1876 for a two year term. At the Republican Convention in Cincinnati in 1876, he was nominated for president and barely won the nomination over the favorite, James Blaine of Maine.

Elected president, Hayes served one term before retiring. During retirement he continued to do public service supporting other Republicans, promoting black education with scholarships, and serving as a trustee of Ohio State University. Hayes opposed woman suffrage.

Hayes died on January 17, 1893. He is buried at his estate of Spiegel Grove near Fremont, Ohio.

Presidential Campaign-1876

In 1876, Hayes barely won the nomination of the Republican Party over James G. Blaine, winning on the seventh ballot by six votes. One of the dominant themes in the presidential campaign was a fair treatment of all people of the South including blacks. Hayes' Democratic opponent was Samuel J. Tilden, governor of New York.

Reform was another theme for both parties. The major scandals of Grant's administration were a dominant theme for the Democrats plus the lasting effect of the 1873 depression, added to the feeling that Hayes would lose. Tilden was the favorite at the campaign's end.

Presidential Election-1876

In early returns, Tilden took a lead. In fact, Hayes saw the early results and retired for the night, certain that he had lost. Tilden was confident of a victory.

However, in one of the most disputed, and at times, confusing election in U. S. history, Rutherford B.

Hayes, Republican from Ohio, was elected by a vote in the House of Representatives. The popular vote was close with Tilden getting 4,288,546 (51%) popular votes to Hayes' 4,034,311 (48%) votes. However, three Southern states, South Carolina, Louisiana, and Florida were Republican controlled and the popular vote and the electoral vote were in question in those states. In addition, one electoral vote from Oregon was disputed. At this point Tilden had 184 electoral votes one short of election; Hayes had 166 votes.

The election was brought to the House where the Democrats had a majority. The Senate had a Republican majority. Moderates from both parties created a commission of fifteen members to arbitrate the election and report to House. The commission consisted of five House members, five Senate members, and five Supreme Court justices. The commission reported and the vote counting began February 1, 1877. The constant objections and need for rulings continued almost to inauguration day, March 4, 1877.

Before the voting, the Democratic controlled House made a tactical error. They voted to admit Colorado to statehood with the expectation that the three electoral votes would go to Tilden. Colorado voted for Hayes instead. In the House, the ruling went for the Republicans with Hayes being granted the electoral votes of the contested states of Louisiana, South Carolina, Florida, and the one electoral vote from Oregon by an 8 to 7 commission vote. Hayes was elected president with 185 electoral votes to 184 for Tilden.

The final tally came down to the moment before inauguration with the threat of a Democratic filibuster past the March 4th deadline. The final electoral vote tally had Hayes winning 21 states and Tilden winning 17 states.

Major Legislation During Presidency

The Bland-Allison Act, 1878, required that the government again begin to purchase silver monthly. It was passed over Hayes' veto.

A resumption of the Specie Act of 1879, which was the redemption of greenbacks for gold and was intended to put the economy on a more solid basis, was passed.

Civil service reform corrected the spoils' system abuses of previous administrations.

In 1879, Chinese immigration to the U. S was restricted. This restriction was instituted by Congress over Hayes' veto. In 1880, a treaty was signed with China, limiting the inflow of Chinese to the U. S.

Hayes set a policy establishing American control of a canal to be built in Panama that would be built twenty-five years later.

Major Events During Presidency

The Reconstruction lasted from 1865 to 1877. It ended with the withdrawal of the last Federal troops from New Orleans on April 24, 1877.

In 1877, a railroad strike because of wage cuts began on the Baltimore & Ohio railroad. It spread to other lines. Federal troops were sent to restore order after strike deaths in West Virginia and Pittsburgh.

James A. Garfield
20th President (1881)

James Abram Garfield brought prestige back to the presidency that had been lost under President Grant. The 6 feet tall, physically impressive Garfield was well prepared to become president. The good natured Garfield showed his ambition and fortitude by rising from poverty to become a college president, state senator, Civil War general, congressman, and president of the nation. He was the last of a line of seven log cabin presidents to be elected. In his four short months as president, Garfield defied the machine politics and made appoint-ments he wanted to run the country. He had the potential for a great presidency when an irate office seeker shot him in the back at the Baltimore and Potomac railroad station in Washington.

Biography

James A. Garfield was born in a log cabin in Orange, Ohio, on November 19, 1831, to Abram and Eliza Garfield. His father died when he was two, so Eliza Garfield was left to raise the four children. Garfield and his brother and sisters had to find work when they were quite young in order to survive.

Garfield learned to read at age three. Formal schooling took place for only a few short months a year. The robust, gregarious James Garfield grew into a stalwart tall young man who wore a beard all his adult life. As a man, he found that he had the gift for oratory, becoming famous for his ability to captivate listeners.

As Garfield grew older, he dreamed of being a seaman. At age 16, he left home for Cleveland, Ohio, to work on the Great Lakes as a sailor. He failed to get the sailing job, but he did find a job guiding the horses that pulled the boats on the Ohio Canal between Cleveland and Pittsburgh. Later when Garfield became ill with malaria, he returned home.

Garfield continued his education at district schools and began teaching in one of them. He enrolled at the Eclectic Institute in Hiram, Ohio, and graduated with honors.

In 1854, he entered Williams College in Williamstown, Massachusetts, as a Junior and perfected his oratory skills. He did lay ministry and for a time considered entering the ministry. Instead he decided to teach. At Williams College, he campaigned in 1856, for Republican presidential nominee, John Fremont.

At age 26, Garfield married a school teacher, Lucretia "Crete" Rudolph, 26, on November 11, 1858. From the marriage, they had seven children with four sons and one daughter living to maturity.

Garfield taught classical languages at the Institute from 1856 to 1857. From 1857 to 1861, Garfield was president of the Institute. During this time he studied law and was admitted to the bar in 1860. The ambitious Garfield became interested in politics and proceeded to use his oratory skills to speak out on the country's problems of slavery and states' rights. With his anti-slavery views, he joined the newly formed Republican party, speaking out against slavery and secession. In 1859, he was elected a state senator, serving until 1861 when he joined the Union army. He was made a colonel and put in charge of recruiting and organizing the Ohio Voluntary Infantry.

During the Civil War, Garfield led his brigade at Middle Creek, 1862; and at Shiloh, 1862. As a Brigadier General, he served as General William Rosecrans' chief of staff at the Battle of Chickamauga in 1863. His valor earned him a major general rank.

In 1862, he was elected to the House of Representatives and Lincoln persuaded him to resign from the army and take his seat. This Garfield did in December, 1863. He was reelected to the House for the next eighteen years where he became the leading Republican legislator.

At the 1880 Republican Convention, Garfield nominated John Sherman, who opposed Grant and Senator John Blaine, for president. When none of the candidates could win a majority, the convention turned to Garfield and nominated him on the 36th ballot. His vice-presidential candidate was Chester A. Arthur, a member of the Stalwart Republicans, conservative backers of former President Grant.

James Garfield, 49, defeated the Democratic General Winfield Scott Hancock by a narrow margin.

As president, Garfield attempted to create a balanced administration. His taking in all factions of the Republican party, angered his most stalwart backer, Roscoe Conkling of New York. However, Garfield managed to get his appointees confirmed by the Congress.

The prime example of Garfield's intentions to form a balanced administration, occurred immediately after his inauguration. He named the Half-Breed liberal James Gillespie Blaine his Secretary of State.

On July 2, 1881, while on his way to a short vacation, Garfield was waiting with Secretary of State Blaine in the Baltimore and Potomac Railroad station in Washington, D. C., when an irate office seeker, Charles J. Guiteau, shot him in the spine, shouting, "I am a Stalwart and Arthur is president now."

After several months, Garfield died on September 19, 1881, of infection brought about by doctors trying to locate the bullet with non-sterile instruments.

Presidential Campaign-1880

The 1880 presidential campaign lacked any real differences between Garfield and Democrat Winfield S. Hancock of Pennsylvania. The only difference was that the Republicans wanted high tariffs on imports and the Democrats wanted enough tariff to cover expenses and a small profit. Because he had been House leader during the Credit Mobilier scandal and had to defend his position on the scandal, Garfield was attacked

on it. The Democrats also attacked Garfield for his vote for Hayes while on the commission that had awarded the presidency to Rutherford Hayes.

Presidential Election-1880

Republican Garfield's popular vote was 4,446,158 (48%), Democrat Hancock's was 4,444,260 (48%), and Greenback party Weaver's was 305,997 (3%). The 9,210,420 voters was the greatest number of voters of any election to that time in United States history. Garfield won by only a margin of 9,464 votes to capture his electoral votes.

While the popular vote was close, the electoral vote was not. Garfield won 19 states and 214 electoral votes. Hancock also won 19 states but with only 155 electoral votes.

Major Events During Presidency

With the assassination of Garfield by Charles J. Guiteau, the Civil Service spoils system, begun during Andrew Jackson's time, came to an end. The assassination ended the Stalwarts reign as the distributors of government jobs.

The public held the Stalwarts indirectly responsible for Garfield's death because of their defense of the spoils system. It brought about Civil Service reform after Stalwart Vice-President Chester A. Arthur became president on September 20, 1881.

Charles Guiteau was tried for the assassination, found guilty, and executed on June 30, 1881.

United States population in the 1880 census was 50,189,209, a growth of over 11 million in a decade.

Chester A. Arthur
21st President (1881-1885)

Chester Alan Arthur was over 6 feet tall and heavily built, weighing over 220 pounds, when he became president. The elegant, handsome president's most distinguishing features were his bushy side whiskers and mustache. The affable, congenial Arthur always appeared the well-dressed gentleman. Honest and straight-forward in his dealings, he proved to be more presidential than anyone had expected, least of all his Stalwart party associates who expected him to further his political life by continuing the patronage system he had learned while working in New York as a protege of Congressional boss, Roscoe Conkling.

When Arthur became president, he was expected to revive the spoils system that Hayes had ended. Instead he repudiated the Radical Roscoe Conkling, and refused to appoint persons to government positions as a political payoff. He revived civil service reform begun by President Hayes and vetoed bills he felt were not in the public interest. Arthur proved to be a purposeful, conscientious president.

Biography

Chester A. Arthur was born on October 5, 1829, in a parsonage in North Fairfield, Vermont. His father, Reverend William Arthur, was an immigrant Irish minister. His mother was Melvina Stone Arthur, a native of Vermont. Arthur's childhood was without roots as his family constantly moved around the state of Vermont.

Arthur, as a young boy, attended local schools, later went on to the Lyceum in Schenectady, New York, and then in 1845, at age 15, he entered Union College in Schenectady as a sophomore. Arthur, an excellent student and a Phi Beta Kappa, graduated with honors in 1848.

After graduation Arthur taught school and began his study of law. He was admitted to the bar in 1854 when he moved to New York.

Both Arthur and his father were opposed to slavery. As a lawyer, Arthur became involved in cases involving blacks and their freedom. In one case Arthur won a monetary settlement for a black woman who had not been allowed to ride the streetcar in New York city.

In 1859, at age 30, Arthur married Ellen "Nell" Lewis Herndon, 22. Although somewhat strained by his political work and the Civil War, theirs was a happy marriage. They had a son and a daughter who lived to maturity. Mrs. Arthur died in 1880, a year before Arthur became president.

In 1860, Arthur helped organize the Republican Party in New York. Then during the Civil War he organized supplies and equipped the New York state militia. His political work was brought to the attention of Representative Roscoe Conkling, the political boss of New York state. As a close friend, Arthur became his lieutenant. Arthur learned the patronage system and gave jobs to deserving Republican supporters during his stint as collector at the New York Port Authority.

After his election, President Hayes ordered an investigation into the spoils system of New York, resulting in Chester Arthur's dismissal from his custom house post in 1878. This caused a split in the Republican party with the supporters of the spoils system called the Stalwarts and the reformers of Hayes called the Half-Breeds.

At the 1880 National Convention the Republicans were divided and nominated Garfield, a Half-Breed. When they looked for a vice-president, the compromise was Chester Arthur, a Stalwart.

After the assassination of James Garfield, Chester Arthur became president on September 20, 1881. He was determined to run a presidency following Hayes' example and have a civil service untainted by the spoils system. He succeeded in his efforts. Because of the prosperity of the country and the over abundance of money, the term "pork barrel" came into being to designate the local projects that a Congressman could get the government to pay for and not have the burden fall on local taxpayers.

Because the Republicans were not pleased with Arthur's stand against the old patronage system, at the Republican National Convention in 1884, they did not renominate Arthur, but instead nominated his rival, James G. Blaine. In the November election Blaine lost to Democrat Grover Cleveland.

In retirement, Chester Arthur suffered from life threatening Bright's disease, a kidney disease. After suffering for months, he died on November 18, 1886

Chester had run a clean and honest administration, refusing to give in to political expediency to remain in office.

Major Legislation During Presidency

By 1882, the great influx of Chinese laborers reached a peak of 39,579 for the building of the Transcontinental Railroad. Consequently, the Chinese Exclusion Act of 1882, passed, suspending Chinese immigration to the United States for a period of ten years.

The River and Harbors Act of 1882, was filled with federally financed local projects. It was vetoed by Arthur because he saw it as a pork-barrel bill, but Congress overrode the veto.

The Pendleton Act of 1883, created the modern civil service system and by law did away with the political spoils' system that had become so much a part of partisan politics. President Arthur signed and enforced the act which provided for a testing system that was fair to all who took it, and provided a basis for fair hiring of those who applied for jobs.

The so-called Mongrel Act of 1883, created a commission that recommended the reduction of tariffs. This laid the groundwork for later tariff disputes between the Republi-cans who wanted higher tariffs to protect the jobs of the American worker and the Democrats who were for freer trade. Over the years each party would use its stand on the tariff as a campaign issue.

Major Events During Presidency

In 1870, the first transcontinental passenger train went from Boston to San Francisco. In 1867, in Chicago, George Pullman developed the first railroad sleeping car and organized the Palace Car Company.

The Northern Pacific Railroad completed its line from Ashland, Wisconsin, to Portland, Oregon in September, 1883.

With the need to set up timetables for the railroads and with the telegraph bringing the country closer together, the time difference between East and West had to be adjusted.

In November, 1883, standard time, invented by Dr. Charles L. Dowd, was adopted. It divided the United States into four time zones: Eastern, Central, Mountain, and Pacific zones, bringing uniformity to transcontinental travel.

For the second time in the nation's history, the country had three presidents in one year. Rutherford Hayes completed his term on March 3, 1881, James Garfield became president on March 4, and on September 19, 1881, Vice-President Chester Arthur became president after Garfield's assassination.

In 1883, the Supreme Court ruled the 1875 Civil Rights Act unconstitutional. Only the rights of blacks to serve on juries was upheld.

Grover Cleveland
22nd President (1885-1889)

Grover Cleveland's first name was Stephen, but he was always called Grover. The 5 feet, 11 inches tall, 250 pound, quick-tempered son of a minister, grew to be an extremely honest and patriotic man. Throughout his life he found himself at odds with associates at work, in government, and in his political party because of his honesty. The reform-minded Cleveland was a large, gregarious man who sought political office for the good that he might do for his fellow man and the country. Cleveland is the only president who had a four year space between his two terms.

Biography

Grover Cleveland was born on March 18, 1837, in Caldwell, New Jersey, to the Reverend Richard F. Cleveland and Anne Neal Cleveland. Until he was 11, his parents taught him to read and write. They instilled in him a strict religious upbringing which might explain his very strict adherence to honesty which he carried over to his later political life. His family moved often. When he was four, they moved to Feyetteville, New York, where he attended a local academy. In 1850, they moved to Clinton, New York, where he attended the Liberal Institute. Plans for college were dropped when his father died in 1853, and he returned home to work.

Cleveland later moved to Buffalo, New York, where he edited a paper, the *American Shorthorn Handbook,* for his uncle. In return, his uncle arranged for Cleveland to study law in a Buffalo law firm. He was admitted to the bar in 1859.

During the Civil War, Cleveland spent the time practicing law. He was drafted for war duty, but under the Conscription Act of 1863, he paid $150 to a Polish immigrant to take his place. He approved of Lincoln's handling of the war, although he remained loyal to the Democratic party.

Early in his law career he was made assistant district attorney for Erie County. He began to earn his reputation for honesty and integrity and was next elected county sheriff from 1871 to 1873.

In 1874, a young woman, Maria Halpin, gave birth to a son and she named Cleveland as the father. As a bachelor, Cleveland took responsibility and supported the son until he was an adult.

By 1881, the Buffalo city government had become so corrupt that Cleveland was elected as a reform mayor. He proceeded to throw out the dishonest office holders and set up an honest government. This election was followed in 1883 by his being elected as governor of New York as a reform Democrat.

Cleveland's record for honesty in government was the quality the national Democrats needed and so in 1884, he was nominated for president. Cleveland won in a close race against James G. Blaine, the Republican candidate. Cleveland became the first Democratic president since James Buchanan in 1857.

On June 2, 1886, Cleveland married Frances Folsom in the only presidential marriage held in the White House. John Philip Sousa's Marine band provided the music. The Cleveland marriage produced five children.

During his term as president Cleveland did not have a good working relationship with the Congress including his own Democratic party. He refused to fill patronage jobs for his party and he vetoed several bills that the Democrats wanted. Consequently, he lost the 1888 election to Republican Benjamin Harrison when New York's electoral votes went to Harrison. Cleveland returned to New York City and practiced law, enjoying semi-retirement.

In 1892, Cleveland once again received the Democratic party nomination even though he had come out against some of the party leaders on tariff and silver coinage issues aligning himself with the conservative wing of the party. He was elected to a new term and returned to the White House on March 4, 1893.

Following his retirement in 1897, Cleveland lived on an estate in Princeton, New Jersey, where he became active in university affairs and in the insurance business.

On June 24, 1908, at the age of 71, Grover Cleveland died after a long illness. He was a man who as he said, "...tried to do right." His life was a testament to that philosophy.

Presidential Campaign-1884

The presidential campaign of 1884 was one based upon the public's perception of the moral character of the candidates. James G. Blaine from Maine was seen as a man who moved in high places with such tycoons as John J. Astor and Jay Gould, who tried to corner the gold market during Grant's administration. Grover Cleveland, Democrat, was pictured as morally corrupt because of an earlier love affair. While never commenting on the event himself, Cleveland advised friends when asked about the child, to tell the truth. Cleveland's honesty prevented it from becoming an issue.

Presidential Election-1884

The election was a close contest with Democrat Grover Cleveland winning with 4,874,621 (49%) popular votes and 219 electoral votes from 20 states. Thomas Hendricks was his vice-president.

Republican James G. Blaine received 4,848,936 (48%) popular votes and 182 electoral votes.

Benjamin Butler of the Greenback party had 175,096 (2%) votes.

Major Legislation During Presidency

The presidential succession was again defined in the Presidential Succession Act of 1886, which stated that should something happen to both the president and vice-president, the cabinet officers would be next in line depending upon the office creation date.

In 1887, the first major Interstate Commerce Act was enacted to regulate railroads and private businesses through the Interstate Commerce Commission that was created.

The Dawes Severally Act, 1887, gave Indians citizenship and title to reservation lands if they renounced tribal allegiances.

The Hatch Act of 1887 created agricultural experimental stations aligned with agricultural colleges in various states.

On January 20, 1887, the U.S.-Hawaiian Treaty for reciprocal trade was renewed and modified. The United States was permitted to build a naval base at Pearl Harbor.

Major Events During Presidency

On October 28, 1886, Cleveland dedicated the Statue of Liberty on Bedloe's Island, a gift of the French people commemorating the 1774 Revolutionary War alliance between France and the United States.

The Statue, a symbol of freedom, was designed by Auguste Bertholdi in France where it was dedicated in Paris on July 4, 1884. It was dismantled and reassembled on Bedloe's Island where it became the symbol of freedom for thousands of immigrants in the coming century.

Samuel L. Gompers was elected president of the newly organized American Federation of Labor in Columbus, Ohio, on December 8, 1886.

Electric power was beginning in the United States. New York city installed electric street lamps in 1880. Electric street cars appeared in Baltimore and Boston by 1888.

Benjamin Harrison
23rd President (1889-1893)

The 5 feet, 6 inches tall Benjamin Harrison, grandson of President William Henry Harrison, was a dignified, intense, articulate public speaker and a successful officer in the Civil War.

Harrison commanded respect because of his independent and forceful personality. This prevented his being highly popular, but his sincerity in what he attempted, commanded the respect of his contemporaries. He was the last of the Gilded Age presidents and by the time he left office, the country was turning to economic expansionism with the industrial changes beginning to be seen and experienced throughout the country.

Biography

Benjamin Harrison was born on a family farm in North Bend, Ohio, on August 20, 1833, one of fourteen children. He was the son of John Scott Harrison, the son of the ninth president, William Henry Harrison, and Elizabeth Irwin Harrison. He lived on the farm until the age of 14, when he left home to attend

101

Farmer's College, a prep school in Cincinnati. Until then he had gone to school in a log cabin school his father had built for the community.

In the fall of 1850, he entered Miami University of Ohio as a junior and graduated with honors in 1852.

On October 20, 1853, Harrison married Caroline Lavinia Scott. Their marriage produced a son and a daughter. They moved to Indianapolis where he studied law until 1854, when he was admitted to the bar. Harrison set up a law office, developing a law practice and became involved in politics as a Republican. In 1857, he was elected city attorney for Indianapolis.

With the outbreak of the Civil War in 1862, the Indiana governor appointed Harrison to the rank of colonel with the duty to activate the 70th Indiana Regiment.

Under General Hooker, Harrison was made a brigadier general because of his ability and courage in battle. He led his brigade into Atlanta with General Sherman in 1864. While still in uniform, he made speeches supporting the Republican Abraham Lincoln for president.

Following the Civil War, Harrison returned to his lucrative Indianapolis law practice and civic work.

By 1876, he had become politically prominent enough to run for governor of Ohio. He did not win, but established himself as one of Indiana's leading politicians. The following year he became leader of the Republican party in Indiana and in 1881, was elected a U. S. senator after turning down a cabinet position under President-elect James Garfield. In 1887, the Democratic controlled state legislature defeated him for another senate term.

A year later, Harrison announced his intention to run for president. At the 1888 Republican Convention, he was nominated on the eighth ballot along with Levi P. Morton of New York for vice-president.

After a low key campaign by both Republicans and Democrats, he was elected president over Grover Cleveland even though he had fewer popular votes. His presidency was an active one. However, Harrison's rather cold and precise administrative manner, as well as the Republican party's failure to support his campaign, brought about defeat by Grover Cleveland in 1892. The death of Harrison's wife in 1892 added to his defeat because he stopped actively campaigning.

On April 6 1896, he married Mary Lord Dimmick, niece of his first wife. They had a daughter the following year.

Harrison continued a successful law practice in Indianapolis acting as a council for Venezuela in a boundary dispute with Great Britain over British Guiana.

Harrison died on March 13, 1901, of pneumonia. At his funeral, the Hoosier poet, James Whitcomb Riley, delivered the eulogy. He was buried beside his first wife in Crown Hill cemetery in Indianapolis.

Presidential Campaign-1888

The campaign of 1888 was characterized by great civility. The only speech that President Grover Cleveland made was his acceptance of the nomination. Benjamin Harrison made no major public appearances, but received visitors at his home in what was called, "front porch" campaigning. James G. Blaine campaigned extensively for Harrison. The issue was the import tariff which Cleveland wanted to reduce, although he was against doing away with it entirely. Harrison wanted a high tariff to protect American goods from foreign competition.

Presidential Election-1888

President Cleveland received a popular vote of 5,534.488 (49%) to Harrison's 5,443,892 (48%), a difference of 90,596 votes. Harrison, however, easily defeated Cleveland in the electoral count, winning 20 states and 233 electoral votes to Cleveland's winning 18 states and 168 electoral votes. New York's Tammany Hall machine disliked the reform-minded Cleveland and managed to keep him from winning his own state of New York with 36 electoral votes and so prevented his election.

Major Legislation During Presidency

The Dependent and Disabilities Act, 1890, extended benefits to Civil War veterans for non-military disabilities.

The Sherman Anti-Trust Act of 1890, prevented monopolies in manufacturing and commercial businesses but was worded in a way that made labor unions and farmer alliances illegal.

Under the Sherman Silver Purchase Act, 1890, the government bought up silver using gold notes, causing a run on the gold deposits of the United States. It was one factor that brought on a depression in 1893.

The McKinley Tariff Act of 1890, raised the tariffs on imports to an historic high, causing a rise in consumer prices which added to the depression.

States admitted to the Union were North Dakota and South Dakota on November 2, 1889, as the 39th and 40th states; Montana on November 8, 1889, the 41st state; Washington on November 11, 1889, as the 42nd state; Idaho on July 3, 1890, as the 43rd state; and Wyoming on July 10, 1890, as the 44th state.

Major Events During Presidency

On April 22, 1889, the Oklahoma Territory was declared, open. Hundreds of acres of Western land were available to land rushers. The Sooners, who had gone into the territory as squatters and then claimed the land after its opening, gave Oklahoma the nickname "The Sooner State." Guthrie and Oklahoma City began as tent cities.

On May 31, 1889, the disastrous Johnstown, Pennsylvania, flood occurred. Over 2,000 lives were lost when a dam broke. Property damage was set at about $10,000,000.

On October 2, 1889, the first Pan-American Conference was held that established the Pan-American Union in 1890, to provide stability in the two Americas .

On December 29, 1892, the last major conflict between U. S. troops and Indians was fought at Wounded Knee.

The 1890 population of the United States was 62,979,766, an increase of 12,790,550 in a decade.

Grover Cleveland
24nd President (1893-1897)

Grover Cleveland is the only two-term president who had a four year gap between terms. He retired for four years and then in 1892, the Democrats nominated Cleveland by a narrow margin. His second term was more tempestuous than the first term. Adlai E. Stevenson of Illinois was vice-president.

Presidential Campaign-1892

The major concern in the 1892 campaign was the on-going debate about the tariff on imports. Cleveland wanted a reduction in the tariff while Benjamin Harrison defended the use of tariffs to protect the American tradesman.

Congress had passed the Sherman Silver Purchase Act of 1890, which put more currency into circulation and increased the inflation. At the same time voters were rather concerned about the free spending of the "Million Dollar Congress" and in the mid-term elections swept Democrats into Congress because of the spending of the Republicans.

The candidates stopped campaigning when Mrs. Harrison suddenly died in the middle of the campaign.

A third party, the Populist, ran James Weaver who called for more silver coins and printed money.

Presidential Election-1892

Grover Cleveland, Democrat, won the election with a popular vote of 5,556,918(46%); Benjamin Harrison, the incumbent Republican, received 5,176,108(43%) popular votes. The Populist, James Weaver, received 1,041,028(9%) votes.

Cleveland received 277 electoral votes from 23 states to Harrison's 145 electoral votes from 16 states. Weaver won 4 states and 22 electoral votes. North Dakota's votes were evenly divided between all three candidates.

Major Legislation During Presidency

Some inflation and a depression had begun prior to Cleveland's second term. This occurred because the prior Congress had passed the Sherman Silver Purchase Act of 1890. The Act put more currency into circulation. In 1893, with Cleveland's backing, major financiers such as J. P. Morgan urged Congress to stay on the gold standard by repealing the Sherman Silver Purchase Act. In turn, this change was blamed for the decrease in the gold reserve because people turned in currency for gold.

Cleveland's anti-silver stand divided the Democratic party. Near the end of his term, Cleveland was almost abandoned by his supporters because of his anti-free silver. It became the major contention between Democrats and Republicans in the next election.

Major Events During Presidency

A four year depression was brought on by the Panic of 1893, lasting Cleveland's entire second term. The ensuing crisis deepened when hundreds of banks failed, railroads went bankrupt, and European banks sold off U. S. stocks and bonds. Congress repealed the Silver Act, but it did little to slow down the coming world depression.

Causes for the depression were low gold reserves brought about by high tariffs, high entitlements paid, and poor foreign trade balance. The failure of the Philadelphia and Reading Railroad was also a cause.

The Pullman Strike of 1884 in Chicago, led by Eugene Debs, lasted for nearly three months with seven men killed during the strike. Railroad workers struck because of wage cuts and unemployment. Using Federal troops, Cleveland broke up the strike and arrested Debs. The strike had tied up the railroads, interrupting mail delivery.

In 1894, Coxey's Army, a group of 500 unemployed Ohioans, marched on Washington, demanding a public works program.

In 1895, Cleveland used the Monroe Doctrine to get Great Britain to accept a resolution to a boundary dispute in Venezuela. It was resolved in Great Britain's favor.

On January 4, 1896, Utah became the 45th state.

On November 7, 1893, Colorado became the second state to adopt women suffrage. Wyoming had granted women the vote on December 10, 1869.

William McKinley
25th President (1897-1901)

An able and conscientious administrator, legislator, and leader, William McKinley represents the coming new age of American enterprise at the turn of the century. A born leader who believed in the American idea of democratic principles, McKinley was able to convey this belief to the voters. He was a new presidential type who had an urbane outlook. His even-tempered, cheerfully optimistic personality endeared him to the electorate that elected him to two presidential terms. McKinley was a living example of the belief in the American democratic ideal in which as he said the people were the rulers and their will the supreme law. At the turn of the century, the 5 feet, 7 inches tall, 200 pound, heavy-set McKinley was a new modern president who ushered in the new century with optimism.

Biography

William McKinley was born on January 29, 1843, in Niles, Ohio. He grew up in the towns of Niles and

Poland a short distance apart. He attended public schools. When he was in his teens, he attended a church seminary and discovered that he had the gift to be an orator, speaking with a clear, strong voice that served him well in his political life. He entered Allegheny College but never finished because of illness and lack of family finances brought about by the Depression of 1857.

McKinley went to work, teaching school and serving as a postal clerk before enlisting in the Union Army during the Civil War. He began as a private in the Twenty-third Ohio Volunteer Regiment

His commander was Rutherford B. Hayes, later president of the United States. McKinley's valor in battle earned him the rank of major. He was discharged after a service of four years.

Following the war, he studied law in the office of Charles Glidden, prominent Ohio lawyer. Later he attended Albany Law School in New York. He was admitted to the Ohio bar in March 1867, and opened a law office in Canton, Ohio. There he became involved in politics as a Republican. This was not unusual because while in uniform he had cast his first presidential vote for Lincoln. He worked in the campaign for the election of Rutherford Hayes for governor and for U. S. Grant for president.

On January 25, 1871, he married Ida Saxon. They had two daughters who died while young. Ida became an invalid whom McKinley took care of all his life.

McKinley's early political career included two separate terms in the House of Representatives between 1877-1883 and 1885-1891. The terms were highlighted by two concerns of 19th century American political agenda, high or low tariffs and the silver or gold standard for U. S. currency.

During the second term in Congress, McKinley showed his leadership and became chairman of the powerful Ways and Means Committee. He wrote and sponsored the highly protectionist tariff act, the McKinley Tariff of 1890. This bill, along with unbridled Congressional spending, cost him and many Republicans their congressional seats in the 1890 elections.

After his defeat, McKinley returned home but remained active in national politics. Then at the 1896 Republican convention, he was nominated for president on the first ballot.

Elected president in one of the most active campaigns since the Civil War, William McKinley, served a full four year term and was reelected for another four year term in 1900.

Less than a year later, on September 6, 1901, while standing in a receiving line at the Pan American Exposition in Buffalo, New York, an avowed anarchist, Leon F. Czolgosz, waited to shake McKinley's hand and when his turn came, fired two shots at McKinley. The second bullet wounded the president who died on September 14, 1901 from a gangrene infection caused by the bullet. McKinley's assassin was later tried and electrocuted without admitting remorse for his act. William McKinley is buried at the McKinley National Memorial in Canton, Ohio.

Presidential Campaign-1896

The 1896 presidential campaign was one of confusion. Free silver Republicans left their party to support the Democrat William Jennings Bryan, of Nebraska, as the nominee of the Democrat Populist. Major themes of the campaign were the Republicans' desire for higher tariffs on imports to protect commercial manufacturers and the Democrats' desire for more currency by minting more silver in response to the Depression of 1893.

It is William Jennings Bryan who is remembered for his cross country campaign when he took a vigorous stand against the gold standard and advocated the minting of silver. In his travel by train, he gave 600 speeches and as many as ten to twenty a day.[1] In his impassioned speech he said "You shall not crucify mankind upon a cross of gold." Bryan with that speech managed to get a Democratic platform plank for free silver passed. During the campaign McKinley hardly ventured from his home, meeting delegations on his front porch. Others carried the McKinley campaign across the country, speaking out for higher tariffs.

Presidential Election-1896

McKinley easily defeated Bryan by almost a half million votes. Analysis indicates that the Republicans raised greater sums of money and so were able to outspend Bryan's campaign in getting their message to the voters.

William McKinley collected 7,108,48 (51%) votes to Bryan's vote

1 Eileen Shields-West World Almanac of Presidential Campaigns p. 125

count of 6,511,495 (47%). In electoral votes McKinley received 271 from 23 states to Bryan's 176 electoral votes from 22 states.

John Palmer, National Democrat polled 133,435 (1%) votes; Joshua Levering, Prohibition Party received 125,072 (1%) votes.

Presidential Campaign-1900

In contrast to the 1896 campaign, the 1900 presidential campaign was clear and direct. McKinley again faced a vigorous opponent in William Jennings Bryan. Bryan's campaign was against the expansion of the United States as a result of the Spanish-American war. Vice-President Theodore Roosevelt did most of the active campaigning for the Republicans with the slogan "Four more years of the Full Dinner Pail." With the return of prosperity, Bryan had lost a campaign issue, free silver. The voters were satisfied and gave McKinley an even greater margin of victory.

Presidential Election-1900

The new century was ushered in with a Republican victory by William McKinley. The popular vote was 7,218,039 (52%) and 292 electoral votes from 28 states for McKinley. Democrat William Jennings Bryan received 6,358,345 (46%) votes and 155 electoral votes from 17 states. John Wooley, Prohibition, 209,004 (2%), Eugene Debs, Socialist, 86,935 (1%).

Major Legislation During Presidency

The Dingley Tariff Act, 1897, restored higher import tariffs on raw and manufactured wool and hides.

Hawaii, Guam, Porto Rico and the Philippines became American territories in July of 1898. The Gold Standard Act of 1900 put the United States on the gold standard with all currency backed with gold reserves.

Major Events During Presidency

The Spanish-American War of 1898, was brought about by the United States' sympathy for the Cuban struggle for independence from Spain and the desire to eject a European power from the hemisphere. American commercial interests were also a factor as the nation's companies had extensive interests in Cuba. Spanish atrocities and misrule were emphasized by journalists led by William Randolph Hearst, thus stirring up public opinion to go to war with Spain and free Cuba.

The final impetus for war occurred on February 15, 1898, with the unexplained explosion and sinking of the U. S. battleship *Maine* in Havana harbor with the loss of 266 men. On April 25, 1898, Congress declared war.

The Treaty of Paris, 1899, ended the four month Spanish-American War. In the treaty, Spain ceded the Philippines, Puerto Rico, and Guam to the U. S. and gave Cuba its independence thus serving the U. S. interests.

In the war in Cuba, Theodore Roosevelt became a national hero with his leadership of a cavalry regiment nicknamed the "Rough Riders."

In the Far East in June, 1900, a group of Chinese nationalists known as the Boxers marched on Peking, killing as they went, and took up siege positions around the foreign embassies and taking personnel hostage.

In August, 1900, armed forces of American, British, French, German, Russian, and Japanese troops attacked and scattered the Boxers. The hostages were released and China agreed to pay relatives for the incident.

Future President Herbert Hoover was in China as an engineer during the Rebellion and helped to defend the foreign community at Tientsin from the Boxers.

On March 20, 1900, Secretary of State John Hay called for all nations that traded with China to respect an equality of trade and to respect China as an independent nation. This established what became known as the Open Door Policy toward China. The United States tried to maintain that all nations have an equal footing in commercial enterprises in China following the Boxer Rebellion.

1900 Census

The 1900 annual census counted the population of the United States at 75,994,575, an increase in the past ten years of almost 21%. New York was the largest city with a population of 3,437,202 with Chicago next with 1,698,575. Movement of the general population was east to west and south to north.

The United States was increasingly becoming urbanized with 40% of the population living in urban areas.

Theodore Roosevelt
26th President (1901-1909)

Theodore Roosevelt, Jr. came to the presidency with fifteen years in public service. At age 42, he was the youngest president in our history. As a man of action with a zest for life, Roosevelt appealed to the adventurous nature in everyone. His infectious smile and his boisterous, happy approach to life endeared him to the people. He lived a life of excitement and fulfillment as a soldier, explorer, author, rancher, and politician. A heavy barrel-chested man 5 feet 8 inches tall, he became a dominant force over Congress and the Western Hemisphere. He wore glasses all his life because of myopia, but he never let it interfere with his adventurous life. Roosevelt was a conservative conservationalist who believed that the environment was to be savored and not abused. He is credited with establishing our national resources policy for land conservation. A nationalist, he believed strongly in a progressive economic system to restrain corporate businesses from taking advantage of consumers.

Biography

Theodore Roosevelt was born on October 27, 1858, in New York City. His father, Theodore, was a wealthy import merchant who helped establish the Metropolitan Museum of Art and the New York Orthopedic Hospital. Theodore Roosevelt's mother was Martha Bulloch Roosevelt from Georgia. He had two sisters and a brother. He was a distant cousin of President Martin Van Buren and Franklin D. Roosevelt, and an uncle to Eleanor Roosevelt.

As a youth, Roosevelt was constantly in poor health, suffering from severe asthma to the point that he was home taught by his aunt. He traveled extensively with his family and was taught languages by tutors. He exercised daily and and when he passed the entrance exams to enter Harvard in 1876, he was a healthy and robust man.

Roosevelt had a successful college career. He excelled in academic courses, applied himself to extensive reading of hundreds of books and participated in the sports of boxing and tennis. He began writing a book on the sea war fought during the War of 1812. He continued to write all his life.

On October 27, 1880, soon after graduation, Theodore Roosevelt, 22, married Alice Hathaway Lee, 19, of Massachusetts. After graduating from Harvard in 1880, Roosevelt entered Columbia Law School. He was diverted from his law studies when he became interested in politics. Roosevelt successfully ran and won three terms in the New York State legislature where he became involved with a group of reform-minded Republican legislators.

In 1884, both his mother and his wife died on the same day. Theodore Roosevelt finished his third legislative term and then retired from politics, living on his ranch located on the Little Missouri River in the Dakota territory. Here he remained until 1886, returning to his writing by completing a biography of Thomas Hart Benton. He outlined and began a series of books published under the title, *The Winning of the West*.

In 1886, he returned to politics, running and losing the race for mayor of New York City. That year he married Edith Carow on December 2, 1886, and moved to Sagamore Hill on Long Island. During their marriage they had four sons and a daughter.

Roosevelt soon tired of the sporting life and again turned to public service for fulfillment. He was appointed to the United States Civil Service Commission. During the six years of service he revised the system, making it a key department in the government.

In 1895, he resigned to become president of the New York Police Board. In two years he totally restructured the police force. Following that he became the assistant secretary of the Navy under President William McKinley. Roosevelt was an active, driving assistant who advocated a larger and well-armed navy. He also wanted the United States to expand and drive Spain from the hemisphere.

With the *Maine* explosion in Havana, Cuba, harbor, Roosevelt resigned and volunteered for army service.

The Spanish-American War brought out Roosevelt's ability to

lead. A lieutenant colonel, he organized the First Volunteer Cavalry Regiment known as the "Rough Riders." His leadership in the charge up San Juan Hill outside of Santiago, Cuba, established Roosevelt as a courageous and bold leader. On his return to New York, the political bosses nominated him for governor. Roosevelt won by a narrow margin. He put in reforms and reorganized city government in much the same way as he had done with the Civil Service, the New York police department, and the Navy. The reorganization angered the city bosses. They arranged for him to be nominated for the vice-presidency on the Republican McKinley ticket against William Jennings Bryan and Adlai E. Stevenson. With McKinley and Roosevelt's election victory, the New York bosses were rid of Roosevelt.

Six months after McKinley's victory, he was assassinated. On September 14, 1901, Theodore Roosevelt was sworn in as the 26th president of the United States in a simple ceremony at the home of Ansley Wilcox.

In 1904, Roosevelt was elected president in his own right. After one term he retired and went to Africa on a safari. Returning in 1910, he was disturbed by the direction of the William Howard Taft administration, and challenged Taft at the Republican convention in 1912. He was defeated and formed his own party which became known as the "Bull Moose Party." This move divided the Republican party and resulted in the election of Democrat Woodrow Wilson

In his retirement, Roosevelt continued his travels as well as writing and serving as editor of the *Outlook* magazine.

Roosevelt died of a blood clot to his heart on January 6, 1919, at Sagamore Hill. He is buried at Young's Memorial Cemetery in Oyster Bay, New York.

Presidential Campaign-1904

The campaign for the presidency in 1904 was one of agreement instead of opposition. Because he became president when McKinley was assassinated, Roosevelt wanted to show that he could win the presidency on his own. As the "Square Deal" president he had wide support with conservationists and labor. Judge Alton Parker, chief justice of New York state court of appeals, Roosevelt's opponent, agreed with Roosevelt on most issues such as the gold standard, Philippine independence, and the rights of labor and consumers. Both took a stand against monopolies. Thus the campaign was rather quiet, with Roosevelt remaining in Washington and not campaigning. Parker remained at home and did not travel to campaign. His support was primarily in the Democratic South.

Presidential Election-1904

The election of 1904 was easily won by Roosevelt and his vice president, Senator Charles Fairbanks of Indiana. Roosevelt was the first successor president to win election in his own right. Roosevelt defeated Judge Parker in the popular vote, winning 7,626,593 (56%) votes and 336 electoral votes from 33 states to Parker's 5,082,898 (38%) votes and 140 electoral votes from 13 states. Eugene Debs, the Socialist candidate, received 402,489 (3%) votes. Silas Swallow, Prohibitionist, had 258,596 (2%) votes.

Major Legislation During Presidency

Theodore Roosevelt declared he would continue the enforcement of the Monroe Doctrine under his "Big Stick" policy. In 1902, when British and German navies threatened Venezuela over disputed debts, Roosevelt quietly informed the government of Germany that they must negotiate with Venezuela or he would use the Navy. After a week, Germany's Kaiser consented to arbitration and the crisis was over.[1]

The Spooner Act, 1902, authorized President Roosevelt to acquire land to build a canal across the isthmus. After Columbia rejected the United States' offer to purchase a ten mile wide strip of land to form the Canal Zone. Panama revolted from Columbia. Days later Panama granted the U. S. a ten mile wide strip of land in perpetuity for $10 million and an annual fee for the creation of a canal by the United States. This agreement remained until 1979, when the ten mile strip was legislatively returned to Panama. They took possession of the Canal at the end of 1999.

The Meat Inspection and the Pure Food and Drug Act passed in 1906, providing federal inspection of meat and proper labeling of foods that move interstate.

The Reclamation Act of 1902 established conservation efforts by

the government. It used the monies from the sale of western land to construct dams for irrigation of arid land. Roosevelt established the first wild life refuge at Pelican Island, Florida, and made Devil's Tower in Wyoming, the first national monument. The National Park Service was established in 1916, the direct result of Roosevelt's conservation efforts

The Hepburn Act of 1906, allowed the Interstate Commerce Commission to regulate railroad rates.

Oklahoma was admitted to the Union on November 16, 1907, as the 46th state in the Union.

Major Events During Presidency

The 1901 Hay-Pauncefote Treaty, an agreement between the United States and Great Britain, gave the United States the right to construct and operate a canal across Central America provided it remain free and open to all countries.

Theodore Roosevelt mediated the peace treaty that ended the Russo-Japanese War of 1904-1905. For this he was awarded the Nobel Peace Prize, the first American to receive this honor.

The Anthracite Coal Strike of 1902, by Pennsylvania miners was settled after Roosevelt threatened to seize the mines. They settled for a small pay raise.

In October and November, the Panic of 1907, brought about bank failures and stock prices dropped. However, the United States government and loans from businessmen such as J. P. Morgan, brought it under control.

On April 18, 1906, the San Francisco earthquake killed 700 people.

[1] Thomas Russell Life of Theodore Roosevelt pp.184-7

William Howard Taft
27th President (1909-1913)

William Howard Taft was a congenial and easy-going conservative who reluctantly accepted the nomination and the election to the presidency. He was large man, standing 6 feet 2 inches tall and weighing over 330 pounds. He felt that to do "something permanently useful to his fellow countrymen" was the fulfillment of his life's work. He did not enjoy the role of president, and his apparent disinterest and reluctance at times to act showed this. Taft showed himself to be a great public servant in the many earlier positions that he held, notably his work as Governor General of the Philippines. His even-tempered nature belied the fervor that he brought to his governing. He viewed government as a functioning organization that needed to be used with efficiency in a specific way in order to serve the people.

Taft's conservative nature did not understand negotiation nor deviousness. He wanted the government to work. He was praised for his directness and sympathy for people.

Biography

William Howard Taft was born near Cincinnati, September 15, 1857, in Mount Auburn, Ohio, to a lawyer, Alphonse Taft and Louisa Torrey Taft. He grew up in Cincinnati, an average baseball playing youth who, as a high school student, graduated second in his class. He attended Yale during the years, 1874-1878, where he again excelled in math and composition, graduating second in his class of 1878.

At 28, he married Helen Herron, 25, from Cincinnati on June 19, 1886. Later as First Lady, she would be the first president's wife to ride down Pennsylvania Avenue with her husband. She was responsible for the planting of the 3000 Japanese cherry trees on the Washington Tidal Basin. They were given to the United States by the Emperor of Japan.

Taft joined a law firm in 1883, and campaigned for the Republican James G. Blaine who was defeated by Chester A. Arthur. It was during this time that Taft decided that the judiciary side of law was his forte, and he set his sights on becoming a Supreme Court Justice. During the following years, he served in Cincinnati as a judge in the Superior Court, in the United States Circuit Court, as United States solicitor general, and ex-officio member of the Sixth Circuit Court of Appeals. From 1886-1900, Taft was a professor of law and dean of the University of Cincinnati Law School.

Taft's experiences as a judge prepared him for his eventual service as Chief Justice of the U.S. Supreme Court following his presidency.

From 1900 to 1904, Taft served as Commissioner and Governor-General of the newly acquired Philippines. He was appointed by President McKinley to set up a civil government in the islands which he proceeded to do with great success. Because of his desire to set up a civil service system, put English language in schools, improve the physical infrastructure such as roads and harbors, make health improvements, and carry out land distribution in the Phillipines, Taft twice turned down President Theodore Roosevelt's offers to appoint him to the Supreme Court.

When Taft returned from the Philippines in 1904, President Roosevelt appointed him to be Secretary of War.

During his term as secretary from 1904-1908, Taft oversaw the beginnings of the building of the Panama Canal. Again in 1906, he declined to serve on the Supreme Court in order to finish his work in the War Department.

It was during this time that Taft declared his desire to eventually be on the Supreme Court, but at the urging of Roosevelt and Taft's wife, who wanted passionately to be First Lady, he declared he would accept a draft to run for president.

In Chicago in 1908, Taft was nominated on the first ballot of the Republican Convention. His vice-presidential running mate was James S. Sherman of New York.

Taft's Democratic opponent was William Jennings Bryan of Nebraska, who advocated a free silver policy. In 1925, Bryan opposed Clarence Darrow, the prosecutor in the Scopes evolution trial.

On November 3, 1908, Taft defeated Bryan and became the 27th president. In the four years as president, Taft attempted to continue the reforms of Theodore Roosevelt. He continually fell short of the goal, and after two years was content to just be president, enjoying golf and afternoon naps. However, Taft successfully oversaw many reforms and important legislation. The most important reform was the income tax.

When Theodore Roosevelt returned from a safari to Africa, he felt that Taft had betrayed his policies and had a falling out with Taft over the firing of Gifford Pinchot, chief forester and conservationist whom Roosevelt had appointed.

Taft had always been obese, but during the years of his presidency, his weight reached 355 pounds. He often declared in public that he did not feel like being renominated.

In 1912, the Republican Convention renominated Taft and ignored Roosevelt who broke with the convention and formed the Bull Moose Party to run for president. This split in the Republican party allowed the election of Democrat Woodrow Wilson to be president.

After his defeat, Taft became a law professor at Yale, lecturing on government and international law. He supported Wilson in trying to keep the country out of the European war. In 1918, Wilson appointed Taft co-chairman of the National War Labor Board. Taft supported Warren Harding for president in 1920. Later Harding appointed Taft to be Chief Justice of the Supreme Court, a goal that Taft had always wanted. He became the only person to serve as president and chief justice. He successfully guided the court until 1930, clearing the backlog of cases, proving to be an efficient administrator and justice. During that time he wrote 253 opinions.

In 1930, Taft's health failed and he resigned early in the year, suffering from high blood pressure, heart disease and poor liver function.

He died on March 8, 1930 at the age of 72.

Taft's wife, Helen Herron Taft, lived until May, 1943, when she died at the age of 82.

Presidential Campaign-1908

The campaign of 1908 was not an exciting one. The Republicans ran the contest basically on the record of Theodore Roosevelt, and not on what they hoped Taft would accomplish. They centered on the need to revise the tariff, establish better anti-trust laws, and revise the nation's monetary system. They wanted citizenship for all residents of Puerto Rico and statehood for New Mexico and Arizona.

The biggest mistake that William Jennings Bryan made was to call for the nationalization of the railroads. This socialistic idea was not well received by the voters, and it proved to be one of the reasons for them to vote for Taft. Taft campaigned rather lazily and indicated that his administration would not be a fast paced one like Roosevelt's had been.

Presidential Election-1908

In the election of 1908, Taft with 7,676,258 (52%) popular votes, won 321 electoral votes from 29 states.

Bryan had 6,406,801 (43%) popular votes and 162 electoral votes from 17 states. Socialist Eugene Debs received 420,380 (3%) votes. Prohibitionist Eugene Chafin 252 821 (2%) votes.

Major Legislation During Presidency

Again the tariff question was given another political face lift. The Payne-Aldrich Tariff Act of 1909 was passed and replaced the Dingley Tariff Act of 1897. The 1909 Act eased some tariffs but raised rates on coal, iron ore, and hides.

The Mann-Elkins Act, 1910, extended the regulatory powers of the Interstate Commerce Commission (ICC). It gave the ICC powers to regulate the railroads and brought the communication industries under the ICC regulation.

In 1911, Taft continued Roosevelt's enforcement of the Sherman Anti-Trust Act, starting over ninety suits and bringing about the end of the monopolies of the American Tobacco Company and Standard Oil Company.

The Webb-Kenyon Interstate Liquor Shipments Act, 1913, halted liquor shipments from wet states to dry states. It was passed over Taft's veto.

On January 6, 1912, New Mexico became the 47th state, and on February 14, 1912, Arizona was admitted to the Union, bringing the United States to forty-eight states.

The Postal Savings Plan system was started and paided small investors 2% interest at some post offices.

In 1909, Congress passed the Sixteenth Amendmen establishing the collection of income taxes by the Federal government. Taxes were collected at 1% on incomes over $3000 and those over $4000 for married persons. The amendment was ratified in 1913.

In 1910, the Mann Act was passed making it a federal offense to transport women across state lines for illegal purposes such as prostitution.

Major Events During Presidency

The four years of Taft's term were years of peace and expansion for the United States and the rest of the world. Taft established what was called the policy of Dollar Diplomacy in which he encouraged American businesses to invest in Central and South American countries. He called it an extension of the Monroe Doctrine.

In 1911, the Progressive Party was formed by Senator Robert F. LaFollett of Wisconsin. When the Republicans failed to nominate Theodore Roosevelt for president, he took over the Progressive party calling it the Bull Moose Party. He then ran for president, splitting the Republican party.

1910 Census

The U.S. census in 1910 showed the population at 91,972,266. The center of the population had moved westward and in 1910 was in Bloomington, Indiana. The population per square mile was 31 persons, an increase of about 4 persons since 1900. About 46% of the population lived in urban areas. Less than half the population had completed elementary school. Only 4% were college graduates.

Thomas Woodrow Wilson
28th President (1913-1921)

As a man of vision and inspiration who had worked tirelessly to bring the vision of a more democratic world to reality, Woodrow Wilson spent his life trying to bring peace to a world bent on conflict. A teacher, scholar, and visionary, he felt the world needed to be governed by the principles of peace and well-being, and to bring this about he led his nation in a world war to uphold these principles. He became a leader in an attempt at establishing a world government.

Woodrow Wilson was a 5 feet, 11 inches tall man with chiseled features, dominated by a thrust out jaw and piercing blue-gray eyes. The pince-nez glasses that he had worn since he was an eight year old, became a trademark. He was an expressive and compelling orator in public, but a shy, retiring person in private. Highly educated with a dozen college degrees, Wilson expressed the view that the president spoke for the nation and his insight of events made him the spokesman for the "whole people," not just for special interest groups.

Biography

Woodrow Wilson was born in Staunton, Virginia, on December 28, 1856, son of Joseph Ruggles Wilson, a Presbyterian minister and Jesse Janet Woodrow Wilson, a theological professor. As a child, Wilson was not well and was taught at home, learning to read at age nine.

Growing up during the Civil War and attending private schools because there were no public schools during the Reconstruction, Wilson eventually attended the College of New Jersey which later became Princeton University.

Wilson studied law on his own and in 1882, he was admitted to the bar. He went on to gain a doctor's degree in political science from Johns Hopkins University, and wrote his first book, *Congressional Government.* He began a career as a college teacher, first at Byrn Mawr College and then at Princeton University.

On June 24, 1885, Wilson, 28, married Ellen Louise Axson, 25. They had three daughters, two of whom were married in White House weddings.

Wilson continued to teach on jurisprudence and political economy at Princeton and served as its president from 1902 to 1910. While serving as president of Princeton, Wilson brought about internal changes in the way courses were taught. He changed the structure of departments and the curriculum. Classes were no longer large lectures but small reading groups

From 1911 to 1913, Wilson was Governor of New Jersey, opposing the political bosses and bringing about progressive changes in state government.

In 1912, Wilson went on a campaign tour for the presidency and was given the Democratic nomination at the convention.

Woodrow Wilson was elected president, defeating incumbent, William Howard Taft. He was inaugurated on March 4, 1913, to become leader of a country that was heavily Republican. He appointed William Jennings Bryan as secretary of state. He resolved to be a strong leader, working with Congress to pass good laws that would give direction to the nation.

Wilson began by reviving an old custom, addressing a joint session of Congress on the state of the Union. As president he frequently met with Congressional committees to devise legislation.

After the death of his first wife, Ellen Axson, in 1914, Wilson, 58, married Edith Bolling Galt, 43, on December 18, 1915. During World War I, she became an active leader in the war effort. It was she who nursed and protected Wilson after his stroke in 1919, while he was still president.

Fighting to stay out of the war in Europe, he led the nation on a path of neutrality. The sinking of the *Luisitania* left Wilson defending his neutrality policy. However, after Germany announced in February, 1917, that they would again sink any ship, enemy or neutral, that they found on the high seas, Wilson had no other choice but to ask Congress to declare war. They did so on April 6, 1917. Wilson had been pursuing a policy of preparedness for several years prior to 1917 and consequently the United States' entrance in the war began to turn the tide against Germany, bringing an armistice on November 11, 1918.

The greatest disappointment of Wilson's presidency occurred after the war ended. After the signing of the Versailles Treaty in 1919, Wilson took up the fight for its ratification by Congress. Its preamble contained a clause for the establishment of a League of Nations, a type of world government. Wilson could not convince the country or Congress to agree to joining the League. He went on a long, arduous speaking tour of the west, seeking to change public opinion.

Overworked, Wilson suffered a third paralytic stroke on October 2, 1919. From 1919, until he the end of his term, Wilson with the help of his wife, Ethel, conducted the country's business from his sickbed. He refused to give up any power to Vice-President Thomas R. Marshall.

After retirement, the former president continued to suffer poor health until he died on February 3, 1924, convinced that eventually a League of Nations for world peace would become a reality. He stated just before his death that he "was not one of those who have the least anxiety about the triumph of the principles that I have stood for."

Presidential Campaign-1912

The Republican Party's division between President William Howard Taft and Theodore Roosevelt, who felt that Taft had not pushed the Progressive program far enough, brought about Woodrow Wilson's election as president. The Progressives held a separate convention

and Roosevelt became the nominee. Roosevelt's Bull Moose Party drew off enough votes from Taft to elect Woodrow Wilson president with less than fifty percent of the vote.

Wilson called his vision of the future The New Freedom. He traveled the country presenting this doctrine. His New Freedom idea was based upon ending big corporation monopolies and thereby freeing up competition, and giving the unions the freedom for collective bargaining. Roosevelt's Progressive program would go even further. However, an attempt on Theodore Roosevelt's life a month before the election gave Wilson an apparent lead. Wilson campaigned for a Democratic congress to carry on his proposed reforms.

Presidential Election-1912

Woodrow Wilson, Democrat from Virginia, drew a popular vote of 6,293,152 (42%) and 435 electoral votes from 40 states to Theodore Roosevelt's 4,119,207 (27%) and only 88 electoral votes from 6 states. President Taft received 3,486,333 (23%), 8 electoral votes from 2 states. The Socialist Eugene Debs polled 900,369 (6%) votes. Wilson's vice-president was Thomas R. Marshall.

Presidential Campaign-1916

Wilson was renominated by the Democrats for president. He ran on the slogan, "He kept us out of war." The other themes that the Democrats used were continued social reform of the prisons, women suffrage, build-up of the military, and tuberculosis hospitals for the poor.

Wilson's Republican opponent was Charles Evans Hughes, former governor of New York and a Supreme Court justice.

Presidential Election-1916

Woodrow Wilson was reelected in a close election. He received 9,129,300 (49%) and 277 electoral votes from 30 states. Charles Evans Hughes' polled 8,546,789 (46%) and 254 electoral votes from 18 states. The Socialist Allen Benson had 589,924 (3%) and Prohibitionist J. Frank Hanly received 221,030 (1%) of the vote. Thomas R. Marshall was vice-president.

Major Legislation During Presidency

The Underwood Tariff Act, 1913, reduced the tariff rates of foreign imports from 41% to 27% and allowed iron, steel, and raw wool free entrance. The act established a new income tax for individual incomes to offset the drop in tariffs.

The Federal Reserve Act, 1913, created the Federal Reserve System, the first overhaul of the banking system since its inception. It established a solid foundation for our banking system.

The Federal Trade Commission, 1914, was an anti-monopoly measure passed to help small businesses.

The Clayton Antitrust Act, 1914, established labor rule for collective bargaining and exempted labor and agriculture from the anti-trust law. The Child Labor Laws were later declared unconstitutional.

The Adamson Act, 1916, established the eight hour day for trainmen. Eventually it was accepted as the standard for all workers.

On April 8, 1917, the 17th Amendment passed. Senators would be elected by popular vote, not appointed by state legislatures.

In 1917, the Selective Service Act became law. It required all men between the ages of 18 and 30 to register for military service.

The 18th Amendment established the Prohibition of liquor nationwide on January 16, 1919.

On August 18, 1920, the 19th Amendment gave women the vote.

Major Events During Presidency

The Panama Canal opened on August 15, 1914.

With World War I in full force, and the threat to U. S. shipping mounting, Wilson ordered the arming of U. S. merchant ships in March, 1917.

On April 2nd, 1917, four merchant ships were sunk. Then the liner *Lusitania* was sunk. Consequently, Wilson asked for a declaration of war. On April 6, 1917, Congress passed a resolution for war which Wilson signed.

The U. S. purchased the Virgin Islands from Denmark in 1917.

The Paris Peace Conference was held from January 18 to May 7, 1919. Peace terms were agreed to thus ending World War I.

World War I ended on November 11, 1918. The Versailles Treaty was signed on June 28, 1919.

Wilson was awarded the 1919 Nobel Peace Prize for his efforts to establish the League of Nations

The Senate did not ratify the Treaty of Versailles because of the clause establishing the League of Nations.

Warren G. Harding
29th President (1921-1923)

Warren Harding was the first senator to move directly from the senate to the presidency. He was the first president elected after women gained the vote. Friendly to the point that he could not disappoint anyone, the conservative Harding avoided any confrontation. He was sincere, handsome, and well-liked by everyone. With the country responding to his "back to normalcy" theme, Harding was elected by a large margin. The six feet tall, ruggedly built Harding had a presidential appearance with silv- er hair and chiseled features. As someone remarked, "He looks like a president." Unfortunately, he did not have the ability to analyze problems and seek solutions. He was a conciliator, not a leader. He relied on others to make decisions, and this led to abuses of power by those around him. He was a positive person who was too trusting during his term, leaving a tarnished reputation about his administration after his death. Harding's legacy is that his administration was filled with scandal.

Biography

Warren Gamaliel Harding was born on November 2, 1865, on a farm in Corsica near what is now Blooming Grove, Ohio. His father, George T. Harding and his mother, Phoebe Dickerson Harding, were doctors. The oldest of six children who lived to maturity, Warren grew up in Caledonia, Ohio, living the typical rural life of a farm community. For a time he was a railroad worker and then worked for a newspaper, learning the printing trade. As a result, he established a campus newspaper while attending Ohio Central College. He graduated in 1882.

Harding tried teaching for one year, then studied law, sold insurance, and finally became a reporter for the Marion, Ohio, *Marion Star*. In 1884, he and two others purchased the bankrupt newspaper, and set out to establish a new publication. Soon Harding owned the entire newspaper which slowly became successful.

On July 8, 1891, Harding, 25, married a widow, Florence Kling DeWolfe, 30, from Marion, Ohio.

In 1899, Harding was elected to the Ohio state senate and served from 1899 to 1903. In 1903, he became lieutenant-governor of Ohio. He continued to seek political offices and run his newspaper until 1915, when he was elected a United States Senator.

As senator, he campaigned with Senator Henry Cabot Lodge against the adoption of the League of Nations. He voted for prohibition, though as president, he kept illegal liquor in the White House.

The 1920 Republican National Convention was held in Chicago and for days, Harding was brokered as the compromise candidate for the party because he had no enemies, was well-liked, and popular. His senate voting record followed accepted party lines. As senator he had voted for prohibition and for women's suffrage. Harding was nominated after two days and several ballots.

On November 2, 1920, Harding won the presidency with Massachusetts Governor Calvin Coolidge as vice-president He was inaugurated, March 4, 1921.

In his three years in the White House, Harding quietly filled the presidential role, unaware of the scandals that were occurring. He was returning from a trip to Alaska when he suffered a stroke and died on August 2, 1923, at the age of 58. He was buried in Marion, Ohio.

It wasn't until after his death that details of the governmental scandals that he may have guessed at finally came out. He expressed it when he said that it wasn't his enemies that he feared, but his friends. Years later his love affairs with Carrie Phillips and Nan Britton by whom he had a daughter came to light.

Presidential Campaign-1920

Warren Harding's Democratic opponent James M. Cox campaigned vigorously for Congress urging that the United States join the League of Nations. In contrast, Harding returned to the McKinley days by campaigning from his front porch for a return to "normalcy."

Apparently the voters interpretpreted this to mean that the U. S. would not join the League and that the country should remain away from the affairs of Europe. In his inaugural address, Harding emphatically advocated that we should not join the League of Nations.

Presidential Election-1920

The election of 1920 was the first time women could vote. It was a landslide for Republican Warren Harding. His popular vote was 16,153,115 (60%) votes to Democrat Cox's 9,133,092 (34%) votes. Harding received 404 electoral votes from 37 states; Cox won 127 electoral votes from 11 states. Socialist Eugene Debs had 915,490 (3%) votes. Parley Christensen, Farmer-Labor, 265,229 (1%) votes.

Major Legislation During Presidency

In 1921, the Budget and Accounting Act established the Budget Bureau to oversee and control the spending of governmental agencies.

In a reversal of previous administrations, the Congress with Harding concurring, raised the tariff on imports with the Emergency Tariff Act of 1921 and the Tariff Act of 1922. They established higher import taxes on manufactured and agricultural products.

The 1921 Emergency Quota Act restricted European immigration to 3% per year of any nationality based on what that nationality's population was in the United States. in the 1910 census. The result of the act was that immigration was reduced by a half in 1922.

The Emergency Tariff Acts of 1921 and 1922 raised duties on imports by 38%. They would be replaced by the Hawley-Smoot Tariff Act in 1930.

Major Events During Presidency

In the Teapot Dome scandal Harding's Interior Secretary Albert Fall was convicted of selling the nation's oil reserves under his control, to oil companies for personal gain.

Harding's Attorney General Harry Daugherty committed suicide after destroying his papers that apparently showed his acceptance of bribes. No evidence was found to link Harding to any of the scandals.

On July 2, 1921, Harding was called off the golf course to sign the document that formally ended the war between the United States and Germany.

The 1921 Washington Arms Limitation Conference was held to limit the expansion of arms by Japan against China. It preserved the China Open Door policy.

In a celebrated murder cases, Nicola Sacco and Bartolomeo Vanzetti, two anarchists, were found guilty of murder. They were executed in 1927.

Harding pardoned Eugene Debs, Socialist, convicted under the 1917 Espionage and Sedition Acts.

The great "Red Scare" occurred in 1920-1921. Attorney General A. Mitchell Palmer made extensive raids in 1919 and 1920 on radical and anarchist organizations, illegally detaining citizens. About 250 were deported. The scare abated and Palmer was discredited.

The 1920 census was 106,021,537, an increase of 13,793,041 over the 1910 population of 92,228,496.

Calvin Coolidge
30th President (1923-1929)

The 5 feet, 9 inches tall Calvin Coolidge was a quiet, unassuming leader during one of America's most turbulent economic booms, the Roaring Twenties. He was able to quietly handle the scandals that appeared from the Harding years. As an administrator he carefully engineered a safe path without fanfare or scandal. His philosophy of government was that the less government, the better for the country. He led the government with a simple and direct style that reflected his upbringing which instilled honesty, thrift, and a solid set of values. He expected that government should serve the people well.

Following a depression in 1920-21, the country revived from the deprivation of World War I with an economic expansion of major proportions. A conservative in his outlook on government and economics, Coolidge became a symbol of this prosperity. His thrifty nature can be summed up in the fact that he never owned an automobile and he did not own his own home until after he retired.

Biography

Calvin Coolidge was born on July 4, 1872, in Plymouth Notch, Vermont. His father, John, a farmer, store keeper, and local politician, came from Plymouth, Vermont, and married Victoria Moor in 1868.

Growing up, Coolidge attended the Plymouth elementary school, the Black River Academy, and a college prep school that qualified him for attendance at Amherst College. He graduated cum laude from Amherst in 1895, and followed this with a study of law in Northampton, Massachusetts. He studied law in Northampton, was admitted to the bar in 1897, and began a law practice. Coolidge became interested in politics while at college. He entered local politics and was elected to the city council in 1895.

On October 4, 1905, a year before he was elected to the Massachusetts legislature, Coolidge, 33, married Grace Anne Goodhue, 26, a lady whose lively personality was the opposite of the stoic Calvin. They had two sons.

In 1906, Coolidge was elected a state representative. After two terms, he returned to become mayor of Northampton where he applied his conservative approach to government by reducing spending and lowering taxes. He later returned to the state legislature, serving three terms as a senator from 1911 until 1915. In the final two years he was president of the senate and the most influential representative in state office.

He left the senate when he was elected lieutenant governor of Massachusetts in 1915, and later governor of the state in 1918.

Coolidge reached national prominence during his term as governor when he quelled a 1919 Boston police strike after days of rioting and looting. For this he became known as a law and order politician. The following year Warren Harding beat out Coolidge for the Republican presidential nomination, but delegates made Coolidge the vice presidential nominee by acclamation. In the 1920, election the team of Harding and Coolidge won a landslide election.

On August 3, 1923, Calvin Coolidge became the 30th president when Harding died. Coolidge was given the oath of office by his father, John, a notary public. After completing Harding's term, Coolidge easily won the 1924 election.

After retiring to Northampton, Massachusetts, in 1928, Coolidge wrote his autobiography and numerous articles for the newspapers. He died on January 5, 1933, of a heart attack. He is buried at Plymouth Notch, Vermont.

Presidential Campaign-1924

In the presidential campaign of 1924, Coolidge's opponent was John W. Davis of West Virginia, a legislator and former ambassador to Great Britain under President Woodrow Wilson. It was Davis who helped write the Treaty of Versailles, ending World War I. He was nominated after 102 ballots after Governor Al Smith of Louisiana and William McAdoo of California had fought for the nomination and had finally withdrawn.

The prosperity replaced the depression years of 1920-21. With prosperity returning and with the promise of good government after the Harding scandals, Coolidge did little campaigning. He gave a major address during the last week of the campaign. His campaign slogan was "Keep cool with Coolidge."

Coolidge supported the party platform against joining the League of Nations, for higher tariffs, more prohibition enforcement, extension of civil service to postmasters, and for creating a cabinet department of education and relief.

Senator Robert M. LaFollette, the Progressive candidate from Wisconsin, campaigned vigorously for president and gained much support.

Presidential Election-1924

Republican Calvin Coolidge received 15,719,921 (54%) votes; Democrat John Davis received 8,386,704 (29%) votes; Progressive Robert LaFollette 4,832,532 (17%) votes. The Electoral vote: Coolidge won 35 states with 382 votes; Davis won 12 states with 136 votes; LaFollette won Wisconsin's 13 votes.

Major Legislation During Presidency

Within a year into his term, Coolidge was able to sign into law several major pieces of legislation.

The first was the Immigration Act of 1924. By using the population base of 1890 instead of 1910 for setting immigration totals, the number of immigrants admitted to the United States was reduced. The percentage entering was cut from 3% to 2% as well. The Act placed a ceiling of 150,000 immigrants that might enter in a given year. It excluded the Japanese entirely.

The Revenue Acts of 1924 and 1926 reduced income and inheritance taxes primarily for the wealthy. It did away with the gift tax and some excise taxes imposed during World War I. This freed capital and brought about speculation in the stock market, a factor in bringing on the Great Depression in the 1930's.

The Veterans Bonus Act of 1924 was passed over Coolidge's veto. It awarded veterans a paid up insurance policy in twenty years. 15,000 veterans marched on Washington in 1932 to demand an early payment of the 1924 bonus from a government mired in economic recession.

The 1924 Snyder Act declared that all American Indians born in the United States were American citizens.

The 1926 Air Commerce Act put commercial aviation under the Commerce Department to regulate the growing airline industry. The Senate ratified the act in 1929.

The Farm Relief Acts of 1927 and 1928 were both vetoed by Coolidge. The bills sought to fix prices on agricultural produce which the government would buy and store for sale to foreign countries at fixed prices.

In 1928, the Kellogg-Briand Pact was signed by fifteen nations in Paris. The signing nations agreed to renounce the use of war as a national policy.

Major Events During Presidency

Investigations into the Harding administration in 1924, brought out many abuses of public trust led by bribery and fraud by the Ohio Gang, all friends of Harding.

The major scandal was about the

Teapot Dome oil reserves that were sold for personal gain by members of Harding's cabinet. Secretary of Interior Albert Fall and Navy Secretary Edwin Denby convinced Harding to transfer oil reserves to Fall's control. Fall took bribes to allow Mammoth Oil to tap the Teapot Dome in Wyoming and Elk Hills in California. He was convicted of fraud and served time in prison.

Senator Thomas Walsh of Wyoming investigated the Veterans Bureau and found fraudulent use of funds. Harding's friend, Director Charles Forbes was found guilty of fraud and sent to prison.

In 1925, Coolidge sent the Marines to Nicaragua to quell the civil war that occurred. Little was accomplished with guerrilla warfare against the government. The United States troops continued occupancy until 1933.

In 1925, the fundamental view of creation versus the scientific view of evolution was put on trial in the "monkey trial" of schoolteacher, John Stokes. Stokes had defied a Tennessee law forbidding the teaching of evolution. Clarence Darrow put defense lawyer, William Jennings Bryan on the stand to defend the fundamental Biblical view of creation. Stokes was found guilty and fined $100. The law remained until 1967.

The alleged robbery and killing of two men in 1920 at a shoe company by two immigrant anarchists, Nicola Sacco and Bartolomeo Vanzetti, grabbed the public's attention. Their trial and conviction in 1921, and execution in 1927, in spite of evidence that many felt was circumstantial, caused street demonstrations world wide. Many people believed Sacco and Vanzetti were convicted because of their anarchistic views. In 1970, an underworld informant revealed that the Morelli gang from Brooklyn, New York, had committed the crime.

On May 20-21, 1927, Charles A. Lindbergh flew non-stop from New York to Paris in the plane *Spirit of St. Louis* in thirty-three and a half hours.

On October 25, 1926, the United States Supreme Court ruled that the Tenure of Office Act of 1867, was unconstitutional. The Court indicated that the president does have the power to dismiss Cabinet members and other executive officials without the Senate's consent. This was the act under which Andrew Johnson was impeached and tried. He had defied Congress, avowing that the act was unconstitutional.

With prohibition in full swing and bootlegging running rampant, the United States was overrun by illegal organizations, domestic and foreign. Crime rose. The most prominent leader was Al Capone of Chicago. His organization's income ran to millions of dollars from bootlegging, gambling, prostitution, and protection rackets. Speakeasies which served the illegal liquor were everywhere.

Congress held hearings on the problems of prohibition. Enforcement of the Volstead Act, the law to enforce the Amendment, was difficult to administrate. Coolidge pledged to continue the enforcement and budgeted $30 million for more and better enforcement.

Herbert Hoover
31st President (1929-1933)

Herbert Hoover spent his entire adult life as a progressive in public service. The 5 feet, 11 inch tall Hoover was a man filled with the desire to serve his country and its people as well as the world. He became a successful engineer and a world humanitarian with great organizational skills who directed food and medical relief to many countries throughout his life. He used his indefatigable energy, his focus on details and his engineering knowledge to bring much needed relief to Europe, aiding the Belgium people during World War I, and all of Europe following the war. As a manager of large enterprises, Hoover had no equal. He was a self-reliant individualist and an organizer who saw the broad scope of a project yet could focus on the details needed to carry on a project to its fulfillment.

It is unfortunate that his name is linked to the one event that he could not control or manage, the Great Depression and the world wide depression that followed the exciting 1920's.

Biography

Herbert Clark Hoover was born in West Branch, Iowa, on August 10, 1874, to Quakers Jesse Hoover and Hulda Minthorn Hoover. By the age of nine, Hoover was an orphan. His father died when he was six, and his mother when he was nine. He was raised first by his uncle, Allan Hoover, near West Branch, Iowa, and during Hoover's teen years by his uncle, Dr. John Minthorn, who lived in Oregon. He learned about the business world from Dr. Minthorn.

Early in life he decided to be a mining engineer and later entered the first class of Stanford University in Palo Alto, California, in 1891, graduating in 1895 as a mining engineer with a major in geology.

After graduation he worked for several companies as a mining engineer, first in Nevada in the gold mines, then California, and in 1897-98, for a British company in Australia.

On February 10, 1899, Hoover, 24, married Lou Henry, 24, in Monterey, California. Immediately following the marriage, they set off for Hoover's new job in China, working for his mining company and for China as chief mining engineer. He helped develop many coal mines in China. While there he helped defend the foreign community during the Boxer Rebellion in 1900. Later while working in the silver mines in Burma, he made his fortune and was worth an estimated four million dollars.

It was during World War I that Hoover gained his reputation for organizing projects on a large scale when he served as head of many relief agencies. First, he was a leader of the American Relief Committee, aiding stranded Americans in Europe in 1914. Following the war, he headed the Commission for the Relief of Belgium, helping hundreds of thousands of people who were without food and shelter.

In the years following his return to the United States in 1917, Hoover's name and reputation made him one of the best known, most popular person in America. Hoover Clubs related to his work as United States Food Commissioner from 1917 to 1919, sprang up across the U. S. When Harding was nominated for president, he asked Hoover to serve either as Secretary of Interior or of Commerce. Hoover chose the Commerce post.

When Coolidge became president in August, 1923, Hoover continued to head the Commerce Department for eight more years.

In 1928, when Coolidge decided not to run for president, the Republican Convention chose Hoover, who promised voters prosperity with the slogan, "A chicken in every pot." Hoover won easily over New York governor, Democrat Al Smith.

About ten months into his term, Hoover faced the financial problem of the century, the beginning of the Depression. The stock market crashed on October 29, 1929, leaving thousands without jobs. It was a world-wide event. Hoover and his advisors were at a loss as to how to remedy the situation. Banks failed. Hoover was reluctant to step in and use the government to try to correct the economy. Instead he appealed to businesses and manufacturers to keep things running. The vicious cycle of no jobs, no income, and no purchasing power spread to Europe and the Depression deepened. By 1932, the federal government established the Reconstruction Finance Corporation to provide loans and relief to local and state governments. It was too late. Hoover's popularity declined as people blamed him for the depression. In 1932, he was defeated by the Democrat Franklin D. Roosevelt, governor of New York.

Herbert Hoover died at the age of 90 on October 20, 1964. He had spent his retirement years doing what he enjoyed most, working with relief organizations and advising Presidents Truman and Eisenhower on reorganizing the executive branch of government.

Presidential Campaign-1928

With Hoover's reputation at its zenith because of his humanitarian work and because of the prosperity the country was enjoying, there were few domestic issues to resolve during the campaign. His Democratic opponent was Alfred E. Smith of New York, the first Roman Catholic ever to run for president. This did become an issue. Hoover himself stayed above the fray of rumors circulated about what would happen if Smith were elected. The issue hurt Smith's chances in the South, normally a Democratic stronghold.

The need for Prohibition was an issue. Hoover defended the Harding administration's actions. Smith had little effect because of his involvement in New York politics and his Tammany Hall connect-

ions. The Republican's slogan, "Let's Keep What We Got" was effective for Hoover.

Hoover and the Republicans were able to take the credit for the good times and prosperity in 1928.

Presidential Election-1928

In what was to be his only elective office, Hoover swept the country by gathering in a popular vote of 21,437,277 (58%) to Smith's 15,007,698 (41%) votes. The electoral vote was a landslide for Hoover with his winning 444 votes from 40 states and Smith winning 87 electoral votes from the 8 states.

Major Legislation During Presidency

The Agricultural Marketing Act, 1929, created the Federal Farm Bureau to help farmers market produce surpluses and form cooperatives. It was abolished in 1933.

Again there was an attempt to protect farmers from foreign competition with the passage and the reluctant signing by Hoover of the Hawley-Smoot Tariff Act of 1930. It raised the tariff on imports to 42%, the highest it had ever been. It caused a world-wide tariff war and contributed to the Depression. It was eliminated in 1934.

The London Naval Treaty of 1930, called for the United States, Britain, and Japan to maintain a navy on a 5-5-3 basis. Japan later renounced the treaty, and an arms race ensued, a factor leading to World War II.

In 1932, labor received a boost with the passage of the Norris-LaGuardia Anti-Injunction Act. It barred the use of injunctions to prevent labor strikes, picketing, and other union job action tactics.

Hoover signed the Emergency Relief Act that authorized $300 million for loans to states to help in the states' relief programs

The 20th Constitutional Amendment was ratified in 1933. It moved the inauguration of the President from March 4 to January 20, to cut the gap between the November election and the late inauguration.

Major Events During Presidency

Black Thursday, October 24, 1929, occurred only a few months after Hoover became president. On that day the stock market began losing value and though a group of business men tried to halt the slide, they could not and on October 29, 1929, the stock market lost millions of dollars in value. The market slide continued until 1932. By 1932, most Americans were out of work and the Great Depression had settled in. In Europe, it brought to power Hitler and the Nazis. Because of the Depression, Hoover, the Great Humanitarian, became a symbol for the country's condition. The unemployed made cardboard shelters and lived in shanty towns called "Hoovervilles." Newspapers became "Hoover blankets," used for warmth by the unemployed .

During September and October, 1931, over 800 banks closed causing financial panic. By the end of 1931, over 2,300 banks closed, causing businesses to close and financial ruin to thousands of citizens out of work. By early 1932, unemployment 12 reached million. In mid-1932, the Bonus March of World War I veterans arrived in Washington, demanding that Congress pay them the bonus promised to them in 1924 during Coolidge's administration. When Congress voted down the bonus, not due until 1945, thousands of the veterans pitched camp in the "Hooverville" in Washington. Hoover ordered Federal troops under the command of General Douglas MacArthur with his staff of Majors Dwight D. Eisenhower and George Patton to clear the make-shift camp away. Cavalry with drawn swords scattered the veterans and burned their "Hooverville." For this, Hoover's humanitarian image suffered.

In 1930, the United States took part in the London Naval Conference which had as a goal the limitation of naval fleets in order to prevent another world war.

In October, 1931, Al Capone, underworld leader, was convicted of tax evasion.

Charles and Anne Lindbergh's infant son was kidnapped and murdered in March, 1932. For this crime, Bruno Hauptman was convicted and executed April 3, 1946..

With unemployment reaching 12 million by 1932, the Reconstruction Finance Corporation was established in January, 1932, to stimulate banking and revive businesses by providing emergency financing to institutions such as life insurance companies, railroads, banking institutions, building and loan companies, and government owned corporations.

The 1930 census set the U. S. population at 123,202,624, a decade gain of 17,181,087 from 106,021,537 in 1920.

Franklin D. Roosevelt
32nd President (1933-1945)

Franklin Delano Roosevelt with his "New Deal," a term he first used when he was governor of New York, changed the course of the United States more than any other president before or since. The 6 feet 1 inch tall Roosevelt was our only handicapped president, having been crippled by polio at the age of 38, after which he had to use arm crutches just to stand.

Roosevelt possessed a great presence and charm that he exuded to all around him. As president, his personal fireside chats on radio pre-sented ideas with a candor that conveyed his genuine concern for people and endeared him to millions. His powers of persuasion helped him get legislation passed to aid the economic recovery from the Great Depression. Roosevelt overcame his crippling disability with determination and humor. He showed that a handicap need not prevent a person from living a full, productive life. Later, as Commander in Chief, Roosevelt skillfully directed the war effort during World World War II.

Biography

Franklin Roosevelt was born at home on January 30, 1882, in Hyde Park, New York, to Sara Delano Roosevelt whose ancestry goes back to one of the first pilgrims to immigrate to Plymouth in 1621. His father, James Roosevelt, was a lawyer, financier, and country squire at Hyde Park. Growing up in Hyde Park and the Roosevelt summer retreat on Campobello Island, Franklin Roosevelt's childhood was quite insulated from the public,

On March 17, 1905, Franklin, 23, married a distant cousin, Eleanor Roosevelt, 20. They had four sons and a daughter. Eleanor became a prominent person in her own right. When Roosevelt became president, she served as his eyes and ears as she traveled the world as his emissary. She had her own liberal agenda and often influenced the President in liberal causes.

Franklin's education consisted of private tutors, private schools, and eventually Harvard. He never completed a law degree, but passed the bar exam in 1907. He entered politics, winning his first election in 1910 as a state senator from New York.

Roosevelt became a supporter of Woodrow Wilson, and upon Wilson's election in 1913, he was appointed assistant secretary of the Navy.

In 1920, Roosevelt ran for vice-president with James Cox but they were defeated in the landslide election of Harding and Coolidge.

Roosevelt was an active sportsman and athlete until he contracted polio in 1921, while vacationing at Campobello. It took three years of rehabilitation to learn to stand with leg braces and canes. Roosevelt reentered the political arena in 1924. He ran for governor of New York and won a narrow victory.

In 1930, he was again elected governor by a large majority. This put Roosevelt in the forefront for the 1932 presidential campaign against Hoover, who was caught up in the Great Depression. Roosevelt's "New Deal" promises to the people won the election decisively.

Franklin Roosevelt went on to serve three full terms and a partial fourth term as president. His dynasty established the Democratic party and its liberal social programs for years to come.

On April 12, 1945, while vacationing at the "Little White House" in Warm Springs, Georgia, where he went to swim in the therapeutic waters for his useless legs, he was sitting for a portrait and suffered a stroke. He died without regaining consciousness. He was buried at his home in Hyde Park, New York.

Presidential Campaign-1932

The campaign of 1932 was dominated by the Great Depression and what should be done in response to it. Roosevelt made over sixty speeches nationwide to show that an invalid had the vigor to be president. In his speeches he spelled out some of the changes he would propose to Congress to end the Depression and put people back to work. He proposed economic remedies for farmers, factory workers, businessmen, and banks. The crowds he spoke to were enthusiastic and receptive. In contrast, the incumbent Hoover did not actively campaign until a few weeks before the election. He tried to defend his administration, but the mood of the country was not receptive. He addressed small and hostile crowds. Roosevelt's theme song, "Happy Days are Here Again," set the tone of the campaign, overwhelming the Hoover slogan, "Play Safe with Hoover."

Presidential Election-1932

Franklin Roosevelt scored a landslide victory, receiving 22,829,501 (57%) popular votes to Herbert Hoover's 15,760,684 (40%) votes. Roosevelt won 472 electoral votes from 42 states; Hoover won the 59 electoral votes of 6 states. Socialist Norman Thomas had 884,649 (2%); Communist William Foster, 103,253 votes.

Presidential Campaign-1936

The 1936 campaign between Democratic ticket of Franklin Roosevelt and John Nance Garner and the Republican ticket of Alf M. Landon and Frank Knox was one that hinged not on the results but on the methods used by the Democrats in the recovery from the Great Depression. Landon agreed with what was done because he was on the progressive side of the Republican party, but he did not agree on the methods. He attacked Roosevelt and Congress, stating that the New Deal was unconstitutional. His campaign slogan was "Life, Liberty, and Landon." The Democrats countered with "Follow Through with Roosevelt." The Democratic party stressed how they were bringing the country back from disaster. Roosevelt did not campaign until October.

Presidential Election-1936

The election of 1936 was another landslide for Roosevelt and the Democrats. In the popular vote Roosevelt received 27,757,333 (61%) over Landon's 16,684,231 (37%). Unionist William Lemke 892,267 (2%); Socialist Norman Thomas had 187,833 votes.

In the electoral vote Roosevelt won 46 states and 523 electoral votes to Landon's 2 states of Maine and Vermont with 8 electoral votes.

Presidential Campaign-1940

Prior to Roosevelt's nomination to run for an unprecedented third term, two of his close associates, Vice-President John Nance Garner and Roosevelt's Postmaster General and former campaign manager, James Farley, wanted to run for president. Roosevelt let the convention know that he was interested when he indicated that the delegates could nominate anyone they wanted. His non-refusal to run resulted in a decisive first ballot nomination.

Roosevelt's opponent, a former Democrat, Wendell L. Wilkie, swept into the Republican nomination on the sixth ballot amid the gallery's cries of "We Want Wilkie."

The two major issues of the campaign were the third term and the volatile situation in Europe with the rise of Hitler and his conquests. Again Roosevelt did not campaign until two weeks before the election and then he attacked the Republicans and pledged to keep the United States out of war. Nearly 75% of the newspapers in the United States backed Wilkie because of his anti-war stance.

Presidential Election-1940

With the threat of war and with the recovery going along well, the voters stayed with Roosevelt and he was again elected by an overwhelming majority of states. The popular vote was Roosevelt 27,313,041 (55%) to Wilkie's 22,348,480 (45%). In the electoral vote count, Roosevelt won 38 states with 449 votes; Wilkie won 10 states with 82 electoral votes. Socialist Norman Thomas had 116,410 votes.

Presidential Campaign-1944

The 1944 Presidential campaign was different from any other. First of all, no nominee had ever run for a fourth term, and in addition, most knew that President Roosevelt was in very poor health with little hope of finishing another term. The war needed to be won and peace established. The adage of not changing horses in the middle of a stream was effectively used by the Democrats, urging Roosevelt's reelection.

Roosevelt's selection of Harry S. Truman for vice-president almost assured Truman that he would be president in the future. Roosevelt was less than prompt in making up his mind about a running mate. He wanted to drop Henry Wallace. He led his advisor, James Byrnes,to believe that he might become his running mate. The selection of Truman at the 1944 Democratic Convention was not concluded until a short time before the nominations on the floor. Truman added a Midwest balance to the ticket as well as adding greater vig-

or to the campaign.

Roosevelt's opponent was Thomas E. Dewey, a New York Republican who gained national fame for his successful campaign against organized crime as a New York City district attorney. The Republicans and Dewey did not attack Roosevelt's foreign policy with the war on, but rather tried to deal with a fourth term and Roosevelt's poor health.

Presidential Election-1944

Although Dewey came closer to Roosevelt than anyone else in the popular voting in previous Roosevelt's elections, the election of Franklin Roosevelt to a fourth term in 1944 was almost a foregone conclusion. Roosevelt received 25,612,610 (53%) votes to Dewey's 22,017,617 (46%) votes. The electoral votes were almost a landslide again for Roosevelt. He received 432 electoral votes from the 36 states; Dewey won 99 electoral votes from the 12 states

Major Legislation During Presidency

Franklin Roosevelt's three complete terms occurred during two of this nation's most turbulent historical periods.

The Great Depression was alleviated to some degree by his proposed legislation aimed at ending the economic and social unrest caused by the event. The total legislation was called the New Deal, which involved the direct intervention of the Federal government in daily life and set the United States on the path to the modern welfare state. Throughout Roosevelt's terms, legislation backed by the Federal government was passed, changing forever how Americans lived, worked, and retired.

The initial step in the economic recovery was the closing of all banks for a governmental audit. The passage of the Emergency Banking Relief Acts of 1933 and 1935 prevented banks from dealing in the stock market and established the Federal Deposit Insurance Corporation (FDIC) with government insured deposits up to $10,000 against loss. In addition, Roosevelt issued an executive order calling in all gold and taking the United States off the gold standard. His order fixed the dollar value at 59.06 cents.

To get men back to work, the Civilian Conservation Corps hired young men to work for a $1 a day in CCC camps run by the military. Most of the money had to be sent home to their families.

The National Industrial Recovery Act brought about price, wage, and production agreements among businesses.

By 1936, the Works Progress Administration put over three million people to work. Under Federal supervision, they built new structures in hundreds of towns, constructed new highways, parks, bridges, and many public buildings. It was phased out in 1943.

Another large natural resource was harnessed by the Tennessee Valley Authority developing dams along the Tennessee River bringing electricity and flood control to the states along the river.

The 20th Amendment was ratified on February 6, 1933. It set January 3rd as the date for Congress to convene, moving the inauguration of the president and vice-president from March 4 to January 20.

The 21st Amendment repealing prohibition was ratified on December 21, 1934.

On July 5, 1935, the National Labor Relations Act or Wagner-Connery Act recognized unions allowing them to organize and participate in collective bargaining. The National Labor Relations Board was established in the act to oversee the collective bargaining.

In 1935, the Social Security Act created unemployment insurance and a tax to establish a retirement fund to be paid to workers when they retired.

In an attempt to stay out of foreign wars, the Neutrality Acts of 1935, 1936, and 1937 were passed. They forbade the United States from aiding any country involved in war or civil war.

On September 16, 1940, the Selective Training and Service Act passed, creating the first peacetime drafting of men between the ages of 21 and 35 into military service. Roosevelt drew the first draft number.

With the Lend Lease Act of 1941, the United States began supporting the European allies with ships, supplies and military equipment. This action was a major strategy for the survival of England and Russia in the early stages of World War II. The United States became "The Arsenal of Democracy."

In 1944, Congress passed the G. I. Bill. It provided money for education and housing to veterans, triggering a post-war economic boom.

Major Events During Presidency

In 1933, Roosevelt exchanged notes with the Soviet Foreign Minister giving the Soviets diplomatic recognition for the first time since the Russian Revolution in 1919.

The major consuming event of Roosevelt's third term was World War II. From 1941 when the United States entered the war after the Japanese attacked Pearl Harbor on December 7, 1941, until his death in 1945, Roosevelt spent the time leading and directing the Allied cause.

D-Day "Operation Overlord" June 6, 1944, marked the beginning of the conquest of the Axis powers of Germany and Italy, when American and British forces under Supreme Commander Dwight D. Eisenhower landed on the beaches of Normandy.

In December, 1944, the Germans made their final effort in the Battle of the Bulge centered at Bastogne in Belgium. The Allied lines bent but didn't break and by January, 1945, the Allies had reestablished their positions.

When the end of the European phase of the war was near, Roosevelt, Stalin, and Churchill met at Yalta in February, 1945, to develop post war plans. For a promise to enter the war against Japan, Stalin was given concessions that he be allowed to draw up boundaries and divide Europe and eastern Europe.

The result was the domination of Poland and Eastern Germany by the Soviet Union. From this came the Cold War that lasted from 1946 to 1976. The Berlin Wall was built in 1961 as the Soviet Union dominated Eastern Europe.

The final phase of World War II, had to be won in the Pacific against Japan. The United States and its allies, principally Australia, waged a war of attrition in order to bring the conflict to the island of Japan. After the Japanese forces drove General Douglas MacArthur from the Philippines at Bataan and Corrigidor in early 1942, there were few bases from which the Allies could launch attacks against the Japanese forces.

The first major naval air battle was fought in May, 1942, in the Battle of the Coral Sea. A June, 1942, naval victory in the Battle of Midway was Japan's first naval defeat.

In late 1942 and into 1943, United States launched the first major offensive at Guadalcanal. In the naval Battle of Guadalcanal, United States forces captured the island by preventing Japanese forces from landing reinforcements.

The United States forces continued to island hop in 1943 and 1944 with landings on Tarawa, Makin, the Marshall Islands, Admiralty Islands, and Burma.

By 1944, United States forces were close enough to begin bombing the island of Japan. By late 1944 and into 1945, American B-29's Superfortresses bombed Japan.

In February, Marines landed on Iwo Jima, 750 miles from Japan. In March, Marines took Okinawa, only 360 miles from Japan.

Roosevelt died April 12, 1945, leaving Truman to find a way to end World War II.

The 1940 census saw the United States population rise 8,961,945 to 132,164,569 from the 1930 count of 123,202,624.

Harry S. Truman
33rd President (1945-1953)

Tackling one of the most momentous periods in our history, Harry Truman, "The Man From Independence," proved to be forthright and decisive in his decisions to end World War II and to begin dealing with the problems of the post-war world. A no-nonsense Truman displayed the Midwestern heritage he grew up in by his "the buck stops here" philosophy. He was a man who did not want to be president, but when it was thrust upon him with Roosevelt's death, Truman plunged into the job with optimism and energy. The 5 feet, 10 inches tall Truman was an experienced politician. He understood American politics, but it was the foreign affairs that were a mystery to him. He was a master at adaptation and within months, he understood the politics of foreign affairs and brought about the end of the war with Japan by making the decision to use the atom bomb. No president had ever had such an awesome responsibility. With candor he made the decision to end the war and save American lives.

Biography

Harry S. Truman was born on May 8, 1884, in Lamar, Missouri, to John Truman, a farmer, and Martha Young Truman. His mother educated him before he attended grade school and high schools in Independence, Missouri. He suffered poor eyesight and wore glasses from age 6. Because of family financial trouble, Truman never attended college, but continued to work in Independence.

Between 1903 and 1906, Truman was a bank clerk in Kansas City. He then moved to a farm near Independence, living there until he was 33 years old. He learned to successfully manage 600 acres

World War I gave Truman the opportunity to show his leadership and management skills. In 1918, as a member of the National Guard, First Lieutenant Truman shipped out to France where he was an artillery commander. In 1919, he was discharged with a rank of major.

Upon his discharge at age 35, he returned to Independence and married Elizabeth Wallace, 34, on June 28, 1919. They had known each other since grade school and had graduated from Independence High School in 1901.

Truman established a men's clothing store in Independence, but lost it in the depression of 1922. In November, 1922, he ran for a judgeship for the Pendergast political machine and won. He was defeated for reelection but even after the defeat, he continued to move up in the Democratic party. In 1926, he was elected a county judge.

Truman's honesty and cost cutting earned him a reputation for good, honest government.

By 1935, he was a well-known politician. He ran for the U. S. Senate and won, serving two terms before he was chosen by Franklin Roosevelt for vice-president. In 1941-1944, he gained national notice as head of a Senate committee investigating the national defense program. The committee exposed military and industrial waste during World War II.

At the 1944 Democratic Convention, Roosevelt wanted to replace Vice-President Wallace either with James Byrnes or Harry Truman. He held his decision in abeyance until the last moment when he chose Truman. Truman reluctantly accepted the nomination.

On April 12, 1945, Roosevelt died and Truman, after only eight weeks as vice-president, became president. After his swearing in, Truman found that he had not been told of the atomic bomb development.

Truman served as president for the conclusion of the term and then in an upset win over Thomas E. Dewey in 1948, served a full term on his own.

By 1949, Truman had decided not to seek reelection to a third term but he did not indicate the fact until 1952.

In retirement, he continued to be active in Democratic politics, campaigning for Adlai Stevenson in 1952 and again in 1956.

Truman's failing health brought about his death on December 26, 1972, at the age of 88. He is buried in the cemetary behind the Truman Library in Independence, Missouri.

Presidential Campaign-1948

In the 1948 presidential campaign, Truman showed the country his mettle by covering the nation with a 30,000 mile campaign trek against the New York Republican, Thomas Dewey. Truman's blunt, plain speech appealed to the common man, who shouted "Give 'em Hell, Harry." He said that he told the truth. Labor supported Truman when he called for a national health program and a repeal of the Taft-Hartley Act that labor hated. Truman called for higher farm supports. By election day, pollsters predicted Dewey's election by a close margin.

Presidential Election-1948

In one of the most dramatic election finishes in our history, Truman defeated Dewey. Truman triumphantly held the *Chicago Tribune* newspaper up for photographers with the headline stating "Dewey defeats Truman."

The popular vote was Democrat Truman 24,179,345 (50%); Republican Dewey 21,991,291 (45%); States' Rights Democrat Strom Thurmond 1,176,125 (2%); Progressive Henry Wallace 1,157,326 (2%).

The Electoral vote was Truman 303 in 28 states to Dewey's 189 electoral votes from 16 states. Thurmond won 39 electoral votes from 4 states.

Major Legislation as President

The most important legislation on labor relations passed over Truman's veto by a Republican Congress when the Labor Management Relations Act, 1947, was enacted.

Known as the Taft-Hartley Act, it prevented a closed shop by unions and put restrictions on strikes. It allowed the federal government to use an injunction to provide an 80 day cooling off period against strikes that might damage the economy.

The Presidential Succession Act, 1947, set the Speaker of the House and President Pro Tem of the Senate in line for the presidency.

In July, 1947, the National Security Act was passed. It set up the Air Force as a separate and equal branch of the armed services with the Army and the Navy. The Act also created the National Security Council and the Central Intelligence Agency.

In June, 1948, the Displaced Persons Act granted visas to over 205,000 Europeans who could not return to their homes in Soviet dominated countries.

The 22nd Amendment provided that the president can only serve two terms or only one if he has served two years of a prior president's term. It became effective February 26, 1951.

Major Events During Terms

The surrender of Germany took place on May 7, 1945, at Reims, France.

On July 16, 1945, the Atomic Age began when the United States exploded the first atomic bomb at Alamogordo, New Mexico.

The atomic bombing of Japan on August 6 and 9, 1945, brought about the end of World War II with the formal Japanese surrender on September 2, 1945, on the battleship *Missouri*. Two hundred thousand persons were killed in the bombing.

The United Nations was created in San Francisco in 1945, at a United Nations Conference. Fifty nations created the UN charter. The charter was later ratified by the United States Senate in July, 1945.

The Nuremburg trials of 22 Nazi leaders took place in 1945-1946. They were tried for war crimes especially the Holocaust which killed thousands of Jews. Nineteen were found guilty with twelve sentenced to death.

In 1946, the United States granted the Philippine Islands their independence. In turn, the United States was given leases for military bases on the islands.

The Truman Doctrine was declared in March, 1947. It stated that the U. S. would not tolerate the subjugation of peoples who wish to be free. It was directed at preventing Greece and Turkey from falling under Communist Soviet control.

The Marshall Plan (1948-1952) provided for monies and material support from the United States for the rebuilding of Europe.

In June, 1948, the United States began the Berlin Airlift, ferrying supplies and food to Germans in Berlin who were isolated by the Soviets when they cut off all highways and railways into and out of Berlin. Over 270,000 flights were made carrying over 2 million tons of food and supplies.

In 1948, Israel was declared a separate state. The United States quickly recognized Israel.

The Korean War (1950-1953) occurred when the North Koreans invaded South Korea. The United States under the United Nations charter resisted the invasion under the command of General Douglas MacArthur. The Chinese entered and drove the United States forces back. The war continued into the next presidential term.

President Truman sent thirty-five military advisors to Vietnam in 1950, to aid the embattled French force fighting Ho Chi Minh and his Communist forces.

An assassination attempt on Truman occurred on November 1, 1950, when two Porto Rican Nationals tried to enter Blair House where the Trumans were staying while the White House was being restored. One was killed and the other convicted and sentenced to die. The Trumans were unharmed.

In 1952, Truman ordered the seizure of steel mills when an impending strike might have hindered the Korean War effort. A judge later ruled that Truman had exceeded his authority.

September 8, 1951, Japan, the United States and other nations signed the peace treaty in San Francisco, giving Japan the right to defend itself.

On July 3, 1952, Truman signed the bill that made Porto Rico a self-governing commonwealth after it voted to support a constitution similar to the United States.

The United States exploded the first hydrogen bomb on the Eniwetok Atoll in the Marshal Islands on November 1, 1952.

Census-1950

The 1950 census showed that the United States population at 150,697,361. This was an increase of over 19 million since 1940, when the population was 132,164,599.

Dwight D. Eisenhower
34th President (1953-1961)

Soldier, statesman, president, and world leader sum up the life of Dwight David Eisenhower. The 5 feet 10 inch Eisenhower was a trim, athletic man whose integrity and honest nature won him friends and the respect of opponents both in war and peace. He was a gregarious man with a wide, infectious smile who genuinely liked people. Eisenhower was often chided for his quiet non-political approach to the presidency. His systematic control of the position was like the other roles in his life including his army career. He viewed the presidency as a means to unify the nation.

Eisenhower delegated authority to those whom he knew and trusted to carry out the true role of government which was to serve the people. It was this managerial style that often earned him the reputation of a passive president because he worked with the media and the Congress in the same way. He was politically a moderate and a fiscal conservative who brought about an era of peace and prosperity following World War II.

Biography

Dwight David Eisenhower was born on October 14, 1890, in Denison, Texas. His parents were David Jacob Eisenhower and Ida Elizabeth Stover Eisenhower. Ike, as he was later called, was the third of six children, all sons.

While Dwight was still an infant, the Eisenhowers moved to Abilene, Kansas, where he grew up as one of the poor in the town, attending grade and high school in Abilene. An average student, he graduated in the class of 1909.

To get a free education, he took the entrance exam for the Naval Academy but at twenty was too old for admission. Instead, he joined the class of 1915 at West Point in 1911, and graduated in 1915, ranking 61st in a class of 164. Upon graduation as a second lieutenant, he was assigned to the 19th Infantry.

On July 1, 1916, Lieutenant Eisenhower, 25, married Marie "Mamie" Geneva Doud, 19, at the bride's home in Denver, Colorado. They had met in 1915 in San Antonio, Texas. Their marriage survived 28 army moves and in 1961, they retired to Gettysburg, Pennsylvania, their first permanent home. They had two sons with only one, John, living to adulthood.

During World War I Eisenhower was assigned duty in the states and rose to Lieutenant Colonel on a temporary basis by 1918. After the war, he was made a permanent captain, and then in 1920 a major.

Later Eisenhower served as a tank commander at several posts in the United States from 1921 to 1922.

From 1922 to 1924, he served in Panama. In 1925-26, Eisenhower attended the Command and General Staff School for officers at Fort Leavenworth, Kansas. He graduated first in a class of 275 officers. He next attended the War College in 1928-29, to complete his officer training.

Eisenhower served under the assistant Secretary of War from 1929 to 1932.

In 1933, Eisenhower joined General Douglas MacArthur as special aide and helped MacArthur clear out the "bonus marchers" who had set up Hooverville in Washington, D. C.

From 1935 to 1939, he served with MacArthur as senior military assistant in the Philippines. He continued to rise in rank. At the beginning of World War II, Eisenhower was serving on a general's staff, receiving a promotion to brigadier general in 1941.

While serving in Washington on military planning at the War Department under Army Chief of Staff General George C. Marshall, he was promoted to major general in March, 1942. Because of his exemplary work, General Marshall recommended him for another promotion, and in June, 1942, President Franklin Roosevelt assigned him commander of U. S. forces in Europe with the rank of lieutenant general.

Because of his success in commanding the U. S. forces in the invasion of North Africa, Sicily, and Italy, Roosevelt named Eisenhower, Supreme Allied Commander to oversee the eventual invasion of Europe against Hitler's stronghold.

Amid conflicting weather forecasts, General Eisenhower gave the order to proceed with "Operation Overlord,"the invasion of Europe. The assault had been scheduled for June 5, but was carried out instead on June 6, 1944, because of poor weather on the 5th.

In December, 1944, Eisenhower was given the rank of five-star general. He directed the final assault on Germany, accepting their surrender on May 7, 1945, at Rheims, France.

When he returned to the United States, he was accorded a hero's welcome. Eisenhower later served as army chief of staff beginning in November, 1945.

In February, 1948, he resigned from the Army, retiring to his Gettysburg farm with his wife, Mamie.

In retirement, Eisenhower painted landscapes and wrote *Crusade in Europe* about his wartime experiences. In 1948, he became president of Columbia University.

By 1950, the Cold War was on and Eisenhower, now a General of the Army, returned to head the allies of NATO, the North Atlantic Treaty Organization.

While both Democrats and Republicans vied to get Eisenhower to run for president, it was the Republicans who got him to commit as a party member. By 1952, he declared that he would run for president as a Republican.

Eisenhower easily won the nomination and the election. After serving two terms as president, he again retired to his Gettysburg farm in 1961 to play golf, paint, and write. He died on March 28, 1969, at the age of 78.

Presidential Campaign-1952

With the campaign slogan of "We Like Ike" ringing across the land during the primaries and after a bitter political battle with Robert Taft at the Chicago Republican nominating convention, Eisenhower easily won the nomination for president. Eisenhower and his running mate, Richard M. Nixon, became front-runners to win the election. Touring the country, Democrat Adlai Stevenson of Illinois and Eisenhower and Nixon conducted a vigorous campaign. The keynote of the campaign was sounded by Joseph McCarthy of Wisconsin with his Communists in government theme. Eisenhower indicated that he would seek out the "pink mess" in Washington.

Television was used extensively for the first time to bring the candidates into the voters' homes. The rather formal, scholarly speech of Stevenson contrasted with Eisenhower's more informal speech and warm smile. Television ads were used extensively to go along with Eisenhower's campaign travels as he visited forty-four states.

During the campaign, a furor was caused by a "secret fund" that Nixon had used for campaign expenses. Nixon went on television and defused the situation with a speech about "Republican cloth coats" and a dog by the name of Checkers. The speech saved him and Eisenhower kept him on the ticket.

Finally, Eisenhower scored with voters when he made a promise to "go to Korea" if elected and bring the Korean War to an end by breaking the deadlocked peace talks.

Presidential Election-1952

On November 4, 1952, Republican Eisenhower swept to an impressive victory over Adlai Stevenson with a popular vote of 33,936,234 (55%) to Stevenson's 27,314,992 (44%) votes. Eisenhower in what would be considered a landslide, won 442 electoral votes from 39 states; Stevenson won 89 electoral votes from 9 states. The election established a two party system in the South with the Republicans winning the key states of Texas, Tennessee, and Florida, states that had been Democratic in the past.

Presidential Campaign-1956

The Republican Eisenhower set out to gain the presidency again in more leisurely way. His campaign's slogan of "Peace, Progress, Prosperity" caught on with the voters. He had closed the chapter on the Korean War as promised and the voters responded. Stevenson again conducted a vigorous campaign, but he could not begin to challenge the popular incumbent.

Eisenhower had suffered a heart attack and major surgery during the preceding year, but the convention nominated him on the first ballot.

Presidential Election-1956

As the first president to run after the amendment that placed the two term limit on the presidency, Eisenhower won by gaining 35,590,472 (57%) votes and winning 41 states with 457 electoral votes to Adlai Stevenson's 26,022,752 (42%) votes and 73 electoral votes from 7 states.

Eisenhower had brought about desegregation in Little Rock, Arkansas, through the use of Federal troops, and the black voters responded in greater numbers than at any other time for a Republican. Eisenhower won the state of Louisiana, becoming the first Republican to win in the Deep South since Rutherford Hayes.

Major Legislation During Presidency

In spite of a Democratic Congress, Eisenhower was able to govern effectively.

In 1960, the Civil Rights Act passed and became law. Leading up to its passage were several earlier events. It had been preceded by the Supreme Court's desegregation decision of 1954, *Brown vs. Topeka Board of Education* which established equality of education regardless of race.

In 1957, Eisenhower sent federal troops to Little Rock, Arkansas, to quell the unrest that occurred when black students tried to attend Central High School. Troops were used to escort black students

In 1954, the St. Lawrence Seaway Act was passed that would provide improvement such as deepening the river channel and building locks so that ocean sailing vessels could use ports on the Great Lakes.

In 1954, the Communist Control Act took various civil rights away from members of the Communist Party in the United States.

On August 30, 1954, Congress passed the Atomic Energy Act which permitted the U. S. to share atomic information with friendly nations. The Act also provided for the development of atomic power plants in the United States.

In 1956, the Interstate Highway System law was passed. When completed, the system would initially provide over 42,000 miles of super highway across the United States and carry Eisenhower's name.

In 1959, Alaska became 49th state on January 3, 1959. Hawaii became the 50th state on August 21, 1959.

Major Events During Presidency

In December, 1952, Eisenhower fulfilled a campaign pledge and went to Korea to get the stalled peace talks started again. By July, 1953, a peace accord was signed. In the war, the United States had over 150,000 total casualties with 34,000 Americans killed.

The Eisenhower Doctrine was proclaimed in response to the Suez Crisis in Egypt in 1956-1957. The doctrine stated that the United States would come to the defense of any country in the area that would be threatened by the Soviet Union and communism.

The 1954 Army-McCarthy hearings were called by Senator Joseph McCarthy of Wisconsin to investigate Communism in government. An enthralled nation watched the daily televised hearings and saw McCarthy's tactics of innuendo and guilt by association in action. He was disgraced and later was "condemned" by the Senate, but not given a censure.

The seeds of the Vietnam War were sown when the United States entered into the Southeast Asia Treaty Organization (SEATO) which later was extended to include Vietnam, Cambodia, and Laos. It stated that the United States would come to the defense of pact countries. In 1955, the first of the American military advisers were sent to Vietnam to train the Vietnamese army.

The Formosa Resolution was passed by Congress in 1955 authorizing the president to use the armed forces to protect Formosa and the Pescadores Islands. This resolution is cited to justify our involvement in Vietnam. Then in 1956, 350 more advisors were sent to Vietnam.

In May, 1955, the Supreme Court ordered the implementation of the *Brown vs. Topeka* decision, preventing racial discrimination in schools. Eisenhower used federal troops in enforce the desegregation of Central High in Little Rock, Arkansas.

On October 4, 1957, the Space age began when the Soviet Union launched a small satellite, *Sputnik 1*, into an orbit around the earth .

In answer to *Sputnik,* on January 31, 1958. the United States launched *Explorer 1,* a small artificial satellite

On November 28, 1959, the United States successfully tested an intercontinental ballistic missile with a range of over 6,300 miles.

The U-2 spy plane incident of 1960, threatened Eisenhower's ability to deal with the Soviets. Pilot Gary Powers was shot down over Soviet territory and captured. Later he was exchanged for a Soviet spy.

In the fall of 1960, the United States placed an embargo on almost all exports to Cuba after Cuba nationalized all industries, many of them American. Later in January 1961, before he left office, Eisenhower broke off diplomatic relations with Cuba.

John F. Kennedy
35th President (1961-1963)

At age 43, John Fitzgerald Kennedy was the youngest elected president, the first Roman Catholic president, and the first president to be born in the 20th century. The handsome Kennedy possessed great charm and wit. He displayed sensitivity to the conditions of the poor. He was a tireless worker and expected that same dedication from those around him in government. His pro-civil rights stand endeared him to millions yet divided the Democrats and brought about a Republican revival in the South.

The six feet tall Kennedy was coldly analytical and a political pragmatist who moved quickly to become a presidential candidate. He was an accomplished speaker who could fix a moment in time with his words. With a Boston Irish intonation, he delivered a short, stirring inaugural address, willing his listeners to "ask not what your country can do for you; ask what you can do for your country."

In his three years as president, he created an aura about the presidency that few others have done.

Biography

John Kennedy was born on May 29, 1917, in Brookline, Massachusetts, to Joseph P. Kennedy, a self-made millionaire by age 35, and Rose Fitzgerald Kennedy. Both parents were from active political families. Rose Kennedy's father was a two term mayor of Boston, later a state legislator and congressman for Massachusetts. John Kennedy's father served under Franklin Roosevelt.

After elementary school in Brookline, Kennedy continued his education at private schools. At 18, he graduated from Choate Academy in Connecticut and entered Harvard in 1936. He showed his ability to write with his first book, a best seller, *Why England Slept*, developed from a thesis he wrote after a summer tour of Europe in 1939. He graduated *cum laude* from Harvard in 1940.

During World War II service, Kennedy was a decorated naval officer, receiving a Naval and Marine Corps medal and a Purple Heart. He commanded a PT boat that was destroyed under him. He and his crew were rescued from a Pacific island. In the incident he received a back injury that was to plague him his entire life. His story became a motion picture, *PT Boat 109*.

John Kennedy's political career began with his election to the U. S. House of Representatives in 1946. He served three terms and then was elected a U. S. Senator in 1952. He married Jacqueline Lee Bouvier, the daughter of a wealthy stock broker, on September 12, 1953. They had two children.

While recovering from back surgery in 1954 and 1955, Kennedy wrote *Profiles in Courage* , a book about senators who took political and moral stands on issues. It won the 1957 Pulitzer Prize for biography.

In 1956, he sought the vice-presidential nomination with Adlai Stevenson, but was defeated by Estes Kefauver of Tennessee.

Reelected to the Senate, Kennedy set his sights on winning the 1960 Democratic nomination for president. He won seven primary contests and went to the 1960 Democratic convention a clear choice, winning on the first ballot. He chose Lyndon Johnson of Texas to be his running mate.

After three years as president, Kennedy was assassinated by Lee Harvey Oswald in Dallas, Texas, on November 22, 1963.

Presidential Campaign-1960

Kennedy's Catholicism was always in the background but was never an open issue in 1960. Kennedy brought up the Communist issue, criticizing the Eisenhower administration for Cuba's fall into the Communist sphere. Both Kennedy and Richard Nixon carried on vigorous campaigns. A new campaign element entered the American political scene. For the first time, rival presidential candidates debated on television.

Presidential Election-1960

The election was extremely close. Kennedy retired on election night, unsure of a victory. Lyndon Johnson, the vice-presidential candidate, had been chosen by Kennedy to balance the ticket and hold the Southern voters. The strategy worked as Johnson carried Texas by a slim margin, helping Kennedy win. Kennedy received 34,226,731 (50%) popular votes and 303 electoral votes from 22 states. Nixon had 34,108,157 (50%) votes and 219 electoral votes from 26 states. The vote difference was 118,574. Two tenths of a percentage point separated the two candidates. Nixon was urged to ask for a recount because of voting irregularities, but declined in the interest of the country. Harry Byrd, while not a candidate, received 15 unpledged electoral votes.

Major Legislation During Presidency

The twenty-third amendment was ratified in 1961, giving residents of the District of Columbia the right to vote in presidential elections.

Major Events During Presidency

On April 17, 1961, with Kennedy's approval, Cuban exiles in the United States launched an invasion of Cuba at the Bay of Pigs. Their expected support from the U. S. did not materialize, and they were unable to establish a foothold on the Cuban mainland. Over 1000 surrendered. Kennedy accepted blame for its failure. In 1962, the United States paid money and food to have the captives released.

In August, 1961, the Alliance for Progress was established by Kennedy to provide billions of dollars in aid to Latin American countries.

In March, 1961, Kennedy established the Peace Corps, a State Department agency that selected volunteers to travel to underdeveloped foreign countries to teach and give technical assistance and to raise the country's standard of living.

Kennedy refused to send armed troops, but followed Eisenhower's lead and increased military advisors to South Vietnam from 1,000 to over 16,000.

On August 13, 1961, the Berlin Wall was erected by the Communists, dividing Berlin, Germany, into East and West Berlin.

In October, 1962, the Cuban Missile Crisis occurred when American reconnaissance discovered that the Soviets were constructing a nuclear missile base in Cuba. Kennedy blockaded Cuba. On October 24, after a tense confrontation with Soviet ships meeting the blockade, Soviet Premier Nikita Khrushchev agreed to dismantle the missiles.

In July, 1963, the Soviet Union, Great Britain, and the United States signed a limited nuclear test ban treaty. It banned the testing of nuclear devices in the atmosphere or in outer space.

In May, 1961, Alan Sheppard, Jr. became the first American in space. On February 20, 1962, John Glenn was the first American to orbit the earth, narrowing the space gap with the Soviet Union.

The spring of 1963 was punctuated by racial riots by blacks demanding equal justice and full integration.

In 1962-63, the Supreme Court ruled that public school prayer and Bible reading was unconstitutional.

On August 28, 1963, 200,000 marched on Washington for civil rights and heard Martin Luther King's "I Have a Dream" speech.

The 1960 census put the nation's population at 179,323,175.

Lyndon B. Johnson
36th President (1963-1969)

Lyndon Baines Johnson was the eighth vice-president to succeed to the presidency because of the death of a president. He was sworn in as president on November 26, 1963, ninety-nine minutes after the death of President Kennedy in Dallas, Texas.

Johnson was the consummate politician, having served in the House and the Senate where at age 46, he became the youngest majority leader. He was a quiet, gentle man around friends, but politically he used his six foot, three inch, 200 pound presence to dominate and manipulate colleagues and Congress to gain his legislative agenda.

Biography

Lyndon Johnson was born on August 27, 1908, in a farmhouse on the Pedernales River near Stonewall, Texas. His father was Sam Johnson, Jr., a farmer and state politician. From him Johnson learned the subtleties of politics at an early age. Johnson's mother was Rebekah Baines Johnson, an educated woman who was a newspaper editor and teacher. Although his mother urged him to attend college, Johnson spent several years after graduating from Johnson City, Texas, High School, working at odd jobs. He returned home to work and attend Southwest Texas State College, excelling in debate and pursuing his interest in politics. In 1928, Johnson ran a friend's successful campaign for the state senate.

He graduated from college and taught speech at a Houston high school during 1931.

The next year he went to Washington D. C., as a secretary to Texas congressman, Richard Kleberg.

While studying law at Georgetown University in Washington, Johnson, 26, met Claudia Alta "Lady Bird" Taylor, 21, in 1934. It was a sudden romance with Lyndon proposing marriage on their first date. She was a graduate of the University of Texas. They were married November 17, 1934. They had two daughters.

From 1935 to 1937, Johnson was Director of the National Youth Administration in Texas.

In 1937, Johnson ran for Congress on the New Deal theme and won, returning to Washington as a congressman. He served in Congress from 1937 to 1948. He was a supporter of Roosevelt's New Deal programs and soon became House Speaker Sam Rayburn's lieutenant.

From December, 1941, to July, 1942, Johnson served as a lieutenant commander in the Navy and was awarded the Silver Star. Roosevelt ordered all congressmen back to Washington in 1942, ending Johnson's naval service.

In 1948, Johnson won the Texas primary for the U. S. Senate. Later elected, he served in the Senate from 1948 to 1961. He did not support Truman on his conduct of the Korean War and he voted to override Truman's veto of the Taft-Hartley bill. He opposed the end of segregation in the armed forces, the anti-lynching bill, and opposed the bill to end the poll tax.

At the 1960 Democratic convention, John Kennedy chose Johnson to be his running mate in order to secure winning Texas, Louisiana, and other southern states. The statagy worked. Johnson served as vice-president from 1961 to 1963, when Kennedy was assassinated on November 22, 1963, in Dallas, Texas.

After completing Kennedy's term, Johnson won the Democratic nomination in 1964, choosing Hubert H. Humphrey, a Minnesota liberal, as his running mate.

After winning a term on his own in 1964, Johnson introduced the program of the Great Society with extensive government programs, deepening the welfare state begun by Franklin Roosevelt and continued by John Kennedy. In the years, 1965-1966, Johnson and a Democratic Congress passed the Great Society programs. It brought about more involvement of the federal government in the American peoples lives.

In the remaining years of his term, Johnson got caught up in the Vietnam War with its thousands of casualties. With little support for the war by the American people, Johnson decided not to run for a second term as president. He had hoped his legacy would be the Great Society, not the Vietnam War.

On January 20, 1969, Lyndon and his wife, Lady Bird, retired to their Texas LBJ Ranch. He suffered a third and fatal heart attack on January 22, 1973. He was buried near Johnson City, Texas.

Presidential Campaign-1964

Lyndon Johnson was the first Southern presidential candidate from a Confederate state since the Civil War and the first Democratic nominee from the South since James Polk in 1844.

Johnson was opposed by Barry M. Goldwater, an Arizona Republican, who opposed the Great Society measures that Johnson proposed. Goldwater was a right wing conservative who felt that too much government was wrong. He wanted cuts in welfare, less federal subsidies for education and agriculture, and a voluntary form of Social Security. In the end, people viewed Goldwater as extreme because of his anti-civil rights stance and his support of states' rights with less federal government control. He did want to increase the budget for national defense. Johnson appeared as the peace candidate after Goldwater off-handedly talked of the use of conventional nuclear weapons. It made Goldwater appear as wanting to widen the Vietnam War. Johnson refused to debate Goldwater, remaining above the fray during the campaign. However, in the final month before the election he went on a 60,000 miles campaign journey in forty-two days.

The Democratic slogan,"All the way with LBJ" was catchy and in the end the voters repudiated Goldwater's conservatism and his criticism of Johnson's Vietnam policy as too extreme.

Presidential Election-1964

Johnson won the election with 43,129,566 (61%) votes to Goldwater's 27, 178,188 (39%) votes.

Johnson won 486 electoral votes from 44 states and the District of Columbia. Goldwater captured 52 electoral votes from six states.

Major Legislation During Presidency

At the beginning of his term in 1965, Johnson began developing the Great Society program and convinced Congress to pass the legislation needed to bring about the government run welfare state.

The Economic Opportunity Act of 1964 was to begin Johnson's war on poverty. It created the Job Corps program to provide vocational training for disadvantaged youths, 16 to 21. It created a domestic peace corps, Volunteers in Service to America (VISTA) and the Work-Study program for youths at poverty level to gain a college education. It also provided the Community Action Program involving the Head Start program for poverty preschoolers as well as the Upward Bound program for high schools. The Foster Grandparents program to help institutionalized children was enacted. Legal aid was provided to the poor.

The Civil Rights Act of 1964 banned discrimination in public facilities.

The Voting Rights Act of 1965 made it illegal to use literacy tests for voters and allowed the federal government to register voters.

By 1965, the Medicare program provided hospital insurance through Social Security and Medicaid provided hospital and medical aid for the poor

A series of environmental acts were passed in 1965 and 1967. These were the 1965 Water Quality Act, requiring states to set water quality standards; the 1966 Clean Water Restoration Act giving matching monies to states to build sewage treatment plants; and the 1965 Clean Air Act and the 1967 Air Quality Act which set emission standards for automobiles and helped states set environmental standards.

Federal acts for helping the consumer became law. The 1966 Fair Packaging and Labeling Act helped consumers identify the contents and nutritional values in food.

The National Traffic Safety Act of 1966 created specific safety standards for cars built after 1968.

The 1966 Highway Safety Act set a national highway safety program and required states to do the same.

Finally, the Wholesome Meat Act of 1967 extended federal meat inspection standards to all meat processing plants.

On February 10, 1967, the 25th Amendment went into effect allowing the Vice-President to take over the duties of the President if the President became disabled. If the Vice-Presidency became vacant, the President could appoint someone with Congress' approval.

The Civil Rights Act of 1968 made it illegal to discriminate in the sale and rental of housing.

Major Events During Presidency

Although advisors were in Vietnam prior to Johnson's presidency, when two United States destroyers were attacked by North Vietnam boats in the Gulf of Tonkin, America became involved in the most disastrous foreign engagement in the nation's history. Johnson ordered air strikes against North Vietnam naval bases, beginning an undeclared war with North Vietnam. On August 7, 1964, Congress passed the Gulf of Tonkin resolution which became the basis for the United States involvement in the eight year war.

The Civil Rights movement accelerated during Johnson's presidency. The Watts riot, August 11-16, 1966, in Los Angeles, resulted in 35 deaths and millions of dollars in property damage.

Between June 5-10, 1967, the Arab-Israeli Six Day War occurred. The Israelis captured Jerusalem, the Sinai Peninsula, and Arab land.

By 1968, the United States had 550,000 troops in Vietnam. Eventually, the American public turned against Johnson and the war which had claimed over 40,000 Americans killed during his presidency.

On January 25, 1968, the North Koreans seized the *Pueblo*, a U. S. spy ship and imprisoned the crew.

By March, 1968, the war was a stalemate. Johnson, noting the anti-war movement, announced that he would not run for reelection.

Martin Luther King was assassinated on April 4, 1968, in Memphis, Tennessee. Riots broke out across the United States in protest.

On June 5, 1968, Robert F. Kennedy was shot while campaigning in California He died on June 6, 1968.

Richard M. Nixon
37th President (1969-1974)

Richard Milhous Nixon was a 5 feet, 11 1/2 inches tall, dark-haired man with a personality that has defied biographers. Some see him as person with a dark, introspective nature, given to paranoid imaginings, while others see him as a shrewd, pragmatic politically astute person. Others view Nixon as a combination of both.

Raised a Quaker, Nixon spent all his life seeking to be accepted as an individual and as a public figure. His determination to serve the public in a political role was a driving force in his roles from congressman to president, surviving defeat several times, only to rise again to become a public political figure.

An introspective person, driven to self-doubts, Nixon used the half-truth and brusque personality, to shield himself from being open to the public that elected him. A scholar of history and brilliant negotiator in foreign affairs, Nixon opened China to the world and brought about peace in Vietnam. The Watergate affair and economic instability marred his presidency.

Biography

Richard Nixon's ancestry goes back to King Edward III of England. He had great-grandfathers who had fought in the Revolutionary and the Civil wars.

Nixon was born on January 9, 1913, in Yorba Linda, California. His father, Francis Nixon, was a worker in many trades during his life, with the principal occupation that of grocer. He owned Nixon's Market. He was married in 1906, to Richard Nixon's Quaker mother, Hannah Milhous Nixon.

Richard Nixon grew up in Yorba Linda working for his father in his market. He attended schools in Yorba Linda, but in his junior year he transferred to Whittier High School where he excelled in oratory. He graduated in 1930, receiving several awards for his scholarship.

Nixon attended Whittier College where he majored in history and captained the debate team. In his senior year he was elected class president and graduated second in his class. Nixon received a scholarship from the Quaker school to attend Duke University Law School, graduating with honors in 1937, third in his class and again class president. He was admitted to the California bar in November, 1937.

On June 21, 1940, at age 27, Nixon and Thelma Catherine "Pat" Ryan, 28, were married in Riverside, California. They had two daughters.

During World War II, Nixon served in the Navy, rising to the rank of lieutenant commander. He was stateside for much of the war, but did serve as officer in charge of the South Pacific Combat Air Transport Command at Bougainville and Green Island in the South Pacific from January to June, 1944. He received a citation for his service.

Nixon's political career began with his election to the Congress in 1946, defeating the five term California Democrat, Jerry Voorhis. Two years later he won reelection. He was an active congressman, helping to draft the Taft-Harley Act of 1947, sponsoring anti-communist legislation and finally, serving as chairman of the House Un-American Activities Committee. This eventually led to the conviction of Alger Hiss, a State Department official, as a spy. It was this case that gained Nixon national prominence.

In 1950, Nixon defeated Democrat Helen Douglas for a California seat in the Senate. His campaign was highlighted by his linking Douglas to goals of the Communist party, using her House votes to make the link. With his election at age 38, Nixon became the youngest member of the Senate, where he continued his opposition to President Truman in his conduct of the Korean War and his firing of General Douglas MacArthur.

In 1952, Republican nominee for president, Dwight Eisenhower, chose Nixon as his vice-president running mate. The news of a Nixon secret campaign fund and his supposed use of it for personal gain, brought about pressure for Eisenhower to drop Nixon. Nixon gave the "Checkers Speech" on television, denying the charges and acknowledged that his little girls had received a dog, Checkers, as a gift and he would not return it.

The emotional speech created a public response so favorable for Nixon that Eisenhower declared the next day, "You're my boy!"

As vice-president, Nixon served the country during President Eisenhower's illness, traveled to South America where he was attacked by a mob, and went to Russia where he had his famous "kitchen debate" with Premier Khrushchev on the merits of communism and democracy.

In 1960, Nixon was the Republican presidential candidate and lost by a narrow margin to John F. Kennedy.

Then in 1962, Nixon lost the governor's race to incumbent California Governor Pat Brown. Nixon showed his bitterness when he stated to the press that they would no longer have him to kick around.

The next five years he practiced law and campaigned for Republicans including presidential candidate Barry Goldwater in 1964.

In 1968, Nixon was the Republican nominee for president, running against Hubert Humphrey. He won in a close election.

Then in 1972, Nixon along with Vice-President Spiro Agnew easily won reelection of almost landslide proportions. Political unrest within the Republican party and investigations by a special Senate committee of political tactics such as the Watergate break-in of Democratic headquarters and the subsequent cover-up of the event and people involved, resulted in resignations of two of Nixon's aides. This led to a special Congressional committee that investigated Nixon's involvement in the coverup of the event

and persons involved. On July 27-30, 1974, the House voted to recommend three articles of impeachment.

With impeachment in the House and conviction in the Senate almost certain, President Nixon became the first president to resign the office. He did so on August 9, 1974. He was succeeded by Vice-President Gerald Ford whom Nixon had appointed after the resignation of Vice-President Spiro Agnew for tax evasion.

On September 8, 1974, President Gerald Ford granted Nixon a full and free pardon for any offenses against the United States.

Richard Nixon retired to San Clemente, California, to write and advise on foreign affairs.

Nixon died of a stroke on April 22, 1994, at the age of 81. He was buried at his library site at Yorba Linda, California.

Presidential Campaign-1968

Richard Nixon held an early lead in the polls and decided not to get too involved in the campaign. He advocated ending the Vietnam War, but kept specific ways a secret. Nixon campaigned on the need for law and order, ending the draft, lowering taxes and getting inflation under control. Hubert Humphrey, Democratic nominee, had little support besides labor and liberal Democrats. In addition, Democrat Henry Wallace siphoned off some of Humphrey's support in the South. Humphrey also wished to end the war, but he never found any other issue that would enliven his candidacy and put him in a position to challenge Nixon's massive lead with the voters.

Presidential Election-1968

Nixon easily won the election, garnishing 31,785,480 (43%) votes and 301 electoral votes from 32 states to Humphrey's 31,275,166 (42%) votes and 191 electoral votes from the District of Columbia and 13 states. American Independent George C. Wallace received 9,906,473 (14%) votes and 46 electoral votes from 5 states.

Presidential Campaign-1972

Richard Nixon won renomination for president. His Democratic opponent was George S. McGovern of South Dakota. The campaign was a lopsided one with McGovern never able to shake his image as a radical leftist. The Nixon campaign was mostly carried on by persons in Nixon's administration. The Vietnam War was a topic, but the Republicans maintained there could be no peace without the return of prisoners. The Watergate break in had occurred, but no one paid much attention to McGovern when he labeled the Nixon administration as corrupt.

For the first time, the 18 year old citizen was able to vote in a presidential election.

Presidential Election-1972

The 1972 election was a total landslide for Nixon. The popular vote for Nixon was 47,165,234 (61%) to McGovern's 29,168,110 (38%). In the electoral vote, Nixon had 520 electoral votes, winning 49 of the 50 states. McGovern had 17 electoral votes from the District of Columbia and Massachusetts.

Major Legislation During Presidency

The 1969 Environmental Quality Policy Act set up environmental impact studies for new federal programs. In addition, far reaching acts on various environmental fronts were enacted dealing with air and water quality along with the Resource Recovery Act of 1970 that is the basis for our extensive recycling efforts today.

In the law and order area three major crime bills were passed in 1970.

The Organized Crime Control imposing greater sentences as well as preventing the use of crime monies in legitimate businesses.

The Drug Abuse Control Act reduced some penalties and allowed authorities to enter suspected drug enterprises without warning. The last act was the District of Columbia Crime Control Act.

The Postal Reorganization Act of 1970, turned the postal department over to a private agency.

In 1970, the Occupational Safety and Health Act set up government standards and enforcement of health and safety of workers in industry and business.

On June 30, 1971, the 26th Amendment to the Constitution gave the vote to 18 year old citizens.

The Water Pollution Act of 1972 provided federal involvement in building waste treatment plants and limiting industrial discharge of waste into rivers and streams.

The Consumer Product Safety Act of 1972 created the agency to oversee product safety standards in order to ban unsafe products.

Major Events During Presidency

On July 20, 1969, Astronaut Neil Armstrong in Apollo 11 became the first man to walk on the moon.

In February, 1972, President Nixon became the first American president to visit China. It opened China trade, cultural, and scientific exchanges with the United States.

The final withdrawal of American troops and the return of prisoners from Vietnam took place in January, 1973, when a peace treaty was signed in Paris. The total United States casualties in the Vietnam War was 46,079 deaths and over 303,000 wounded.

The Seabed Treaty of 1970, signed with Russia, banned nuclear weapons testing on the ocean floor. The Chemical Weapons Treaty of 1971 put a ban on new chemical weapons and arranged for the destruction of stockpiles of chemical weapons.

A limit on nuclear weapons was agreed to between the Soviet Union and the United States in the 1972 Strategic Arms Limitations Talks (SALT) agreement.

On June 17, 1972 a break-in at Democratic headquarters in the Watergate Hotel by the "Plumbers," White House Special Investigation unit, occurred. The Congressional inquiry into the Watergate affair and the cover-up of White House involvement was played out on television to the American public.

On December 6, 1973, Nixon appointed Gerald Ford vice president after Spiro Agnew resigned because of income tax evasion.

In 1973, Nixon's close aides, Bob Haldeman, John Ehrlichman, and

Attorney General Kleindienst resigned. Nixon had recorded oval office conversations. A special prosecutor, Archibald Cox, asked for the tapes to prove Nixon's involvement in a cover-up.

Nixon tried to use executive privilege to avoid turning them over and failed. A House Judiciary Committee concluded that the tapes confirmed his attempts at obstruction of justice by using the FBI and the CIA. They recommended three article of impeachment.

The three articles of impeachment brought to the full House by the Judiciary Committee were passed by the House on a vote of 412 to 3. The first article was personal misconduct leading to obstruction of justice. The second, charged abuse of power and failure to fulfill his Presidential oath. The third article recommended by the committee was the closest vote and the weakest article. It charged that Nixon defied the subpoena power of the House committee.

Under the threat of an impeachment trial by the Senate, Nixon resigned on August 9, 1974, the first American president to leave the Presidency on his own volition.

Vice-President Gerald Ford was sworn in as the 38th president on August 9, 1974.

Nixon's aides, H. R. Halderman, John Ehrlichman, former Attorney General John Mitchell, Robert Mardian, and Charles Colson were convicted on various charges for their roles in the Watergate scandal.

The 1970 census counted the United States population at 203,302,031, an increase of 23,978,856 in the decade since 1960.

Gerald R. Ford
38th President (1974-1977)

Gerald Rudolph Ford, Jr.'s rise to the presidency was unusual because he did it without being elected. He was the first vice-president chosen under the 25th amendment. President Nixon chose him after the resignation of Spiro Agnew, Nixon's vice-president. The 6 feet tall, blond, athletic Ford had been a Michigan congressman for 25 years, nine of them as Republican minority leader, when Nixon chose him as his vice-president.

As a congressman, Ford used his political negotiating skills to get programs he favored passed. Ford became president when Nixon resigned on August 9, 1974.

Voters came to view him as a transition president. His honest, conciliatory and forthright approach to government made him few if any political enemies and many political friends in his years as a congressman. He believed strongly in compromise and consensus on government matters. As Ford said in accepting a Democratic bill that he did not totally want, "A half loaf is better than no loaf at all."

Biography

Gerald R. Ford, Jr. was born on July 14, 1913, in Omaha, Nebraska, to Leslie Lynch King and Dorothy Gardner King. When he was two years old, his parents divorced, and his mother and young Leslie, named after his father, moved to Grand Rapids, Michigan. She married Gerald Rudolph Ford, who then adopted her son and named him after himself.

Ford attended the public schools in Grand Rapids and later attended the University of Michigan where he majored in economics and political science. He enjoyed sports with football his major interest. As a senior he was the most valuable player and played against the Chicago Bears in the 1935 All-Star game. He turned down professional football contracts and instead, was an assistant football coach at Yale where he studied law, graduating in the top third of his class. He received his law degree in 1941, and was admitted to the bar in Michigan in June, 1941.

During World War II, Ford was an ensign in the Navy and eventually served as gunnery officer on the aircraft carrier, *Monterey*, participating in most of the major battles in the Pacific. For this service he was awarded ten battle stars. Following the war, Ford joined a Grand Rapids law firm.

On October 15, 1948, Gerald Ford, 35, married Elizabeth Anne Bloomer, 30, in Grand Rapids, Michigan,. They had three sons and a daughter.

In 1948, Ford ran for Congress, winning the Fifth Congressional seat. He served in the Congress from 1948 until 1973. As a congressman, he displayed his ability to organize and lead, serving as Republican minority leader from 1965-1973. Ford was a member of the Warren Commission that investigated the assassination of President Kennedy. He supported President Truman on many issues, but did not support the Great Society of President Johnson's administration because Ford believed strongly that less government was good government.

When Spiro Agnew resigned the vice-presidency on December 6, 1973, Ford became the first appointed vice-president under the provision of the 25th Amendment.

One year later, Ford was president without being elected. Nixon resigned on August 9, 1974, and Ford took the oath moments later. He named the veteran moderate Republican from New York, Nelson A. Rockefeller as his vice-president.

While president, Ford's life was threatened twice in assassination attempts by women. On September 5, 1975, Lynette Fromm drew a gun that did not fire; then on September 22, 1975, Sara Jane Moore fired one shot that missed Ford by several feet. Both women were convicted and sentenced to life in prison.

In his short term, Gerald Ford restored some of the prestige of the presidency that had eroded during the Watergate scandal. Ford's approach to his role as president was to heal the nation. However, the recovery was not enough for Ford to overcome the stigma of the scandal. Seeking a term of his own,

Ford was defeated in his campaign for the presidency in 1976, by Jimmy Carter. Ford retired to California enjoying golf and spending winters in Vail, Colorado, skiing.

Major Legislation During Presidency

In 1974, Ford signed the law creating the Nuclear Regulatory Commission as well as a law to deregulate United States oil prices.

The Campaign Reform Law of 1974 was put into effect limiting individual campaign contributions and providing public support of presidential campaigns.

In 1975, four bills were passed that were to help consumers. They were the Fair Credit Billing Act, the Real Estate Settlement Procedure Act, the Equal Credit Opportunity Act, and the Magnuson-Moss Warranty Act.

The extension of the 1975 Voting Rights Act gave voting rights to Spanish minorities and other foreigners who did not speak English.

By 1975, inflation and unemployment indicated that the country was in a recession. Large cities such as New York were on the brink of bankruptcy. Ford signed a bill to authorize short term loans to help New York avoid default.

Major Events During Presidency

In September, 1974, President Ford granted a "full, free, and absolute pardon" to Richard Nixon for crimes he might have committed while in office. Because of this action, Ford's approval rating with the voting public dropped by 20%.

Later, Ford granted clemency to draft evaders and deserters from the Vietnam War period. This was not accepted by the general public and Ford, who wanted to heal the wounds of the war, lost more credibility with the voters.

On December 9, 1974, Nelson A. Rockefeller was appointed and sworn in as Vice-President.

In the spring of 1975, the United States evacuated the last Americans from Saigon, South Vietnam, as the military collapse of the South government was eminent. On July 2, 1976, North Vietnam had gained control of the South and unified the country into the Socialist Republic of Vietnam. Hanoi became the capital and Saigon was renamed Ho Chi Minh City.

The Cambodians seized the American merchant ship *Mayaguez* and took 39 crew members captive. Ford ordered U. S. Marines to act to free the crew. The military action brought about their release and the return of the ship. Forty-one Americans were killed in the action.

In a new era of Soviet and United States cooperation, the United States space craft, Apollo 18 and the Soviet space craft Soyuz 19 linked up in space.

The Helsinki Accords, 1975, between the United States, Soviet Union, and 33 other nations prevented the United States from interfering in Eastern Europe. It recognized the boundaries of Iron Curtain countries and the need for human rights in all countries. Travel restrictions were eased for travelers into Eastern Europe .

On July 4, 1976, the United States celebrated its Bicentennial nationwide. The major event was the Tall Ships sailing into New York harbor.

James E. Carter
39th President (1977-1981)

Rising from a small Georgia town and a farm family to become president of the United States, James (Jimmy) Carter, Jr., embodies the American Dream. A naval veteran of World War II, Carter held to simple moral truths, to peace, to dedication to serve his fellow man, and to moral honesty. In an age of material comforts and a cynical view of politicians, Carter's open religiosity was a change. It made him seek public office to serve his fellow citizens. This clear, direct approach by Carter was often exploited by those domestic and foreign powers who disagreed with him. The 5 feet, 9 inches tall smiling Carter was often called naive, as he tried to bring peaceful solutions to world problems that have plagued mankind for centuries. His low-key approach to the present was a refreshing change for many. For others this laid back style was questioned as he dealt with domestic and foreign problems. Economic inflation and the Iran hostage crisis near the end of his first term caused voters to deny him a second term.

Biography

James Earl (Jimmy) Carter, Jr., was born on October 1, 1924, in Plains, Georgia. His parents were James E. Carter, Sr., a merchant and farmer, and Lillian Gordy Carter, a registered nurse.

After graduation from Plains High School in 1941, Carter received an appointment to the United States Naval Academy in 1942. He spent a year at college preparing for the entrance exam, passed, and entered the Academy in 1943. He graduated 59th of 820 graduates in June, 1946.

On July 7, 1946, Ensign Carter, 21, married Eleanor Rosalynn Smith, 18, in Plains, Georgia. Following the wedding, Carter went on active duty in the Navy for seven years, rising to the rank of lieutenant senior grade while in submarine duty.

After his father died in 1953, Carter returned to Plains and the family peanut farm. Carter enlarged the operation of the peanut farm until he was a wholesaler and warehouse owner. He became involved with local civic affairs.

By 1962, Carter had his first political office, a seat in the Georgia senate from 1963-1967.

In 1966, in his bid for the governorship, he came in third. He continued to run his business, but in 1970, he again became a candidate for governor of Georgia. He was elected and served as governor from 1971-1975.

As governor, Carter earned the attention of national leaders by his drive for greater efficiency in government. He reduced state agencies from 300 to 22. With the governorship as a stepping stone, Carter began his drive for the presidency in 1974, working tirelessly toward the goal, seeking the support of his fellow Democrats. By 1976, he arrived at the Democratic Convention with enough delegates to be chosen the party's candidate.

With Walter Mondale, the liberal senator from Minnesota as his running mate, Carter defeated incumbent Gerald Ford for the presidency in November, 1976.

After four years as president, Carter found himself at odds with the electorate because of high inflation and an energy crisis. In the Iranian hostage crisis, Carter appeared ineffective as the crisis continued into the November election. It was one of the reasons for his defeat by Ronald Reagan in 1980.

Carter retired to Plains, Georgia, but remained active in national and international affairs. He and his wife, Rosalynn, became active participants in the Habitat for Humanity, the housing for the poor program. They physically worked on construction crews building or remodeling houses. Carter continued to work for a peaceful world, acting as an emissary for President Clinton to North Korea. Internationally, Carter was a monitor for a number of elections in foreign countries.

Presidential Campaign-1976

The 1976 presidential campaign was largely a personality contest. Carter was a fresh face with fresh ideas of government, while Ford had to combat a sluggish economy and high unemployment. Carter made the theme of the status quo into a negative factor for Ford. In the televised debates, Carter appeared just as able to run the country as Ford. He displayed self-confidence and stressed that the country needed change. Ford was put in the position of defending a weak economy and his pardoning of Nixon

Presidential Election- 1976

The election was close. President Ford won 27 states to Carter's 23 and the District of Columbia.

In the popular vote, Carter received 40,825,839 (50%) and 297 electoral votes to Ford's 39,147,770 (48%) and 240 electoral votes. Washington State cast 1 vote for Ronald Reagan.

Major Legislation During Presidency

Deregulation legislation took top priority during Carter's presidency. Industries deregulated were cargo airlines (1977), commercial airlines (1978), natural gas prices (1978), and commercial trucking (1980).

Legislation such as the creation of the Department of Energy focused the administration's efforts at energy conservation. An energy bill decontrolled natural gas prices and required companies to convert to coal. In 1980, a wind-fall profits tax on companies was enacted.

Several conservation legislation bills became law. The 1977 Strip Mining and Reclamation Act set standards for land use. The 1980 Alaska Land Act set aside 104 million acres in national parks, wilderness areas, and wild life refuges.

The Humphrey-Hawkins Full Employment Act of 1978 set a goal of 4% unemployment by 1983.

The Panama Canal Treaty of 1977, set the return of the canal and the Canal Zone to Panama on December 31, 1999.

The Strategic Arms Limitations Treaty II (Salt II) was signed by Carter and Premier Leonid Brezhnev of the Soviet Union. Senate conservatives saw the treaty as unfair to United States interests because it put greater limits on the U. S. than on the USSR. Their opposition to it and the invasion by the Soviets into Afghanistan brought about the treaty's defeat.

Major Events During Presidency

In 1978, with Carter as negotiator, the Camp David Accords were signed by Egyptian President Anwar Sadat and Prime Minister Menachem Begin of Israel, ending thirty years of hostility between Israel and Egypt.

In 1978, Carter created the Department of Education.

In 1979, Carter established diplomatic relations with China withdrawing U. S. forces from Taiwan.

In 1979. after U. S. Ambassador Dubs was killed in Afghanistan, Carter stopped aid to that country. A United States fuel shortage resulted. Russia invaded Afghanistan and refused Carter's request to leave. He cut off the sale of technological equipment to Russia. The United States and 63 other nations boycotted the 1980 Olympic games in Moscow. In 1989, the Soviets withdrew from Afghanistan in defeat.

In November 4, 1979, Iranian militants led by the Ayatollah Khomeini, seized the American embassy and held 52 American personnel hostage for 444 days before their release on January 20, 1981.

Ronald W. Reagan
40th President (1981-1989)

The optimistic, patriotic stance of Ronald Reagan was a reflection of his life. Rising from humble Midwest life, the 6 feet, 1 inch tall Reagan embodied the work ethic and moral standards of the average American. Direct in his approach to life, Reagan sought to relieve Americans of the burden of government while it served people who needed help. Unpretentious in his attitude and demeanor, the former actor used his acting experiences to deliver forthright, stirring speeches, earning him the nickname of "the great communicator." He used television and live audiences to deal with the problems and concerns of the nation. He reestablished the United States as a world power, using the presidency to respond to volatile global political changes. He believed in a strong military force, echoing Theodore Roosevelt.

At age 69, Reagan was our oldest president, leaving office when he was almost 78 years old. Throughout his terms he was vigorous and out-going, dealing actively with foreign and domestic affairs.

Biography

Ronald Wilson Reagan was born to John Reagan, a shoe salesman, and Nelle Wilson Reagan on February 6, 1911, above a Main Street bakery in Tampico, Illinois. Although he was of Irish-Scotch-English ancestry, his nickname of "Dutch," given to him by his father at birth, stuck.

Reagan enjoyed a typical Midwestern childhood as he grew up in several Illinois towns, earning money with various childhood jobs, enjoying sports, especially football, and attending the motion picture theater. As a lifeguard at a swimming beach, he rescued 77 people.

Reagan graduated from Dixon, High School in Illinois in 1928. He participated in football, baseball and track. After high school he went on to Eureka College in Illinois, where he majored in economics and was involved with football, swimming and track. He acted in college plays, continuing his interest in acting that began in high school. As president of the student council, he became a political student leader, leading a student strike protesting cuts in curriculum. It led to the resignation of the college president.

After his graduation in 1932, Reagan became a $100 a week radio broadcaster at an Iowa station. By age 25, he was a leading sports broadcaster in the Midwest, doing football games and Chicago Cub baseball games with station WHO in Des Moines, Iowa.

As the Cub announcer he had the opportunity to go on a spring training trip with the Cubs to California. There he had the chance to do a screen test with Warner Brothers Studios. He accepted the offered contract to act in motion pictures.

For nearly the next twenty years, Reagan appeared in over fifty motion pictures. The most famous was *Knute Rockne, All American,* playing the part of George Gipp, Notre Dame halfback, and picking up a new nickname, the Gipper.

On January 24, 1940, at age 28, Reagan married actress Jane Wyman, 26. They had met on the set of *Brother Rat* (1938) and fell in love. They had a daughter and adopted son. They divorced in 1948.

During World War II, Reagan entered the Army, but because of poor eyesight, he began wearing contact lens, making him unfit for combat. He spent the war making military training films.

Reagan had been a life-long Democrat, believing in their liberal agenda, but his army experience made Reagan more conservative.

Following the war, he returned to acting. He served as president of the Screen Actors Guild from 1947 to 1952 and again in 1959-60. In addition to his film acting, Reagan became a television personality, serving as host of "General Electric Theater" and "Death Valley Days."

During the mid to late 1950's his change to conservatism became more apparent. He became the spokesman for the General Electric Corporation, speaking out against the "welfare state" and the New Deal programs that he had supported during Franklin Roosevelt's presidency.

On March 4, 1952, Reagan, 41, married actress Nancy Davis, 30. They had two children.

In 1952 and in 1956, Reagan campaigned as a Democrat for Eisenhower, and although he earlier had campaigned against Nixon in Nixon's bid for the Senate in 1950, in 1960, Reagan gave over 200 speeches for Nixon. In 1962, Reagan formally registered as a Republican.

In 1964, after a speech on television, Republican political leaders urged Reagan to run for California's governorship. He easily defeated popular Democratic governor, Edmund Brown. Reagan was reelected and served as California governor until 1975. During his terms as governor he instituted many conservative programs.

On two different occasions, Reagan lost the Republican nomination for president. In 1968, he lost to Richard Nixon and to Gerald Ford in 1976. Finally in 1980, after winning 24 of 34 primaries, Reagan went to the Republican Convention in Detroit, assured of the nomination. He gained the nomination on the first ballot and chose George Bush as his vice-presidential running mate.

Reagan was elected president by a landslide over incumbent, Jimmy Carter in 1980.

During his presidency, Reagan survived an assassination attempt when on March 30, 1981, John Hinckley, Jr., fired six shots at the president. One shot ricocheted and struck Reagan, the bullet lodging only an inch from his heart. His press secretary, James Brady, was wounded in the head but survived.

As president, Reagan continued his theme of less government and continued the long process of deregulation of business. The arms buildup added to the deficit, but it provided jobs amid an economy recovering from a deep recession in 1982. Inflation eased, more jobs were available, and a large income tax reduction helped the American worker gain a better financial position.

Reagan's second term was marked by better relations with the Soviet Union and its leader, Mikhail Gorbachev. Reagan found uses for the enlarged armed forces. Marines were sent to Lebanon as a peace keeping force but were withdrawn in 1984, after their barracks was destroyed by terrorists and over 241 perished .

In October, 1983, he ordered the invasion of Grenada to overthrow the anti-American dictatorship.

Reagan's second term was marred by the Iran-Contra affair in which monies from the secret sale of weapons to Iran was diverted to support the Contra rebels in Nicaragua. Reagan testified that he knew nothing of the event.

Following his leaving the presidency at age 78, Ronald Reagan and his wife, Nancy, retired to their California ranch near Santa Barbara and a home in Bel Aire.

Reagan developed Alzheimer's during the last years of his life.

Presidential Campaign-1980

Reagan at 69 was thirteen years older than Carter, but because of high inflation, gas shortages, and the Iranian hostage crisis, President Carter had little chance against the rigorous onslaught of Reagan who wanted fewer government restraints on oil companies.

Reagan came out against abortion and the Equal Rights Amendment and called for greater defense spending. Reagan campaigned for a supply-side economic policy which espoused tax cuts which would increase savings that in turn would be invested in industry and create more jobs. It was a cyclical theory that depended on no interruptions in the process in order to work. It was an inflation fighting strategy that eventually would reduce inflation.

Presidential Election-1980

Reagan received 43,904,153 (51%) popular votes and 489 electoral votes from 44 states to Carter's 35,483,883 (41%) votes and 49 electoral votes from the District of Columbia and 6 states. John Anderson, Republican, running as an independent received 5,719,437 (7%) votes. The election was a commentary on the what the electorate wanted in the presidency, a reestablishment of the United States as a nation and world military power.

Presidential Campaign-1984

The 1984 campaign was different because the Democrats nominated Walter Mondale with Geraldine Ferraro as his running mate. She was the first woman to run for the national office of vice-president.

Reagan pushed his "supply-side economics" by stating that the deficit spending of his administration would eventually lead to greater economic prosperity and more jobs.

The other major topic was the call by Reagan for open world trade. Mondale, backed by unions, wanted tariffs and import quotas. The military build-up that brought about greater deficits during Reagan's first term was attacked by Mondale as wasteful.

Reagan's age never became an issue even though he was the oldest president in United States history. He left office nearly 78 years old.

Presidential Election-1984

It was a major landslide for Ronald Reagan in the 1984 election over Walter Mondale. Reagan received 54,455,075 (59%) to Mondale's 37,577,185 (41%) in the popular vote. Reagan collected 525 electoral votes from 49 states. Mondale received 13 electoral votes from Minnesota and the District of Columbia. Reagan's total popular vote was the largest in the nation's election history.

Major Legislation During Presidency

The most significant legislation enacted was the 1983 Social Security Act which would provide for the fund's solvency to the year 2050. It did this by a raise in Social Security taxes, taxing some retirees' Social Security payments, bringing federal workers into the system, and raising the retirement age to 67 by the year 2027.

The Tax Reform Act of 1986 made significant changes in the income tax. It dropped many low income earners from the tax rolls, shifted more of the tax burden to corporations and reduced the use of many tax shelters.

In December, 1987, Mikhail Gorbachev of the Soviet Union and Ronald Reagan agreed to a nuclear-arms reduction agreement when they signed the INF Treaty to reduce intermediate-range nuclear weapons.

In 1988, the cabinet post of Department of Veteran Affairs was created.

Reagan and Canadian Prime Minister Brian Mulroney signed a trade pact in 1988 that literally created free trade between the two nations until 1999.

Major Events During Presidency

In 1981, the United States launched the space shuttle, *Columbia*, the first reusable spacecraft. Then in 1986, the space program was halted for a time after the space shuttle, *Challenger*, blew up killing six astronauts.

The Israeli invaded Lebanon in June, 1982. This brought a United States response with a Marine peace keeping force sent to Lebanon. Reagan's proposal for a Palestine state was rejected by Israel.

In October, 1983, American forces invaded Grenada to rescue hundreds of United States citizens who were threatened by a Communist coup. With Grenada residents support, the United States forces helped rid the country of the Communist regime and establish a democracy.

Reagan had said that he would never deal with terrorists. However, the Iran-Contra scandal occurred in 1985, when Reagan agreed to sell arms to Iran in its war with Iraq in exchange for American hostages. Members of his administration diverted monies from the covert sale to help the Contra forces opposing the Nicaraguan government in Central America. Reagan created a commission to ferret out the diversion and the subsequence cover-up. The report of the investigation cleared the president of knowing about the diversion. A special prosecutor brought criminal charges against Colonel Oliver North, Admiral Poindexter, and Robert McFarland. Charges against North were later dropped in January, 1989.

The 1980's brought increased terrorist acts against Americans. An April, 1983, explosion at the United States embassy in Beirut, Lebanon, killed 16 Americans and others. Then in October, 1983, the Marine barracks in Beirut was bombed, killing 241 servicemen. In 1985, Palestine Liberation Organization terrorists hijacked a cruise ship *Achille Lauro*, killing an American tourist.

In April, 1986, a bomb in a German disco killed an American serviceman and injured 60 others.

Palestinian terrorists killed five Americans in the Rome and Vienna airports.

Two Libyan terrorists bombed a Pan Am passenger jet over Lockerbie, Scotland, in December, 1988, killing all 259 aboard. One Libyan was tried and found guilty in January, 2001.

In retaliation, the United States put sanctions and cut off trade with Libya. It bombed the Libyan capital and President Qaddafi's residence.

The United States census of 1980 put the country's population at 226,542,203, an increase of 23,240,172 since 1970. The center of the United States was near De Sota, Missouri. The foreign born population had risen from a 1970 low of 4.7% to 6.2% of the population.

George Bush
41st President (1989-1993)

George Bush bought to the presidency the experience of a lifetime devoted to government. The 6 feet 2 inches tall Texan was an experienced legislator with four years of service in the House and eight years as vice-president. His directorship of the CIA gave him needed administrative experience in government while his chairmanship of the Republican party gave him the political experience.

The affable, well-educated Bush was direct in his dealings with colleagues and with the voting public.

Bush was cast in the role of a transition president because of the public's economic concerns at the end of his first term.

In world affairs, Bush showed his ability to unify divergent forces, when under his leadership and his use of the United Nations organization, he united European and Arab countries into a single war-time force to successfully conduct the Gulf War against Saddam Hussein and the Iraqi army.

Bush displayed the easy calm of a man certain of his life's mission, leaving his vice-presidency role with quiet determination to fulfill his promise of a "thousand lights" of good will and harmony.

Biography

George Herbert Walker Bush was born June 12, 1924, in Milton, Massachusetts, to Prescott S. Bush, a banker and United States Senator from Connecticut, and Dorothy Walker Bush. George Bush grew up in wealth, but his mother went to great lengths to order her children's lives so as not to spoil them. Summers were spent at Walker's Point in Kennebunkport, Maine, where Bush enjoyed fishing. Bush later purchased the property and used it as a presidential retreat.

Bush was educated at Greenwich, Connecticut Country Day School, taking an active role in all sports, especially baseball, soccer, tennis, and football.

At age 13, he attended Phillips Academy, an elite boys' prep school in Andover, Massachusetts.

With the world at war, as soon as he became 18, Bush enlisted in the Navy as a second class seaman I. He entered flight training and in June, 1943, Bush earned his wings and was commissioned an ensign. He was the Navy's youngest pilot at that time.

During World War II, Bush flew a Grumman Avenger torpedo bomber on 58 combat missions off the carrier, San Jacinto. He escaped two downed aircraft and was twice rescued at sea. He was awarded the Distinguished Flying Cross for completing a mission after he was struck by enemy fire and before going down at sea.

The submarine Finback rescued Bush. He spent a month with the ship before going ashore. Rotated back to the States, he awaited duty to fly missions against Japan but the use of the atomic bomb and the end of the war brought about his discharge.

Lt. George Bush (j.g.) and Barbara Pierce had become engaged prior to his Pacific service. On January 6, 1945, George, 20, and Barbara, 19, were married. They had six children.

Following the war, Bush enrolled at Yale and graduated in 1948 with a degree in economics. At Yale, he engaged in sports, excelling in baseball and soccer. He was elected president of his senior class.

Not finding the world of finance in his father's investment banking to his liking, he decided to learn the oil business. With his wife, Barbara and son, George, he moved to Odessa, Texas, and began to learn the oil business by sweeping floors and doing field work at a salary of $375 a month.

Over the next two years, Bush worked in the oil fields, and then in 1950, struck out on his own and formed his own company, the Bush-Overbey Oil Development Company. By 1953, his company merged with another and the Zapata Petroleum Corporation was formed. The company developed and sold oil drilling equipment as well as drilling oil wells.

The Zapata Corporation brought in fifty-four oil rich wells near Abilene, Texas. Bush became president of a subsidiary company, Zapata Off-Shore, which he eventually sold. With his wealth from the oil interests, he ran for the United States Senate in 1964 and lost. Then in 1966, Bush became the first Republican to represent the Houston area as a congressman.

In 1970, Bush again ran for the Senate and lost. Following his defeat, President Nixon appointed him as the United States ambassador to the United Nations. Then in 1972, Nixon named him chairman of the Republican National Committee. As chairman, he toured the country, defending Nixon and the GOP against the what was seen as a major embarrassment to Republican candidates, the Watergate scandal. Bush joined others in urging Nixon to resign. Nixon did so on August 8, 1974.

In 1975, President Ford sent Bush to China as the U. S. representative. Late in the year, Ford recalled him to become head of the Central Intelligence Agency which needed reorganization to correct abuses of power. Bush spent the next year reorganizing and revitalizing the CIA.

Bush resigned from the CIA when Carter was elected president in 1976. By 1980, Bush was making a serious bid for the presidency in the state primaries, but withdrew when Ronald Reagan began leading. He accepted the vice-presidency nomination to run with Reagan.

During his eight years as vice-president, 1981-1989, Bush gained broad experience, serving as Reagan's envoy to foreign governments, heading a National Security Council task force, and presiding over the Senate. Bush was the first vice-president to receive the presidential power when it was transferred to him by Reagan when Rea-

gan underwent cancer surgery in July, 1985. In 1987-88, Bush won most of the primaries, and was the only viable candidate at the Republican National Convention. He was nominated on the first ballot.

On November 8, 1988, George Bush was elected president over his Democratic opponent, Michael S. Dukakis, governor of Massachusetts. Bush's vice-president was Senator Dan Quayle of Indiana.

After an eventful first term with an economy that did not move forward and a challenge from a conservative third party, Bush was defeated for a second term by Democrat Governor William Clinton of Arkansas in the 1992 election.

Following the defeat, Bush and his wife, Barbara, retired to Houston, Texas.

Presidential Campaign-1988

In what has been described as a vicious and negative presidential campaign, Republican George Bush and Democrat Michael Dukakis spent millions of campaign dollars attacking each other. Bush attacked Dukakis on the law and order issue, depicting him as soft on crime because of a prison furlough system in Massachusetts. Bush was anti-abortion to Dukakis' pro-abortion. The major issue was the huge government deficit from the Reagan years. Dukakis indicated that he would increase tax collection and close tax loop holes, while Bush said repeatedly, "Read my lips. No new taxes!" Bush managed to tie Dukakis to the far left liberal branch of the Democratic party and align himself with the more conservative Republican right.

The entire campaign was a television media ad war that did little to clarify the real issues. Consequently, only 57% of voters voted in the election. This was the lowest voter turnout since 1964 when records of voter participation were started. A majority of newspapers refused to endorse either Bush or Dukakis.

Presidential Election-1988

George Bush won a lop-sided victory in the popular vote, receiving 48,886,097 votes (54%) and 426 electoral votes from 40 states to Dukakis' 41,809,074 (46%) votes and 111 electoral votes from 10 states and the District of Columbia.

Bush was the first sitting vice-president to be elected president since Martin Van Buren in 1836.

Major Legislation During Presidency

The single most important legislation early in George Bush's term was a tax increase to fight the deficit that had accumulated during Reagan's terms. The increase was aimed at the middle class by tax increases on gasoline, cigarettes, and beer along with an increase in Medicare premiums. The wealthy had to pay more taxes on many luxury items plus an increase in income taxes in the top tax bracket.

In 1989, legislation was passed in which the Federal government would pay off the failed savings and loan institutions because of bad loans.

An agency, the Resolution Trust Corporation would oversee the closing and selling of the saving and loan assets. The estimated cost would be about $500 billion over 40 years. The bill also put new regulations and restrictions on banks and thrift institutions.

The Americans with Disabilities Act of 1990 required businesses, public facilities, and public transportation to make their facilities accessible to people in wheelchairs and other disabilities.

The Clean Air Act of 1990 set stricter requirements for emissions for everyone from industry to automobiles. It was aimed at reducing pollution of air the by the manufacturing industry in order to cut down smog and acid rain.

Major Events During Presidency

On December 20, 1989, in a move that was highly criticized by other countries but endorsed by the Panamanian people, American armed forces invaded Panama and captured Communist dictator, General Manuel Noriega, accusing him of drug smuggling and other crimes. He was later tried, found guilty, and sent to prison in the United States.

In early 1990, with the aid of the Bush administration which had abandoned the Reagan support of the Contras rebels, a democratic vote was held in Nicaragua and the contra rebels were defeated. Bush promised to support the new government by lifting the embargo and giving material and monetary aid to the Nicaraguan government.

The collapse of communism across Europe and the Soviet Union was the greatest international event of Bush's term. In Poland, Czechoslovakia, Hungary, Yugoslavia, Rumania, Albania, and in the Soviet Union movements for democratic elections and the break-up of communistic alliances took place.

Instrumental in bringing about these events were meetings that took place between President Bush and Soviet Premier Mikhail Gorbachev. The Soviets no longer wanted to impose Communism by force and Eastern European countries took advantage of this policy, revolted and instituted pro-Western governments.

The greatest change came about in the unification of East and West Germany on October 3, 1990. This had been brought about by the tearing down of the Berlin Wall in November, 1989.

The end of the Cold War occurred in Paris in November, 1990 when Premier Mikhail Gorbachev of the Soviet Union, President Bush, and the leaders of 20 nations of the North Atlantic Treaty Organization (NATO) and the Warsaw Pact signed a non-aggression pact. In addition, treaties were signed to limit the number and size of nuclear arms and conventional weapons in Europe.

The Persian Gulf War was the defining international event for George Bush. On August 2, 1990, Iraq armed forces invaded oil rich Kuwait in the Persian Gulf.

The United States and Britain went before the United Nations assembly, asked for economic sanctions and an embargo of supplies to Iraq. The sanctions failed to halt Iraq President Saddam Hussein. With his threat to overrun Saudi Arabia, European and Arab countries under President Bush's urging,

banded together and joined American forces to fight and drive Iraqi forces out of Kuwait. The operation was called Desert Storm. The war began on January 17, 1991.

Under United Nations sanctions, the coalition forces led by United States air power and directed by Generals H. Norman Schwarzkopf and Chief of Staff Colin Powell, defeated the Iraqi forces between January 19, 1991 and February 27, 1991.

The actual ground offensive lasted six days with the United States losing 148 killed out of 400,000 American troops that were sent to the Persian Gulf to defend Saudi Arabia. Coalition forces occupied southern Iraq. United States aircraft bombed Iraqi targets. Retreating Iraqis set fire to 742 Kuwait oil wells that burned for weeks. The United Nations with United States support, imposed sanctions as cease fire conditions on Iraq, conditions that Hussein later broke.

The worst oil spill in U. S. history occurred at Prince William Sound in Alaska on March 24, 1989, The *Exxon Valdez* ran aground, spilling nearly 11 million gallons of crude oil.

Bush granted pardons to six former members of Reagan's administration who had been implicated or investigated in the Iran Contra arms for hostages deal.

The 1990 United States census put the population at 248,765,170, an increase of 22,222,967 since 1980. The center of population had moved west about forty-nine more miles to near Steelville, Missouri.

William Clinton
42nd President (1993-2001)

William (Bill) Clinton was the first elected two term Democrat since Franklin Roosevelt's four terms. As a teenager, Clinton after meeting and shaking hands with the 35th president, John Kennedy, vowed that someday he would be president of the United States.

Experienced in governing after serving as governor of Arkansas for twelve years, Clinton demonstrated a personality that could change with the situation, adapting his position on social and economic issues.

Throughout his presidency, Bill Clinton proved to be an elusive political target for opponents. His terms were filled with scandal after scandal, personal and administrative. Despite these, Clinton enjoyed great voter popularity and high job performance ratings because of his constant TV presence and a good economy. He used the the media to further his programs as well as himself by almost daily use of the medium. When proposed programs did not materialize, he shifted positions and proposed new approaches. In this way,

Clinton brought about many social programs in an incremental fashion, using executive orders and piecemeal legislation to achieve his goals in spite of a Republican Congress during the last two years of his first term and the entire second term.

Biography

William Clinton was born William Jefferson Blythe IV on August 19, 1946, in Hope, Arkansas. His father, William Jefferson Blythe III, was killed in an automobile accident before his birth. For a time Clinton lived with his maternal grandparents while his mother, Virginia, studied nursing.

In 1950, when he was four, his mother married Roger Clinton. When he was sixteen, Bill Clinton took his step-father's name

While Clinton grew up in a home filled with the tension of an alcoholic step-father, his early life was normal. Besides the normal activities such as Boy Scouts and music summer camp, Clinton played the saxophone in a jazz trio called the Three Blind Mice.

After attending various elementary schools when they moved to Hot Springs, Arkansas, Clinton attended Hot Springs High School where he held a number of student elected offices. In high school, he was an outstanding student and a member of the National Honor Society and a National Merit Scholarship semi-finalist.

Clinton enrolled in the foreign service course at Georgetown University in Washington, D. C. There he was president of the freshman and sophomore classes. During his junior year he worked in Senator William Fulbright's office. During the Vietnam War, Clinton took a stand against the war. He graduated with a degree in international affairs in 1968.

In October, 1968, Clinton sailed to England to attend Oxford University on a Rhodes Scholarship. He studied politics, economics, and the politics of the communist countries.

At Oxford, Clinton took part in several demonstrations against the United States' involvement in the Vietnam War. There he passed the Army induction physical and was listed as 1-A in the draft. He signed a letter of intent to join the Army Reserve Officers Training Corps at the University of Arkansas.

Later he wrote and told authorities that he would not be joining the program. In the December, 1969, draft, his number was 311, safely above the 195 limit for induction.

In his junior year, Clinton returned to the United States and attended Yale University, taught at a community college and worked in political campaigns. He received his law degree in 1973 and joined the University of Arkansas law faculty.

On October 11, 1975, Clinton, 29, married Hillary Rodham, 27. Following their marriage, they moved to Fayetteville, Arkansas, where he was teaching. They had one child, daughter, Chelsea.

Clinton was defeated in his first run for political office in the Arkansas Third Congressional District. Then in 1977, he won his first public office as Arkansas' Attorney

General. Clinton directed the successful state campaign for Jimmy Carter for president.

In 1978, Clinton ran for governor of Arkansas, saying he was a "compromise progressive." He supported women's right and stricter gun control. At age 32, Clinton was elected the youngest governor in the United States. He instituted vigorous reforms and tax increases to try to improve Arkansas roads and quality of life. He moved too quickly and four years later, lost his reelection bid.

Returning to law practice, Clinton analyzed his loss and planned another run for governor. He ran in 1984 and won handily. In 1986, with the governorship extended to four years, Clinton won again. Then in 1990, as a member of the Democratic Leadership Council and chairmanships of the education and health reform task forces for the National Governors Association, Clinton returned for a fifth term, promising to fill out his four year term. In 1991, Clinton toured the state, asking to be released from his promise in order to run for president.

Clinton conducted a vigorous presidential campaign against incumbent President George Bush. Clinton won the presidency. He resigned as Arkansas governor on December 12, 1992.

Clinton won a second term and was inaugurated on January 20, 1997. He served as president until January 2001, never letting his 'lame duck' status deter him.

Presidential Campaign-1992

The 1992 presidential campaign was an unusual election. In it, a third party, Ross Perot, led the Republican President George Bush and the Democrat Governor Bill Clinton in the polls. It was Perot's dropping out of the race just prior to Clinton's convention acceptance speech that turned the tide in favor of the Democrats and Clinton.

Bill Clinton and his running mate, Tennessee Senator Al Gore, conducted a bus tour of the country, appearing together to offer a generational change from the Reagan and Bush years. Clinton was able to cast doubts about an economic recovery, citing the growing deficit and the need to deal with it.

George Bush reacted to the attacks slowly. His campaign attacked Clinton on his youth, his anti-war record, and his ambiguous stands on national issues.

Meanwhile, Perot, while not a candidate, spoke out on the need to cut the deficit and raise taxes on gasoline, cigarettes, and Social Security benefits. In October, Perot again declared himself a candidate, totally muddying the political waters, taking the initiative and the attention away from President Bush. He charged Bush with being weak on Saddam Hussein at the end of the Gulf War as well as not finding a solution for the savings and loan crisis.

Presidential Election-1992

Because of the presence of Ross Perot, Americans voted in greater numbers than previous elections. Clinton's popular vote was 44,908,233 (43%) votes and 370 electoral votes from 32 states and the District of Columbia. President

Bush received 39,02,282, (37%) votes with 169 electoral votes from 17 states. Ross Perot received 19,741,048 (19%) votes. The election made Clinton a minority president.

Presidential Campaign-1996

In the 1996 campaign the incumbent Clinton was opposed by Senate Majority leader, Robert Dole. The Republican Contract with America initiative of 1994 had lost its momentum, and President Clinton, learning from his political mistakes, had moved toward a centralist position, taking the initiative on many of the issues such as saving social security and balancing the budget away from the Republicans. A year earlier Clinton had stayed fast in his opposition to the Republican budget to the point that on two occasions the government was shut down. In spite of this, his approval ratings rose with the voting public.

Dole's campaign rested solely on his promise to cut taxes by 15 percent. A skeptical public did not trust or else saw no need for it. Because of this, Dole's campaign floundered.

Presidential Election-1996

On November 5, 1996, Bill Clinton was reelected by a margin greater than his first election. He won 379 electoral votes receiving 47,402,357 (49%) votes to Dole's 159 electoral votes and 39,198,755 (41%) popular votes. Perot had 8,085,402 (8%) votes. Perot's role deprived Clinton of a majority.

Major Legislation During Presidency

The Senate voted approval of the Second Strategic Arms Reduction Treaty signed by Russia's Boris Yelsin and President Bush in January, 1993.

The Brady Handgun Violence Prevention Act (1993) required gun dealers to do background checks on gun buyers. In 1997, the Supreme Court declared it unconstitutional.

The 1994 Violent Crime Control and Law Enforcement Act banned the manufacture and use of 19 specific assault weapons.

The North American Free Trade Agreement (NAFTA) between the United States, Canada and Mexico was signed in the Bush presidency. Trade barriers were lowered and reciprocal tax breaks became part of the agreement that took effect January 1, 1994.

On August 22, 1996, the Welfare Reform Bill became law. It provided welfare block grants to be administrated by the states. The minimum wage was raised.

The 1996 Farm Bill replaced farm subsidies with final declining payments and idled land.

Two other bills that passed in 1996 were sanctions against Cuba and the Health Insurance Act that made insurance portable for workers changing jobs.

On April 9, 1997, Clinton signed the Line Item Veto bill. He used it for one budget before it was declared unconstitutional.

On January 1, 2000, the Panama Canal and the Canal Zone was returned to Panama, completing the agreement signed in the Carter Administration.

Major Events During Presidency

A great earthquake occurred in Los Angeles, California, on January

17, 1994, killing 61 people and causing extensive damage to buildings and highways.

In the 1994 mid-year elections, the Republicans led by future Speaker Newt Gingrich, won both the Senate and the House and controlled Congress for the first time in 40 years. His "Contract with America" became the creative blueprint for GOP led legislation to lower taxes, enact welfare reform and create a balanced budget.

In June, 1995, President Clinton and the House continued their confrontation on the budget. Clinton vetoed budget cuts and the crisis escalated. The recriminations on both sides resulted in two partial government shut-downs in the fall of 1996. Clinton weathered the crisis and the GOP Congress lost its initiative for reform.

On July 18, 1995, with the Independent Counsel in place, the Senate began hearings on the Whitewater land deals and Clinton's involvement while Arkansas governor.

In his final two years of his second term, Clinton faced the most serious threat to his protean presidency. On December 19, 1998, Clinton became only the second president to be tried by the Senate on Articles of Impeachment voted on by the House of Representatives. The trial took place during the third week in January, 1999.

The two articles concerned his sexual involvement with an intern, Monica Lewinsky. The first article stated that Clinton "willfully provided perjurious, false and misleading testimony to Special Prosecutor Kenneth Starr's grand jury on August 17, 1998."

The second impeachment article stated that Clinton "prevented, obstructed, and impeded the administration of justice," by advising Lewinsky to lie and give false testimony to a grand jury in the earlier Paula Jones sexual harassment suit.

President Clinton was acquitted on both articles with the vote following party lines. Under 50% of the Senators voted for conviction.

In the spring of 1999, Serbian strong man, President Slobodan Milosovic continued the "ethnic cleansing" policy that he began in Bosnia in 1997, by turning to the Yugoslavian province of Kosovo. His forces burned, killed, and drove out the ethnic Albanians across borders into Albania, Macedonia, and Montenegro, creating hundreds of thousands of refuges.

NATO forces led by the United States bombed Milosovic's forces and strategic buildings and supplies, with the purpose of bringing Milosovic to the point where he could no longer make war. It was a containment policy. In October, 2000, after Milosovic lost the election, he refused to leave. Citizens rioted and drove him out of office.

In April, 1999, Clinton became the first president to be cited by a Federal judge for contempt of court for "giving false, misleading, and evasive answers that were designed to obstruct the judicial process" in the Paula Jones harassment case.

On Friday, January 19, 2001, exiting President Clinton, in order to avoid a future indictment, reached an agreement with the independent council, admitting giving false testimony in the Lewinsky affair.

George W. Bush
43rd President (2001-)

The 6 feet tall George Walker Bush is a management style individual who views the leadership role of the president as a management position. He sees the role as one that establishes goals and objectives and then delegates responsible individuals to carry out the goals. He is low keyed about the assertion of authority, but will demand dedication and responsibility of the people he appoints.

Bush is a serious, yet gentle family man who can and often does assert himself when he wants things done according to a plan. He calls himself a compassionate conservative who believes that government is important as long as there is not too much of it in peoples' lives. He values individual initiative and feels that individuals can and should make decisions and accept responsibility for those decisions. He sees the presidency as a role to set an example of moral values and work related integrity.

Biography

George Walker Bush was born

on July 6, 1946, in New Haven, Conneticut, to George Bush, a future Texas oilman and the 41st president of the United States, and Barbara Pierce Bush.

In the 1950's and 1960's George W. grew up in Midland and Houston, Texas. His family was always in politics. His paternal grandfather Prescott had been a banker and a United States senator from Connecticut from 1952 to 1962. His father began his political career in 1966, representing the Houston area as a congressman.

In 1960, George W. attended San Jacinto Junior High School in Midland before entering Andover, a prep school in Massachusetts where his father had gone. Following graduation, Bush entered Yale where his one accomplishment was to be elected president of his fraternity. He graduated in 1968. With the Vietnam War on, George felt compelled to avoid hurting his father's political fortunes in his run for Congress. He enlisted in the Texas Air National Guard and spent almost a year learning to pilot F-102 interceptors in preparation for a tour in Vietnam. His unit never was called and his tour of duty ended in June, 1970.

In 1973, at age 27, Bush decided to attend the Harvard Business School and work toward a MBA degree. After graduation in 1975, Bush moved back to Midland, Texas.

In 1977, Bush entered the race for Congress from his district. He was joined by his wife of three months, Laura Welsh Bush, 31, a former Austin librarian. She and Bush had met on an arranged date three months before. They were married on November 5, 1977. Twin daughters were born in 1981. The Bushes spent 1978 campaigning for Congress. Conservative Bush lost the 1978 election to a conservative Democrat, Kent Hance.

When the Iranian oil crisis occurred and the need to find oil in this country grew, George W. was in the forefront establishing his company Arbusto, which is Spanish for bush. Later he renamed his company Bush Exploration Oil and Gas Company, which researched mineral and land records. He eventually merged with Spectrum Company and became its president. By the 1980's the oil industry declined, Spectrum was bought out by Harken Energy Company, bringing a large profit to Bush while he remained a consultant with the company.

In 1987 Bush moved to Washington to help his father in his successful run for the presidency.

After the 1988 election, George W. returned to Dallas, Texas, where he wanted to get into a new business. He, along with other local investors, bought the Texas Rangers baseball team. He owned only 5% of the franchise, but became the managing partner and involved himself in the day to day operation of the team. He became the spokesman for the partners and was seen at the ballpark almost daily, mingling with fans. He served in that position until he was elected Governor of Texas on November 8, 1994. He defeated Ann Richards and became only the second Republican governor since Reconstruction.

Beginning in 1999, Bush entered the primaries and garnished enough support to easily win the nomination at the Republican National Convention in 2000.

Presidential Campaign-2000

Campaign 2000 began with fiercely fought primaries in both the Republican and Democratic parties. Democrat Vice-President Al Gore was strongly challenged by Senator Bill Bradley. Governor George W. Bush, the front runner for the Republicans, locked-up in a free-for-all battle with Senator John McCain.

Following the nationwide primaries, both Al Gore and George W. Bush went to their respective National Nominating Conventions with enough delegates to be nominated on the first ballot.

The 2000 presidential campaign was totally different from recent presidential campaigns. There were few if any personal attacks between the candidates. For the first time in the past three or four campaigns, issues that were important to the voters and the country were addressed directly. One of the issues was use of the projected budget surplus in the years ahead. Another issue that voters felt important was the need to provide a program to help senior citizens with payments for needed prescription drugs. The saving of Medicare for future retirees and medical costs for long term illnesses was another issue. Finally, Bush proposed an income tax revision that would make the income tax a simpler and more equitable one. He proposed a tax cut for all taxpayers by bringing percentage equity to all tax brackets.

Gore accused Bush of overspending the surplus and Bush of returning tax money to the rich. Bush maintained that it was unfair to single out one group and all who pay taxes should receive a tax cut. Bush maintained that Gore's added programs involved more Federal government intervention into peoples' lives and making decisions for them instead of allowing them to make decisions for themselves.

The three debates prior to the election helped to define both candidates who were within one or two percentage points of one another. It projected the 2000 election to be one of the closest in years.

Presidential Election-2000

After weeks of court challenges, long nights and days of uncertainty as Florida poll workers counted and recounted ballots, or partial ballots, and tried to decide a voter's intent as they scrutinized thousands of ballots, the Supreme Court of the United States ended the marathon. After 36 days, the election was settled on a 5 to 4 decision. It declared that the question of recounting ballots was too spurious and not done with any set procedure. It stopped Al Gore from having the votes in four primarily Democratic Florida counties totally recounted. The result was that the certification on November 26 of George W. Bush as the winner of Florida's 25 electoral votes was final and made him the president-elect.

The final results of the 200 presidential election gave Vice-President Al Gore 50,158,094 (50%) to George W. Bush's 49,820,518 (49.8%), a difference of 337,576 votes nationally or .03% of the votes cast.

Bush won 30 states and 271 electoral votes to Gore's winning in 20 states and the District of Columbia and 267 electoral votes.

The confusion and uncertainty began on election night, November 7. Television analyses correctly called that Florida would be the state to determine the winner of the presidency. Early in the evening they projected Bush as the winner. They were so convincing that early the next morning, Gore called Bush and conceded the election.

Only an hour later at 3:30 a.m. on Wednesday, Gore again called Bush and stated that circumstances had changed and that he retracted his concession.

In the days ahead, discoveries of voting irregularities, including uncounted ballots, brought calls for manual recounts of the ballots. Both Bush and Gore went into publicity mode, Bush low-keyed and presidential and Gore in battle mode and directing the battle for votes from his Vice-Presidential office. Each candidate had a team of lawyers who prepared strategies for all possible contingencies.

Ten days after the election, Florida Secretary of State Katherine Harris said she could not certify the hand recounts that had already begun because the recounts could not be completed before the legal deadline. Gore went on the offensive and made a nation-wide address that he was willing to abide by a statewide recount. Bush refused the offer. A Florida judge refused to include the recounted votes. Bush's team was ecstatic. Gore indicated he would appeal to the Florida Supreme Court. On November 21, they ruled that the recounts could continue. The Bush team felt that the rules had been changed by the court and the Democratic dominated county boards. Bush decided to appeal to the U. S. Supreme Court.

On November 26, Harris certified Bush the winner in Florida by 537 votes, but it was not over. The absentee ballots were challenged and Gore picked up votes.

On December 4, the U. S. Supreme Court sent the case back to Florida for clarification. Florida Judge Sauls rejected Gore's protest of the certified election result. The Florida Supreme Court overturned his ruling and ordered a statewide recount.

The U. S. Supreme Court halted the recount and heard the case for Gore. On Tuesday, December 11, their 5 to 4 decision rejected Gore's appeal and remanded the case back to the Florida court with the admonition that the recounts did not follow a predetermined set of guidelines. The December 13th decision ended the recount process, solidified Bush's narrow lead and made certification of Bush's Florida electoral vote stand up. Gore conceded the election and ordered the recount stopped.

George W. Bush was the president-elect, making the Bushes the first father and son president combination since John and Quincy Adams in 1824.

The U. S. population was reported at 281,421,906, up 13.2 percent from 1990. The population was shifting from the North and Midwest to the South and West.

Presidents

#	President	Party	Years
1	George Washington	N Pt(F)	1789-1797
2	John Adams	Fed.	1797-1801
3	Thomas Jefferson	D-Rep.	1801-1809
4	James Madison	D-Rep	1809-1817
5	James Monroe	D-Rep	1817-1825
6	John Quincy Adams	D-Rep	1825-1829
7	Andrew Jackson	Dem.	1829-1837
8	Martin Van Buren	Dem.	1837-1841
9	William Henry Harrison	Whig	1841
10	John Tyler	Whig	1841-1845
11	James K. Polk	Dem.	1845-1849
12	Zackery Taylor	Whig	1849-1850
13	Millard Fillmore	Whig	1850-1853
14	Franklin Pierce	Dem.	1853-1857
15	James Buchanan	Dem.	1857-1861
16	Abraham Lincoln	Rep.	1861-1865
17	Andrew Johnson	Rep.(D)	1865-1869
18	Ulysses Grant	Rep.	1869-1877
19	Rutherford B. Hayes	Rep.	1877-1881
20	James A. Garfield	Rep.	1881
21	Chester A. Arthur	Rep.	1881-1885
22	Grover Cleveland	Dem.	1885-1889
23	Benjamin Harrison	Rep.	1889-1893
24	Grover Cleveland	Dem.	1893-1897
25	William McKinley	Rep.	1897-1901
26	Theodore Roosevelt	Rep.	1901-1909
27	William H. Taft	Rep.	1909-1913
28	Woodrow Wilson	Dem.	1913-1921
29	Warren G. Harding	Rep	1921-1923
30	Calvin Coolidge	Rep.	1923-1929
31	Herbert Hoover	Rep.	1929-1933
32	Franklin D. Roosevelt	Dem.	1933-1945
33	Harry S. Truman	Dem.	1945-1953
34	Dwight D. Eisenhower	Rep.	1953-1961
35	John F. Kennedy	Dem.	1961-1963
36	Lyndon B. Johnson	Dem.	1963-1969
37	Richard M. Nixon	Rep.	1969-1974
38	Gerald R. Ford	Rep.	1974-1977
39	James (Jimmy) E. Carter	Dem.	1977-1981
40	Ronald Reagan	Rep.	1981 -1989
41	George Bush	Rep.	1989-1993

Vice-Presidents

Vice-President	Party	Year
John Adams	Fed.	1789
Thomas Jefferson	D-Rep	1797
Aaron Burr	D-Rep	1801
George Clinton	D-Rep	1805
George Clinton	D-Rep	1809
Elbridge Gerry	D-Rep	1813
Daniel Tompkins	D-Rep	1817
John C. Calhoun	D-Rep	1825
John C. Calhoun	D-Rep	1829
Martin Van Buren	Dem.	1833
Richard M. Johnson	Dem.	1837
John Tyler	Whig	1841
George M. Dallas	Dem.	1845
Millard Fillmore	Whig	1849
William R. King	Dem.	1853
John C. Breckinridge	Dem.	1857
Hannible Hamlin	Rep.	1861
Schuyler Colfax	Rep.	1869
Henry Wilson	Rep.	1873
William A. Wheeler	Rep.	1877
Chester A. Arthur	Rep.	1881
Thomas A. Hendricks	Dem.	1885
Levi P. Morton	Rep.	1889
Adai E. Stevenson	Dem.	1893
Garret A. Hobart	Rep.	1897
Theodore Roosevelt	Rep.	1901
Charles W. Fairbanks	Rep.	1905
James S. Sherman	Rep.	1909
Thomas R. Marshall	Dem.	1913
Calvin Coolidge	Rep.	1921
Charles D. Dawes	Rep.	1925
Charles Curtus	Rep.	1929
John Nance Garner	Dem.	1933
Henry A. Wallace	Dem.	1941
Harry S. Truman	Dem.	1945
Alben W. Barkley	Dem.	1949
Richard M. Nixon	Rep.	1953
Lyndon B. Johnson	Dem.	1961
Hubert H. Humphrey	Dem	1965
Spiro T. Agnew	Rep.	1969
Gerald R. Ford	Rep.	1973
Nelson A. Rockefeller	Rep.	1974
Walter F. Mondale	Dem.	1977
George Bush	Rep.	1981
Dan Quayle	Rep.	1989

42 William J. Clinton   Dem.   1993-2001   Al Gore   Dem.   1993
43 George W. Bush   Rep.   2001   Richard Cheney   Rep.   2001

Presidential Elections by State and Party 1789-1848

STATES	1789	1792	1796	1800	1804	1808	1812	1816	1820	1824	1828	1832	1836	1840	1844	1848
Alabama									D-R	D-R	D	D	D	D	D	D
Alaska																
Arizona																
Arkansas													D	D	D	D
California																
Colorado																
Connecticut	F	F	F	F	F	F	F	F	D-R	D-R	NR	NR	D	W	W	W
Delaware	F	F	F	F	F	F	F	F	D-R	D-R	NR	NR	W	W	W	W
District of Col.																
Florida																W
Georgia	F	F	D-R	D-R	D-R	D-R	D-R	D-R	D-R	D-R	D	D	W	W	D	W
Hawaii																
Idaho																
Illinois									D-R	D-R	D	D	D	D	D	D
Indiana								D-R	D-R	D-R	D	D	W	W	D	D
Iowa																D
Kansas																
Kentucky		F	D-R	D-R	D-R	D-R	D-R	D-R	D-R	D-R	D-R	ND	W	W	W	W
Louisiana							D-R	D-R	D-R	D-R	D	D	D	W	D	W
Maine									D-R	D-R	ND	D	D	W	D	W
Maryland	F	F	F	F	D-R	D-R	D-R	D-R	D-R	D-R	ND	ND	W	W	W	W
Massachusetts	F	F	F	F	D-R	F	F	F	D-R	D-R	ND	ND	W	W	W	W
Michigan													D	W	D	D
Minnesota																
Mississippi									D-R	D-R	D	D	D	W	D	D
Missouri									D-R	D-R	D	D	D	D	D	D
Montana																
Nebraska																
Nevada																
New Hampshire	F	F	F	F	D-R	F	F	D-R	D-R	D-R	ND	D	D	D	D	D
New Jersey	F	F	F	F	D-R	D-R	F	D-R	D-R	D-R	ND	D	W	W	W	W
New Mexico																
New York		F	F	D-R	D-R	D-R	F	D-R	D-R	D-R	D	D	D	W	D	W
North Carolina		F	D-R	D-R	D-R	D-R	D-R	D-R	D-R	D-R	D	D	D	W	W	W
North Dakota																
Ohio					D-R	D-R	D-R	D-R	D-R	D-R	D	D	W	W	W	D
Oklahoma																
Oregon																
Pennsylvania	F	F	D-R	D-R	D-R	D-R	D-R	D-R	D-R	D-R	D	D	D	W	D	W
Rhode Island		F	F	F	D-R	F	F	D-R	D-R	D-R	ND	ND	D	W	W	W
South Carolina	F	F	D-R	D-R	D-R	D-R	D-R	D-R	D-R	D-R	D	ID	D	D	R	R
South Dakota																
Tennessee			D-R	D-R	D-R	D-R	D-R	D-R	D-R	D-R	D	D	W	W	W	W
Texas																D
Utah																
Vermont		F	F	F	D-R	D-R	D-R	D-R	D-R	D-R	NR	AM	W	W	W	W
Virginia		F	D-R	D-R	D-R	D-R	D-R	D-R	D-R	D-R	D	D	D	D	D	D
Washington																
West Virginia																
Wisconsin																D
Wyoming																

F-Federalist   D-R-Democrat-Republican   ND-National Democrat   W-Whig
NR-National Republican   AM-Anti-Mason   ID-Independent Democrat

Presidential Elections by State and Party 1852-1912

States	1852	1856	1860	1864	1868	1872	1876	1880	1884	1888	1892	1896	1900	1904	1908	1912
Alabama	D	D	ND	C	R	D	D	D	D	D	D	D	D	D	D	D
Alaska																
Arizona																D
Arkansas	D	D	ND	C	R	O	D	D	D	D	D	D	D	D	D	D
California	D	D	R	R	R	R	R	D	R	R	D	R	R	R	R	P
Colorado							R	R	R	R	P	D	D	R	D	D
Connecticut	D	R	R	R	R	R	D	R	D	D	D	R	R	R	R	D
Delaware	D	D	ND	D	D	R	D	D	D	D	D	R	R	R	R	D
District of Col.																
Florida	D	D	ND	C	D	D	D	D	D	D	D	D	D	D	D	D
Georgia	D	D	ND	C	D	D	D	D	D	D	D	D	D	D	D	D
Hawaii																
Idaho											P	D	D	R	R	D
Illinois		D	R	R	R	R	R	R	R	R	D	R	R	R	R	D
Indiana	D	D	R	R	R	R	D	R	D	R	D	R	R	R	R	D
Iowa	D	R	R	R	R	R	R	R	R	R	R	R	R	R	R	D
Kansas				R	R	R	R	R	R	R	P	D	R	R	R	D
Kentucky	W	D	CU	D	D	D	D	D	D	D	D	R	D	D	D	D
Louisiana	D	D	ND	C	R	O	D	D	D	D	D	D	D	D	D	D
Maine	D	R	R	R	R	R	R	R	R	R	R	R	R	R	R	D
Maryland	D	W	ND	R	D	D	D	D	D	D	D	R	D	R	D	D
Massachusetts	W	R	R	R	R	R	R	R	R	R	R	R	R	R	R	D
Michigan	D		R	R	R	R	R	R	R	R	R	R	R	R	R	P
Minnesota		D	ND	C	C	R	D	D	D	D	D	D	R	R	R	P
Mississippi	D	D	D	R	R	D	D	D	D	D	D	D	D	D	D	D
Missouri	D	D	D	R	R	D	D	D	D	D	D	D	D	R	R	D
Montana											R	D	D	R	R	D
Nebraska				R	R	R	R	D	R	R	P	D	R	R	D	D
Nevada		R	R	R	R	R	R	R	R	R	P	D	D	R	D	D
New Hampshire	D	R	R	R	R	R	R	R	R	R	R	R	R	R	R	R
New Jersey	D	D	R	D	D	R	D	D	D	D	D	R	R	R	R	D
New Mexico																D
New York	D	R	R	R	D	R	D	R	D	R	D	R	R	R	R	D
North Carolina	D	D	ND	C	R	R	D	D	D	D	D	D	D	D	D	D
North Dakota											R	R	R	R	R	D
Ohio	D	R	R	R	R	R	R	R	R	R	R	R	R	R	R	R
Oklahoma															D	D
Oregon						D	R	R	R	R	R	R	R	R	R	D
Pennsylvania	D	D	R	R	R	R	R	R	R	R	R	R	R	R	R	P
Rhode Island	D	R	R	R	R	R	R	R	R	R	R	R	R	R	R	D
South Carolina	D	D	ND	C	R	R	R	D	D	D	D	D	R	R	R	P
South Dakota											R	D	R	R	R	P
Tennessee	W	D	CU	C	R	D	D	D	D	D	D	D	D	D	D	D
Texas	D	D	ND	C	C	D	D	D	D	D	D	D	D	D	D	D
Utah												D	R	R	R	R
Vermont	W	R	R	R	R	R	R	R	R	R	R	R	R	R	R	R
Virginia	D	D	CU	C	C	R	D	D	D	D	D	D	D	D	D	D
Washington											R	D	R	R	R	P
West Virginia				R	R	R	D	D	D	D	D	R	R	R	R	D
Wisconsin	D	R	R	R	R	R	R	R	R	R	D	R	R	R	R	D
Wyoming											R	D	R	R	R	D

W-Whig   ND-National Democrat   P-People's   C-Confederate state Did not vote
CU-Constitutional Union   O-Electoral College refused to count votes

Presidential Elections by State and Party 1916-1968

States	1916	1920	1924	1928	1932	1936	1940	1944	1948	1952	1956	1960	1964	1968
Alabama	D	D	D	D	D	D	D	D	SR	D	D	D	D	AI
Alaska												R	D	R
Arizona	D	R	R	R	D	D	D	D	D	R	R	D	R	R
Arkansas	D	D	D	D	D	D	D	D	D	D	D	D	D	AI
California	D	R	R	R	D	D	D	D	D	R	R	D	D	R
Colorado	D	R	R	R	D	D	R	R	D	R	R	D	D	R
Connecticut	R	R	R	R	D	D	D	D	R	R	R	D	D	D
Delaware	R	R	R	R	R	D	D	D	R	R	R	D	D	R
District of Col.														
Florida	D	D	D	D	D	D	D	D	D	R	R	D	D	R
Georgia	D	D	D	D	D	D	D	D	D	D	D	D	R	AI
Hawaii												D	D	
Idaho	D	R	R	R	D	D	D	D	D	R	R	D	D	R
Illinois	R	R	R	R	D	D	D	D	D	R	R	D	D	R
Indiana	R	R	R	R	D	D	R	R	R	R	R	D	D	R
Iowa	R	R	R	R	D	D	R	R	D	R	R	D	D	R
Kansas	D	R	R	R	D	D	R	R	R	R	R	D	D	R
Kentucky	D	D	R	R	D	D	D	D	D	D	R	D	D	R
Louisiana	D	D	D	D	D	D	D	D	SR	D	R	D	R	AI
Maine	R	R	R	R	R	R	R	R	R	R	R	D	D	D
Maryland	D	R	R	R	D	D	D	D	R	R	R	D	D	D
Massachusetts	R	R	R	D	D	D	D	D	D	R	R	D	D	D
Michigan	R	R	R	R	D	D	R	D	R	R	R	D	D	D
Minnesota	R	R	R	R	D	D	D	D	D	R	R	D	D	D
Mississippi	D	D	D	D	D	D	D	D	SR	D	D	D	R	AI
Missouri	D	R	R	R	D	D	D	D	D	R	D	D	D	R
Montana	D	R	R	R	D	D	D	D	D	R	R	D	D	R
Nebraska	D	R	R	R	D	D	R	R	R	R	R	D	D	R
Nevada	D	R	R	R	D	D	D	D	D	R	R	D	D	R
New Hampshire	D	R	R	R	R	D	D	D	R	R	R	D	D	R
New Jersey	R	R	R	R	D	D	D	D	R	R	R	D	D	R
New Mexico	D	R	R	R	D	D	D	D	D	R	R	D	D	R
New York	R	R	R	R	D	D	D	D	R	R	R	D	D	D
North Carolina	D	D	D	R	D	D	D	D	D	D	D	D	D	R
North Dakota	D	R	R	R	D	D	R	R	R	R	R	D	D	R
Ohio	D	R	R	R	D	D	D	R	D	R	R	D	D	R
Oklahoma	D	D	D	R	D	D	D	D	D	R	R	D	D	R
Oregon	R	R	R	R	D	D	D	D	R	R	R	D	D	R
Pennsylvania	R	R	R	R	R	D	D	D	R	R	R	D	D	D
Rhode Island	R	R	R	D	D	D	D	D	D	R	R	D	D	D
South Carolina	D	D	D	D	D	D	D	D	SR	D	D	R	R	AI
South Dakota	R	R	R	R	D	D	D	R	R	R	R	D	D	R
Tennessee	D	R	D	R	D	D	D	D	D	R	R	D	D	R
Texas	D	D	D	R	D	D	D	D	D	R	R	D	D	D
Utah	D	R	R	R	D	D	D	D	D	R	R	D	D	R
Vermont	R	R	R	R	R	R	R	R	R	R	R	D	D	R
Virginia	D	D	D	R	D	D	D	D	D	R	R	D	D	R
Washington	D	R	R	R	D	D	D	D	D	R	R	D	D	D
West Virginia	R	R	R	R	D	D	D	D	D	D	R	D	D	D
Wisconsin	R	R	P	R	D	D	D	R	D	R	R	D	D	R
Wyoming	D	R	R	R	D	D	D	R	D	R	R	D	D	R

D-Democrat R-Republican SR-States Rights P-Progressive

Presidential Elections by State and Party 1972-2000

States	1972	1976	1980	1984	1988	1992	1996	2000
Alabama	R	D	R	R	R	R	R	R
Alaska	R	R	R	R	R	R	R	R
Arizona	R	R	R	R	R	R	D	R
Arkansas	R	D	R	R	R	D	D	R
California	R	R	R	R	R	D	D	D
Colorado	R	R	R	R	R	D	R	R
Connecticut	R	R	R	R	R	D	D	D
Delaware	R	D	R	R	R	D	D	D
District of Col.	D	D	D	D	D	D	D	D
Florida	R	D	R	R	R	R	D	R
Georgia	R	D	D	R	R	D	R	R
Hawaii	R	D	D	R	D	D	D	D
Idaho	R	R	R	R	R	R	R	R
Illinois	R	R	R	R	R	D	D	D
Indiana	R	R	R	R	R	R	R	R
Iowa	R	R	R	R	D	D	D	D
Kansas	R	R	R	R	R	R	R	R
Kentucky	R	D	R	R	R	D	D	R
Louisiana	R	D	R	R	R	D	D	R
Maine	R	R	R	R	R	D	D	D
Maryland	R	D	D	R	R	D	D	D
Massachusetts	D	D	R	R	D	D	D	D
Michigan	R	R	R	R	R	D	D	D
Minnesota	R	D	D	D	D	D	D	D
Mississippi	R	D	R	R	R	R	R	R
Missouri	R	D	R	R	R	D	D	R
Montana	R	R	R	R	R	D	R	R
Nebraska	R	R	R	R	R	R	R	R
Nevada	R	R	R	R	R	D	D	R
New Hampshire	R	R	R	R	R	D	D	R
New Jersey	R	R	R	R	R	D	D	D
New Mexico	R	R	R	R	R	D	D	D
New York	R	D	R	R	D	D	D	D
North Carolina	R	D	R	R	R	R	R	R
North Dakota	R	R	R	R	R	R	R	R
Ohio	R	D	R	R	R	D	D	R
Oklahoma	R	R	R	R	R	R	R	R
Oregon	R	R	R	R	D	D	D	D
Pennsylvania	R	D	R	R	R	D	D	D
Rhode Island	R	D	D	R	D	D	D	D
South Carolina	R	D	R	R	R	R	R	R
South Dakota	R	R	R	R	R	R	R	R
Tennessee	R	D	R	R	R	D	D	R
Texas	R	D	R	R	R	R	R	R
Utah	R	R	R	R	R	R	R	R
Vermont	R	R	R	R	R	D	D	D
Virginia	R	R	R	R	R	R	R	D
Washington	R	R	R	R	D	D	D	D
West Virginia	R	D	D	R	D	D	D	R
Wisconsin	R	D	R	R	D	D	D	D
Wyoming	R	R	R	R	R	R	R	R

D-Democratic R-Republican AI-American Independent

The First Ladies

The Roles of the First Ladies

Over the years the role of First Lady of the United States as the president's wife is called has changed. Each wife has defined her role as she saw fit. Some women have been almost reclusive, not enjoying the role of First Lady while others have wholeheartedly plunged into the role often in a political fashion.

The role of First Lady is one that the American public is much aware of and is concerned how the woman in that position carries out the role. First ladies are often criticized, looked up to for fashion, and setting a social clime. The public is aware of their conduct of family life, and in general, they are seen as representatives of American life.

It is a difficult role because often the wife of the president has never had such a great responsibility. Therefore, more often than not, the woman arriving in Washington as the president's wife comes unprepared for the public focus given her.

The early first ladies of the presidents were closely tied to the home. The first to break out into the public arena was Dolley Madison. She became the social leader of Washington with her parties and receptions. She served not only as the social leader during President Madison's term, but she was hostess for White House functions under President Jefferson when his daughter could not serve as hostess after the death of his wife.

Dolley even saw war at close range when she fled the White House moments before the British arrived and burned it. She was able to save the portrait of Washington before she fled.

Later there was "Lemonade Lucy" as Lucy Hayes, wife of Rutherford Hayes was derisively called because of her ban on alcohol in the White House. She was a simple, direct woman who loved children and established the White House Easter tradition of the egg roll on the lawn. She was the first to be called "First Lady." Prior to becoming First Lady, Lucy Hayes had served many months as comforter and nurse of Civil War woun-ded in order to be near her husband during his service in the Union army.

Youthful Frances Cleveland, married Grover Cleveland, 49, to become the youngest First Lady at age 21. Their marriage is the first and only presidential wedding to occur in the White House. Cleveland had been her guardian since her father had died when she was a teenager. He saw to her schooling and college education. Upon graduation, he proposed marriage and she accepted. She proved a brilliant hostess and the press made her a person of prominence. In later years she devoted much of her time to helping the poor.

No First Lady appears more outgoing and life engaging than Eleanor Roosevelt. Tall, awkward appearing, she strode through life with vigor and enthusiasm. To the polo-strickened President Franklin Roosevelt, Eleanor became his eyes, ears, and legs as she moved around in the world of politics and international relations, reporting back to him and advising him of actions to take. The shy, "ugly duckling," as Eleanor characterized herself, grew to be a self-assured and dynamic personality with a deep sense of social justice for all people. Her greatest service was her work as chairperson of the United Nations Commission on Human Rights.

Helen Taft knew what she wanted and that was for her husband, William Howard Taft, to become president. She worked constantly toward that end in much the same fashion as Hillary Rodham Clinton did for President Clinton. In similar fashion when their husbands became president, both participated to some extent in activities of the office. Hillary was appointed by President Clinton to head a committee to fashion a health care plan. Helen Taft would often sit in on cabinet meetings and participate in the discussions. After leaving the White House, she emersed herself in education, becoming dean of Byrn Mawr. It was Helen who was responsible for bringing the 3000 Japanese cherry trees from Japan in 1912. They are a Washington spectacular every spring.

Mrs. Edith Galt Wilson, President Wilson's second wife, took a more active role in her husband's life after he had a stroke. She filtered all correspondence and contacts with Wilson in the last year of his presidency. She decided what was important for him to see and what was not.

The appearance and use of the White House have always been the First Lady's concerns. Caroline Harrison, wife of Benjamin Harrison, saw the Executive Mansion in 1889, as too crowded and in need of enlargement. She immediately had plans drawn up for the renovation. She was given $35,000 to redo the present structure's interior. This she did, adding bathrooms. She had the first Christmas tree put up in the White House in 1889. It was Caroline Harrison who started the White House china collection for future generations.

Jacqueline Kennedy, wife of John Kennedy, also took on the task of renovating and redecorating the interior of the White House. The completed redecoration became a television tour of the White House hosted by Mrs. Kennedy. Jacqueline also inspired the fashion world which created the "Jackie" look in clothes and women's hats.

Her poise and calm dignity during the funeral of President Kennedy was an inspiration to people of the United States.

Quite the opposite experiences as First Ladies were women such as Lelita Tyler and Margaret Taylor. Neither was happy about her husband becoming president. Lelita was shy and retiring, became an invalid and remained out of public view. She died after two years as First Lady.

Margaret Taylor also refused to participate in White House functions and remained a recluse on the second floor. Her daughter, Mrs. Betty Bliss, acted as hostess.

Pat Nixon generally stayed out of the limelight, though she often went with President Nixon on foreign trips such as to China. She was responsible for raising millions of dollars to refurnish the White House with antiques.

Martha Washington enjoyed the privacy of Mount Vernon and reluctantly followed President Washington to New York and Philadelphia when he became president. She was hostess to many gatherings and receptions.

Another facet of a First Lady's life is her becoming a leader for a specific cause. This has become very prevalent since the 1980's and continues today. Women like Betty Ford established a drug rehabilitation foundation to help people with addiction. Barbara Bush organized and was head of the Barbara Bush Foundation for Family Literacy. Laura Bush, a former teacher and librarian, will continue with a reading program. Rosalynn Carter became involved with the Habitat for Humanity program with her husband, former President Carter. Lady Bird Johnson went on a crusade to beautify America with an extensive program of seeding wild flowers along the highways of America. Testimony to her program can be seen every spring in her state of Texas that is resplendent with the red Indian Paint Brush flower and Texas state flower, the Blue Bonnet. Other states have followed her leadership and planted acres of flowers along their highways.

Other First Ladies such as Mamie Eisenhower and Bess Truman believed that it was not their role or place to try to influence their husbands in the job as president. They remained aloof and simply had little contact with the press. They still fulfilled their roles as hostesses to White House functions and actively saw to White House affairs.

Many find just participating in the many social demands as White House hostess as well as overseeing the myriad aspects of White House life, enough. They have to prepare budgets, do correspondence, deal with their families, and oversee the many other minute details needed to run the White House.

Ida McKinley carried out these activities despite her subjectivity to seizures. Julia Grant oversaw elaborate dinners and receptions.

As each First Lady comes to be the hostess of the White House, she brings her ambitions and interests that are as varied as the personalities of the women. Some First Ladies are political and are active in their husband's job as president. Others bide their time until their husband is no longer in office.

It remains for each First Lady to define the position as she sees it. Americans expect the First Lady to act as hostess and as a feminine representative of the United States at home and abroad.

Facts About the First Ladies

Interesting and unusual facts about First Ladies:

Ann Harrison's life spanned the American Revolution, War of 1812, Mexican War, and the Civil War, yet she never lived in the White House. She was the wife of one president and the grandmother of another.

Louisa Adams was the only foreign born First Lady. John Quincy

Adams met her in London while on a diplomatic mission. Her father was an American consul to England.

Edith Wilson was the great-granddaughter (seven times removed) of Pocahontas.

Hillary Rodham Clinton is the only First Lady to run for and win public office. She is a Senator from New York.

Mamie Eisenhower and Abigail Adams are two First Ladies honored by an historical site.

Eleanor Roosevelt served the British monarchs, George VI and Queen Elizabeth, hot dogs at a picnic in Hyde Park on their 1939 visit. Her private retreat, Val Kill, is the now an historic site.

Helen Taft was the first First Lady to ride along with her husband down Pennsylvania Avenue to his inauguration .

Lucy Hayes forbid the use of alcohol in the White House and earned the nickname, Lemonade Lucy. Her full-length portrait commissioned by the Women's Temperance Association hangs in the White House.

Abigail Fillmore was a teacher and her oldest student was Millard Fillmore. Their love of books drew them together. As First Lady she established the first permanent library in the White House.

Anna Harrison did not travel to Washington with William Henry Harrison, but stayed in Indiana to make plans to become the First Lady. Harrison died before she could come to Washington so she never lived in the White House.

Because of their living in China for several years, both Herbert and Lou Hoover became proficient in Chinese and often conversed in the White House in Chinese to avert eavesdroppers.

Eleanor Roosevelt was the first First Lady to vote for president on Election Day, 1920. Her husband was running for vice-president. Later in 1942, she was the first First Lady to testify before a congressional committee.

Bess Truman was an excellent athlete. In school she won the shot put in a field event. She was a good tennis player.

Lucy Hayes had the Capitol egg roll for the children moved to the White House lawn.

Lucy Rutherford was the first First Lady to be a college graduate. She graduated with high honors from Ohio Wesleyan Women's College in 1880.

Hillary Rodham Clinton was a Republican and supported Barry Goldwater for President. The Vietnam War caused her to become a Democrat. In 1991, Mrs. Clinton was named one of "100 Most Influential Lawyers in America" by the *National Law Journal*. She is the first lawyer to be First Lady.

Lady Bird Johnson traveled over 200,000 miles promoting the improvement of America's landscape. She helped to gain passage of the Highway Beautification Act of 1965.

Nancy Reagan acted in 11 films. She met Ronald Reagan in 1949, when he was president of the Screen Actors Guild. They appeared together in the film, *Hell Cats of the Navy* (1957).

Dolley Payne Todd Madison

The First Ladies

Martha Dandridge Custis Washington
(1731-1802)
Marriage: January 6, 1759
Children: None

Abigail Smith Adams
(1744-1818)
Marriage: October 25, 1764
Children: Abigail Amelia, John Quincy, Susanna, Charles, Thomas Boyson

Patsy Jefferson Randolf
Jefferson's daughter was his official hostess

Dolley Payne Todd Madison
(1768-1849)
Marriage: September 15, 1794
Children: None

Elizabeth Kortright Monroe
(1768-1830)
Marriage: February 16, 1786
Children: Eliza Kortright, Maria Hester

Louisa Catherine Johnson Adams
(1775-1852)
Marriage: July 26, 1797
Children: George Washington, John, Charles Francis, Louisa Catherine

Rachel Donelson Robards Jackson
(1767-1828)
Marriage: August, 1791
Children: Andrew (Adopted)

Hannah Hoes Van Buren
(1783-1819)
Marriage: February 21, 1807
Children: Abraham, John, Martin, Smith Thompson

Anna Tuthill Symmes Harrison
(1775-1864)
Marriage: November 25, 1795
Children: Elizabeth, Bassett, John Cleves Symmes, Lucy Singleton, William Henry, John Scott, Benjamin, Mary Symmes, Carter Bassett Anna Tuthill, James Finley

Letitia Christian Tyler
(1790-1842)
Marriage: March 29, 1813
Children: Mary, Robert John, Letitia, Elizabeth, Anne Contessem Alice, Tazewell

Julia Gardiner Tyler
(1820-1889)
Marriage: June 26, 1844
Children: David Gardiner, John Alexander, Julie, Lachlan, Lyon Gardiner, Robert Fitzwalter, Pearl

Sarah Childress Polk
(1803-1891)

Marriage: January 1, 1824
Children: None

Margaret Mackall Smith Taylor
(1788-1852)
Marriage: June 21, 1810
Children: Anne Margaret Mackall, Sarah Knox, Octavia Pannill, Margaret Smith, Mary Elizabeth, Richard

Abigail Powers Fillmore
(1798-1853)
Marriage: February 5, 1826
Children: Millard Powers, Mary Abigail

Jane Means Appleton Pierce
(1806-1863)
Marriage: November 19, 1834
Children: Franklin, Frank Robert, Benjamin

Mary Todd Lincoln
(1818-1882)
Marriage: November 4, 1842
Children: Robert Todd, Edward Baker, William Wallace, Thomas

Eliza McCardle Johnson
(1810-1876)
Marriage: May 17, 1827
Children: Martha, Charles, Mary Robert, Andrew

Julia Boggs Dent Grant
(1826-1902)
Marriage: August 22, 1848
Children: Frederick Dent, Ulysses Simpson, Ellen Wrenshall, Jesse Root

Lucy Ware Webb Hayes
(1831-1889)
Marriage: December 30, 1852
Children: Birchard Austin, JamesWebb Cook,RutherfordPlatt, Joseph Thompson George Crook, Frances (Fanny), Scott Russell

Lucretia Rudolph Garfield
(1832-1918)
Marriage: November 11, 1858
Children: Eliza Arabella, Harry Augustus, James Rudolph, Mary, Irvin McDowell, Abram, Edward

Ellen Lewis Herndon Arthur
(1837-1880)
Marriage: October 25, 1859
Children: William Lewis Herndon, Chester Allen, Ellen Herndon

Frances Folsom Cleveland
(1864-1947)
Marriage: June 2, 1886
Children: Ruth, Esther, Marion, Richard Folsom, Francis Grover

Caroline Lavinia Scott Harrison
(1832-1892)
Marriage: October 20, 1853
Children: Russell Benjamin, Mary Scott

Ida Saxton McKinley
(1847-1907)
Marriage: January 25, 1871
Children: Katherine, Ida

Edith Kermit Carow Roosevelt
(1861-1948)
Marriage: December 2, 1886
Children: Theodore, Kermit, Ethel Carow, Archibald Bulloch, Quentin

Helen Herron Taft
(1861-1943)
Marriage: June 19, 1886
Children: Robert Alphonso, Helen Herron, Charles Phelps

Ellen Louise Axson Wilson
(1860-1914)
Marriage: June 24, 1885
Children: Margaret Woodrow, Jessie Woodrow, Eleanor Randolph

Edith Bolling Galt Wilson
(1872-1961)
Marriage: December 18, 1915
Children: None

Florence Kling DeWolf Harding
(1860-1924)
Marriage: July 8, 1891
Children: None

Grace Anna Goodhue Coolidge
(1879-1957)
Marriage: October 4, 1905
Children: John, Calvin

Lou Henry Hoover
(1875-1944)
Marriage: February 10, 1899
Children: Herbert Clark, Allan Henry

Anna Eleanor Roosevelt Roosevelt
(1884-1962)
Marriage: March 17, 1905
Children: Anna Eleanor, James, Franklin, Elliott, Franklin Delano, John Aspinwal

Elizabeth Virginia "Bess" Wallace Truman
(1885-1982)
Marriage: June 28, 1919
Children: Margaret

Marie "Mamie" Geneva Doud Eisenhower
(1896-1979)
Marriage: July 1, 1916
Children: Doud Dwight, John Sheldon Doud

Jacqueline Lee Bovier Kennedy
(1929-1994)
Marriage: September 12, 1953
Children: Caroline Bovier, John Fitzgerald Patrick

Claudia "Lady Bird" Alta Taylor Johnson (1912-)
Marriage: November 17, 1934

Children: Lynda Bird, Luci Barnes

Thelma Catherine Patricia Ryan Nixon
(1912-1993)
Marriage: June 21, 1940
Children: Patricia "Tricia," Julie

Elizabeth Bloomer Warren Ford
(1918-)
Marriage: October 15, 1948
Children: Michael Gerald, John "Jack"Gardner, Steven Meigs, Susan Elizabeth

Rosalynn Smith Carter
(1927-)
Marriage: July 7, 1946
Children: John "Jack"William , James "Chip" Earl, Donnel "Jeff" Jeffery, Amy Lynn

Anne Frances "Nancy" Robbins Davis Reagan
(1921-)
Marriage: March 4, 1952
Children: Patricia "Patti," Ann, Ronald "Skip" Prescott

Barbara Pierce Bush
(1925-)
Marriage: January 6, 1945
Children: George Walker, Robin, John "Jeb" Ellis, Neil Mallon, Marvin Pierce, Dorothy Pierce

Hillary Rodham Clinton
(1947-)
Marriage: October 11, 1975
Children: Chelsea

Laura Welsh Bush
(1946-)
Marriage: November 5, 1977
Children: Barbara and Jenna (Twins)

Presidential Libraries, National Historic Sites, Private Centers, and Homes of Presidents.

References:

Hyland, Pat <u>Presidential Libraries and Museums</u> Congressional Quarterly, Washington, DC 1995

<u>2000 World Almanac</u>, Primedia Reference, Inc., Mahwah, New Jersey

American Automobile Assoc. Tour books 1000 AAADrive, Heathrow, FL 32746-5063 Pamphlets, brochures, and materials

Presidential Libraries and Sites

Adams, John Quincy, Historical Society, Adams Academy Bldg., 8 Adams St., Quincy, MA 02169 (617) 773-1144

Adams, John, National Historic Site 1250 Hancock St., Quincy, MA 02169 (617)770-1175

Buchanan, James , See Wheatland

Bush Presidential Library and Museum, The, George, 1000 George Bush Drive, College Station, Texas 77843 (409)260-9552; Fax: 409-260-9557; E-Mail: library@bush.nara.gov Web: www.csdl.tamu.edu/bushlib

Coolidge, Calvin Plymouth Notch Historic District, Plymouth, VT 05056

Carter Library, The Jimmy, One Copenhill Ave., Atlanta, Georgia 30307 (404) 331-3942; Fax:404-7830-2215; E-Mail: library@carter.nara.gov

Carter, Jimmy, National Historic Site, P.O. Box 392 100 Main St., Plains, GA 31780-0392 (912) 824-3413

Coolidge Birthplace, Calvin, Plymouth Notch Historic District-Plymouth, Vermont

Eisenhower Center, The Dwight D. , 200 E. 4th St., Abilene, Kansas 67410 (785) 263-4751; Fax: 816-833-4368; E Mail: library@eisenhower.nara.gov

Eisenhower, Dwight National Historic Site Gettysburg, PA 17325 (717) 338-9114 or 334-4474

Ford Library, The Gerald R. , 1000 Beal Ave. , Ann Arbor, Michigan 48109-2114 (313) 741-2218; Fax: 734-741-2341; E-Mail: library@fordlib.nara.gov

Ford Museum, The Gerald R., 303 Pearl St NW, Grand Rapids, MI 49504 (616) 451-9263

Grant Home, Ulysses S., 908 3rd St., Galena, IL 61036 (815) 777-0248

Harding, Warren , The President Harding Home and Museum 380 Mount Vernon Ave., Marion, OH 43302 (740) 387-9630

Harrison Home, President Benjamin, 1230 N. Delaware St., Indianapolis, IN (317) 631-1898

Hayes Presidential Center, The Rutherford B., Spiegel Grove, 1337 Hayes Ave., Fremont, Ohio 43420 (419) 332-2081 (800) 998-7737

Hoover National Historic Site, The Herbert, P.O. Box 488, West Branch, Iowa 53258 (319) 643-5301 Fax 319-643-5825 E-Mail: library@hoover.nara.gov

Jackson, Andrew, The Hermitage (Andrew Jackson's home, tomb of Andrew and Rachel Jackson) Hermitage, Tennessee 37076 (615) 889-2941

Johnson, Andrew, National Historic Site , College & Depot Sts., Greenville, TN 37743 (423) 638-3551

Johnson Library, The Lyndon B., 2313 Red River Street, Austin, Texas 78705 (512) 482-5137; Fax: 512-478-9104; E-Mail: library@Johnson.nara.gov

Kennedy, John, National Historic Site 83 Beals St., Brookline, MA 02446 (617) 566-7937

Kennedy Library, The John F., James Columbia Point, Boston, Massachusetts 02125 (785) 263-4751 http://www.cs.umb.edu/jfklibrary/museum.htm

Madison Museum , James 129 Caroline St., Orange, VA 22960 (703) 672-1776

Monroe Historic Fredericksburg Foundation, Inc.,James 129 Caroline St., Fredericksburg, VA 22401 (703) 371-4504

Monroe Museum and Memorial Library, James, 908 Charles Street, Fredericksburg, VA 22401 (540) 654-1043 The largest collect of Monroe materials in the United States

Pierce, Franklin, Homestead National Historic Landmark, Hillsborough, NH 03244 (603) 478-3165

Pierce Manse, Franklin 14 Penacook St., Concord, NH (603) 225-2068 or 224-7668

Polk Home,The James K., 301 W. 7th. Street, P.O. Box 741, Columbia, Tennessee 38401 (615) 388-2354

Polk, James K., Memorial State Historic Site, Pineville, NC (704) 889-7145

Lincoln Birthplace National Historic Site, Hodgenville, KY 42748 (502) 358-3137

Lincoln's Home National Historic Site, 8th. & Jackson St., Springfield, IL (217) 492-4241

Lincoln's Tomb State Historic Site, Oak Ridge Cemetery, Springfield , IL (217) 782-2717

Lincoln's New Salem Historic Site, Petersburg,IL (217) 632-4000 or 632-5440

Mount Vernon, Washington, DC. (Washington's home) (703) 780-2000 or (703) 799-8697

Monticello, Charlottesville, VA 22902 (Jefferson's Home) (804) 984-9800 V. Center (804) 977-1783

Nixon Library and Birthplace, The Richard M. 18001 Yorba Linda Boulevard, Yorba Linda, California 92686 (714) 993-3393; Fax: 714-528-0544; Fax: stedman@chapman.edu Web: http://www.nixonfoundation.org

Presidential Museum,The, 622 North Lee, Odessa, Texas 79761 (915) 332-7123 Museum on the office of the President

Reagan Presidential Library, The Ronald 40 Presidential Drive, Simi Valley, California 93065 (805) 522-8444; Fax: 805-522-9621; E-Mail: library@reagan.nara.gov

Roosevelt, Franklin Little White House State Historic Site, Warm Springs, GA 31830 (706) 655-5870

Roosevelt Library and Museum, The Franklin D. 511 Albany Post Road, Hyde Park, New York 12538 (914) 229-8114; Fax 914-229-0872; E-Mail: library@roosevelt.nara.gov

Roosevelt Memorial, Franklin Delano, West Potomac Park , Washington, D. C. (202) 619-7222 (800) 337-8474 hhtp//www.academic.marist.edu/fdr/

Roosevelt , Theodore   Birthplace National Historic Site,   28th E 20th St., Buffalo, NY 10003   (212) 260-1616

Roosevelt, Theodore   Sagamore Hill National Historical Site, Oyster Bay, NY 11771 (516) 922-4447

Taft, William Howard   National Memorial Site   2038 Auburn Ave.   Cincinatti, OH 45219 (513) 684-3262

Taft Museum, William H.   316 Pike St., Cincinatti, OH 45215 (513) 241-0343

Tyler, John, Home of President   Sherwood Forest Plantation, P. O. Box 8, 14502 John Tyler Memorial Highway, Charles City, VA   23030   (804) 829-5377   Fax (804) 829-2947 http://www.sherwoodforest.org

Truman Library and Museum, The Harry S. 500 W. U. S. Highway 24 , Independence, Missouri 64050 (816) 833-1400; Fax: 816-833-4368; E-Mail: library@truman.nara.gov

Truman, Harry National Historical Site, Delaware St., Independence, MO   (816) 254-9929

Truman, Harry S. Birthplace State Historical Site 1009 Truman St., Lamar, MO 64759 (417) 682-2279

Van Buren , Martin   National Historical Site Kinderhook, NY 12106 (518) 758-9689

Washington, DC
    Franklin Roosevelt Memorial
    Jefferson Memorial (202) 426-6821
    Lincoln Memorial (202)426-6895
    Theodore Roosevelt Island, McLean, VA (703) 285-2598
    Washington Monument (202) 426-6841

Washington, George   Headquarters State Historical Site   Liberty & Washington Sts. Newburgh, NY (914) 562-1195

Wheatland (Historic Mansion of James Buchanan) 1120 Marietta Ave.,Lancaster, PA 17603 (717) 392-8721 w ww.wheatland. org

Wilson Birthplace and Museum, Woodrow 18-24 N. Coalter and Frederick Sts., Staunton, VA 24401 (540) 885-0897 (888) 496-6376

Rutherford Hayes Home, Fremont, Ohio

Bibliography

<u>American Headlines Year by Year</u>   Calvin D. Linton, Ph.D. Editor; Walter A. Payne,Ph.D. Thomas Nelson Publishers, New York, 1985

Atkins, Ollie <u>The White House Years</u> Playboy Press Chicago 1977

<u>American Presidents, The,</u> Golier Inc. Danbury , CN, 1992

Anderson, Judith <u>William Howard Taft: An Intimate History</u> W. W. Norton & Comp   Axelrod, Dr. Alan and Charles Phillips

<u>What Every American Should Know About American History</u>   Bob Evans, Inc. Holbrook, MA   1992

Barzman, Sol <u>The First Ladies</u> Cowles Book Company, Inc., New York

Boller, Jr., Paul F. <u>Presidential Campaigns,</u> Oxford University Press New York 1984

Burner, David <u>Herbert Hoover: A Public Life</u>   Alfred A. Knopf   New York 1979<u>American Presidents</u> Golier Inc. Danbury , CN, 1992

Caroli, Betty Boyd <u>Inside the White House</u> Canopy Books New York 1992

<u>Choosing the President</u> League of Women Voters 1968

<u>Congress and the Nation</u> Vol. IX 1993-1996 Congressional Quarterly Inc. Washington, D. C. 1998

DeGregorio, William A., <u>The Complete Book of U. S. Presidents</u> Random House New York   1993

Ferrell, Robert H. <u>Choosing Truman: The Democratic Convention of 1944</u> University of Missouri Press, Columbia, 1994

Frank, Sid and Arden Davis Melick <u>The Presidents Tidbits & Trivia</u> Greenwich House New York 1984

Freidel, Frank   <u>The Presidents of the United States of America</u> White House Historical Association Washington, D. C. 1969

Freidel, Frank   <u>Our Country's Presidents</u>   National Geographic Society,Washington D.C. 1966

Garraty, John <u>The American Nation</u> Harper & Row, New York 1971

Goodwin, Doris K. <u>No Ordinary Time: Franklin and Eleanor Roosevelt: Home Front in World War II</u> Simon & Schuster New York 1994

Graff, Henry F. Editor <u>The Presidents: A Reference History</u> Simon & Schuster Macmillan, New York 1997

Hillman, William <u>Mr. President</u> Farrar, Straus and Young New York 1952

Jensen, Malcolm C. <u>America in Time</u> Hougton Miffllin Co., Boston, 1977

Kane, Joseph Nathan <u>Facts About the Presidents</u> H. W. Wilson Co. New York 1989

Kunhardt, Jr., Philip, Philip B, Kunhar dt III, Peter W. Kundhardt <u>The American President</u> Riverhead Books, New York, 1999

Lorant, Stefan <u>The Glorious Burden: The American Presidency</u> Harper

& Row, New York 1968

McDonald, Forrest The American Presidency University of Kansas Press 1994

Morris, Richard B., Ed. Encyclopedia of American History Harper & Brothers, New York 1953

Parmet, Herbert S., Richard Nixon and His America Konecky & Koneckym New York 1990

Peare, Catherine Owens The Herbert Hoover Story Crowell Co. 1966

Presidents, The 2 Vols., American Heritage Publishing Co. 1968

Presidency, The, American Heritage Publishing Co. 1968

Presidential Elections-1789-1996 Congressional Quarterly Inc. Washington, D. C. 1997

Remini, Robert V. Andrew Jackson Twayne Publishers New York 1966

Shields-West, Eileen World Book Almanac of Presidential Campaigns World Almanac New York 1992

Shepherd, Jack The Adams Chronicles Little, Brown and Co. Boston 1975

Newsweek November 20, 2000 Pp.10-38; November 27,2000 Pp.30-41; December 4, 2000 Pp. 20-26, 28-34; December 11, 2000 Pp. 26-43; December 25, 2000 Pp.28-37

Time June 21, 1999 Pp.24-31; November 6, 2000 Pp.48-56; November 27, 2000 Pp.28-40; December 4, 2000 Pp. 30-35; December 11, 2000 Pp. 42-51

U.S. News October 2, 2000 Pp. 20-6; November 20, 2000 Pp. 22-35; November 27, 2000 Pp. 24-33

USA Today "An overtime election: 36-day saga" Pp. 8A-9A

Wisconsin State Journal December 14, 2000; December 20, 2000

White, Theodore H., The Making of the President 1960, Atheneum Publishers, New York 1961

Whitney, David C., The American Presidents 8th. Edition, Guild America Books, Garden City, New York 1993

World Almanac 2000 Primedia Reference, Inc. New Jersey, 1999

Photo Credits

W. Ehlert Pp. 13, 25, 27, 52, 199; W. Ehlert Collection Pp. 27, 31, 35, 104, 118, 122, 125, 129, 151, 190, 197; 199; Library of Congress Pp. 139, 163; Messages and Papers of the Presidents Pp. 13, 27, 35, 42, 45, 48, 53, 56, 58, 61, 64, 67, 70, 73, 77, 82, 85, 89, 92, 95, 98, 101, 106, 110, 114; P.133 Franklin Roosevelt Library; P. 143 Dwight D. Eisenhower Library; P. 148 John F. Kennedy Library; P. 155 Richard Nixon Library; P.160 Gerald Ford Library; P. 166 Ronald Reagan Library; P. 171 George Bush Presidential Library; P.176 White House; P.181 George W. Bush

Index

Order Form

Presidents of the United States: America's Heritage $16.95 plus $2.50 for
    postage and handling. $2.00 per book postage for additional copies.

America's Heritage: Capitols of the United States $10.95 plus $2.00 for
    postage and handling. $1.75 per book postage for additional copies.

Please send _____copy(ies) of **Presidents of the United States: America's**
Heritage

Please send _____copy(ies) of **America's Heritage: Capitols of the United**
States

Combination Order: one copy each book....$25 plus $3 postage.

Enclosed is a ___ check or ___money order. **Send no cash.**

        No. of copies Presidents_____@$16.95 = _____
                    Postage & Handling   _____
        No. of copies Capitols   _____ @$10.95   _____
                    Postage & Handling   _____
        Combination-1 Copy each book @ $25.00 _____
                    Postage & Handling   _____
        Wisconsin residents add 5% sales tax   _____

                    Total Enclosed   _____

Send order to: Willis J. Ehlert
        State House Publishing
        4022 Paunack Ave.
        Madison, WI   53711-1625

Discounts on four or more books. Call 608-233-3012 for information.

America's Heritage: Capitols of the United States

Learn more about our nation's capitols. All states capitols are covered plus our nation's National Capitol. Each is pictured with a large black and white photo plus many photos of details of the capitols. Information about the architectural details, construction history, as well as a synopsis of each state's history and symbols are given.

It's a great book for young and adult readers interested in our nation's capitols. Travelers find it perfect for visiting capitols and having information at their finger tips. In its seventh year, the latest edition was published in 2000. Order several for gifts!